In the Red Corner

The Marxism of José Carlos Mariátegui

Mike Gonzalez

Haymarket Books
Chicago, Illinois

Published in 2019 by
Haymarket Books
P.O. Box 180165
Chicago, IL 60618
773-583-7884
www.haymarketbooks.org
info@haymarketbooks.org

ISBN: 978-1-60846-915-4

Distributed to the trade in the US through Consortium Book Sales
and Distribution (www.cbsd.com) and internationally through Ingram
Publisher Services International (www.ingramcontent.com).

This book was published with the generous support of Lannan
Foundation and Wallace Action Fund.

Special discounts are available for bulk purchases by organizations and
institutions. Please call 773-583-7884 or email info@haymarketbooks.
org for more information.

Cover design by Eric Kerl.

Library of Congress Cataloging-in-Publication data is available.

Entered into digital printing March, 2021.

Praise for *In the Red Corner*

"Mariátegui's Marxism involved a deep, almost archaeological appreciation for the deposition and accumulation of Peruvian history's sedimentary layers. In his brief life he probed the complex particularities of that social formation across economics, history, politics, literature, and ideology. He intervened tirelessly in local affairs. At the same time, he knew these immediate, local concerns did not exist in pristine isolation from wider relations. With unparalleled determination, he insisted Peruvian reality could only be grappled with insofar as its innumerable entanglements with the rest of Latin America, and indeed the world—through the history of colonialism and capitalism—were fathomed and assimilated into revolutionary strategy. Latin America's socialist revolutions would never be a mere copy of European traditions, but they were nevertheless bound up in a shared universal project of emancipation. Mariátegui's heretical Marxism involved a utopian-revolutionary dialectic, in which select elements of indigenous communal traditions of the pre-capitalist past were combined with a forward-looking post-capitalist future, where the difference of the particular wasn't cancelled by the project of the universal. This impressive book by Mike Gonzalez turns Mariátegui's dialectic back on its author, parsing Mariátegui's life and work with all the necessary attentiveness to time and place, while simultaneously borrowing selectively from its riches to help reinvent a living Marxism and revolutionary politics adequate to our present."

—Jeffery R. Webber, author of *The Last Day of Oppression,*
and the First Day of the Same: The Politics and Economics
of the New Latin American Left

"It used to be said that Mariátegui was the Latin American Gramsci. But today, from a perspective defined by postcolonialism, it might be more pertinent to think of Gramsci as the European Mariátegui. Mike Gonzalez's new book offers a vividly detailed, eminently readable account of Mariátegui's life and times, with special attention to the formation of his unique form of Marxism. Gonzalez argues that Mariátegui remains crucially relevant to the development of forms of struggle and resistance in the Americas within the new framework of globalization."

—John Beverley, professor emeritus, University of Pittsburgh,
and author of *Latin America After 9/11*

For my dear friend and comrade Peter Archard

Contents

A Revolutionary Rediscovered

José Carlos Mariátegui has suffered badly at the hands of those who have claimed his political inheritance since his death in 1930. Yet the celebration of his centenary, in 1994, marked a kind of resurrection—the rediscovery of Latin America's most creative Marxist,[1] at a time, it might be said, when it was most necessary. His name had often been used as a reference point for very different positions and currents of thought, and this obscured rather than illuminated his complex body of ideas.

Mariátegui described himself as a "marxista, convicto, y confeso." And his Marxism was what Gramsci later described as a "philosophy of praxis." He was a Marxist in thought and practice; his ideas evolved and grew in a specific time and place, and responded to the political demands of both. The evolution of his ideas began in Peru in the conditions of a semicolonial society still stamping at the threshold of modern capitalism. But, as he discovered, Peru was not one world but two; in the encounter between indigenous Peru and *criollo* Peru, he found new challenges and the human and historical material for a creative new vision of how revolutionary change could occur in Latin America. A forced exile to Europe in 1919, principally in Italy, launched him into the fervor of a post-October world, where he acquired, as he put it, "a wife and

1

some ideas." Those ideas were Marxism—a Marxism still absorbing the implications of the Bolshevik Revolution in the fervid atmosphere of a revolutionary West.

Upon returning to Peru in 1923, Mariátegui shared the excitement and the inspiration of the revolutionary movement with his own generation. At home, he engaged with his own reality to expand and deepen the Marxism he had encountered in Italy. This was not simply an intellectual exercise. He was an organizer, a builder of movements, a teacher, and an agitator. In the unpromising conditions of 1920s Peru, Mariátegui interpreted Marx as his eleventh thesis on Feuerbach enjoined—not just to interpret the world, but to change it. And the world he addressed was not only Peru; it was also a Latin America in dialogue with itself and the wider world of revolutionary ideas in the North and West. He formed and led a growing trade union movement; he built a radical press. He saw the formation of a revolutionary party as critical, but he fought hard against sectarianism on the one hand (in particular, the class-against-class positions of the Comintern), and on the other against what he saw as the dangerous populism represented by the American Popular Revolutionary Alliance (APRA), with which he broke during a heated public debate.

Mariátegui encountered Marxism for the first time in an Italy that had recently seen the occupation of the factories and which was locked in debate about the formation of the Communist Party. There, Bordiga represented a closed and sectarian vision that Mariátegui rejected, just as the internal battle within the Communist Party of Italy (Partito Comunista d'Italia, PCI) was engaging Gramsci and others. It is not clear whether Mariátegui knew Gramsci in any real sense, though they certainly met. What is most striking, however, and in a sense most revealing, is how the trajectory and political development of both men ran in parallel. It would be tempting to try to establish some mutual influence, but it would also be fruitless since Mariátegui could not have had access to the key writings, like the *Prison Notebooks*, of the imprisoned Italian. What we can say, however, is that, for reasons that will be touched on later in the book, their frameworks and understandings of Marxism had much in common. Mariátegui never used the term "hegemony," for example, yet his cultural analysis is of extraordinary depth and perception, and his insistence on the interpenetration of politics and culture addresses the impact of ideology as a material factor in the evolution of the class struggle. The embodiment of that insight is the magazine *Amauta*, which he founded and which lasted until shortly after his death. *Amauta* was an extraordinary journal that drew together revolutionary thinkers and artists in an ongoing and open dialogue. Its functions were to inform, to educate, and to stimulate discussion within the Left, while refusing to hold a line that would have excluded the possibility of real debate. The journal was, in some senses, a reflection of the kind of political organization that Mariátegui set out to build, the "frente único," or "the united front," which had been his central organizing principle since 1924. At the same time, its breadth and emphasis on art and culture echoed another central theme—his opposition to mechanical Marxism and sectarianism. He would trace that line of argument in two of his works: *Ideología y política* and the polemic against reformism published after his death as *Defensa del Marxismo*.

The best known and most commonly quoted aspects of his work, and perhaps the most original, were his approach to "the Indian question" and his engagement with the indigenous world. A range of misunderstandings of this aspect of his work will be addressed here. He was quite specifically *not* an indigenista, a movement he analyzed critically in great detail. He saw the indigenous populations as an exploited and propertyless class, and he recognized the right to land as the key to its future liberation. Cultural traditions had survived among them which could allow for Marxism in the Andean context.

Mariátegui lived only into his thirty-sixth year, and he spent most of his years in considerable pain and the last six in a wheelchair. Yet his energy and productivity were breathtaking. The result is a body of political writing and a record of political work that would have left someone in good health and with a longer life exhausted. But what is most important about Mariátegui is not simply his personal achievement, but the immediacy and relevance of his legacy.

In a post-Stalinist world, both conservatives and reformists have been quick to attempt to discredit Marxism. They do this, in many cases, to cover their retreat into a compact with neoliberalism, but the voice of resistance has not been silent. Struggles across the world persist, and

Hugo Chávez's declaration of a "socialism of the twenty-first century" has evoked massive enthusiasm among those who confront neoliberalism. The paradox is that many of those movements have simultaneously expressed both a commitment to revolution and a general suspicion of Marxism and the socialist tradition. It is not hard to understand why Stalinism, in its many manifestations, produced such profound skepticism. It is our responsibility to make Marxism meaningful to a new generation and to demonstrate its capacity to respond to the political demands of a changing world both in theory and in practice. Mariátegui, rescued from his erstwhile friends, has an enormous contribution to make to that discovery. In an era of indigenous mobilizations and resistance, his explorations of the relationship between their traditions and the revolutionary organizations of the working class are unequaled. In the business of clarifying the extent of the mechanical Marxism of the Second International, or of the sectarian currents that have evolved across the Left, his trenchant critiques of both remain as relevant as they were in his time. This is not to pretend that the transformations of a capitalist world have not happened, but only to highlight that the understandings born of specific circumstances remain meaningful beyond them.

Mariátegui's incisive explorations of the relationship between politics and culture connect directly with the cultural critiques born out of Marxism in recent years; he was a Marxist in the richest sense, writing before Lukács, Gramsci, Benjamin, or Guevara were known, least of all in Latin America. Most significantly, all of this meshes with his central and repeated principle of political organization—the united front —long before it was articulated by Trotsky, though the two visions have much in common. The key issue for revolutionary socialists today is how to work, as revolutionaries, with social movements whose horizons are very different. Mariátegui has much to offer in that discussion.

Chapter One

The Resurrection of José Carlos Mariátegui

As "actually existing socialism," which described the Soviet Union and its satellites in eastern Europe, was progressively unmasked—exposed as a cover for regimes that wore socialist clothing while pursuing capitalist ends—a new generation was confronted with a confident capitalism that drove across the planet, exposing its nature. In the face of neoliberalism, what had once seemed to be an alternative system collapsed. Capitalism now operated in a global market, driven by institutions, including the World Trade Organization (WTO) and the International Monetary Fund (IMF)—institutions tasked with preventing any "obstacles" like trade unions, measures to protect national economies, state subsidies, and so on from inhibiting the free movement of capital. Neoliberalism was not new, but it was a particularly ruthless form of global exploitation, as Naomi Klein's *No Logo: No Space, No Choice, No Jobs* demonstrated forcefully to a generation of urban youth who had absorbed, without due scrutiny, the consumerism of the previous two decades. In the West, the protests against the system were driven by a moral outrage—a force that for Mariátegui was or could be revolutionary. In Latin America and the rest of the less developed world, it was the reality of austerity programs and structural adjustments that produced resistance. The fragile protections rarely and minimally provided by the local state left communities vulnerable in the face of the wrecking machine called multinational capital—the giant firms that dominated industries like oil, mining, and export agriculture, backed by global banks and financial agencies were hard to resist. As this wave of anti-capitalism spread, questions were raised: What alternative to this cruel and antihuman system might there be, and how might that other possibility be attained? It was, of course, a question of vision—of the collective imagination—but it was also a question of method, of organization. The myth of progress must be replaced with the myth of revolution. Marx said it very clearly: a universal future can only be forged by a universal class, a class that does not require inequality and exploitation for its very existence, a class whose consciousness is forged in collaboration and community rather than competition and individualism. This was what Marx meant by the "proletariat," those who have nothing to lose but their chains.

The capitalist class had a range of instruments to defend and veil their class rule; these include not just the control of capital, or the deployment of armies, but ideas too—false universals (like the myth of progress itself) religion, common sense, ideology. Its favored instrument was division, a fragmentation of the working class into warring parts by gender, by race, and by belief. It was part of the revolution's task to identify those divisions and overcome them. But that was only half the job. The other part was to create a new class identity, a unified proletariat, multiple and diverse, that would construct the new world. Of course, the bourgeoisie was divided against itself too, just as the working class, by sectarianism, racism, sexism, and all the other ways in which it could be weakened in the face of the class struggle. But when its system was challenged, that dominant class would find its shared commitment and work together.

Mariátegui's resurfacing came as a consequence of an emerging new political consciousness in search of an ancestor. The fall of the Berlin Wall had left the revolution without a language, or indeed a reference point. The Russian Revolution, which had been the lodestar of revolutionary movements for two generations, now had to be rescued from the distortions to which it had been subjected. Karl Marx, in whose name so many falsehoods had been uttered, emerged apparently unscathed. A British Broadcasting Company (BBC) poll found him to be the most important figure of all time for a majority of its listeners. The problem was that the discourse of revolutionary Marxism had been so misused and discredited that it was discarded, or at the very least seriously questioned, for a time, by those resisting capitalism and its depredations. Other proposals came to fill the vacuum. Hardt and Negri's "multitude" described the shifting and unstable world of labor in a global environment, but they did not indicate which instruments should be forged to fight that global force. Anarchism found a wide range of new enthusiasts. John Holloway generalized from the specific experience of the Zapatistas, whose rebellion ultimately expressed itself in the metaphor of the snail—enclosed within its own house. But how could coordination and solidarity—the concepts at the heart of Mariátegui's thinking—be achieved among self-isolating units within a region or a nation, let alone within a global system? And how could unification occur, as Holloway argued it could in his widely read book *Change the World without Taking Power*, without addressing the issue of the state?

Marxism as it had evolved, particularly in the 1980s and 1990s, had also enclosed itself within the universalization of the European experience, or taken refuge in a theory disengaged from practice. The different representatives of the revolutionary tradition, meanwhile, fought one another for dominance across the world and as a result weakened the movement. Dogmatism, a battle for the possession of the revolutionary grail, often supplanted both dialogue and common struggle.

The new movements turned away from a history and an experience that had an enormous amount to offer the renewed struggle, but that seemed unable to address the new movements' multiple characters. Across the planet, issues of class, race, gender, and environmental destruction were addressed by activists marching together. Yet they needed to find defining ideas, identify unifying strategies, and develop common organs of struggle.

There was another facet of the new movements, beyond their specific anti-capitalist purposes that connects with Mariátegui's writings. Global warming was entering the popular consciousness despite the enormous resources injected into climate change denial by the big corporations in oil, gas, and coal. The privatization of water launched by Margaret Thatcher in 1989 was producing a world in which over a billion people were without drinking water and over two billion were denied it for washing and sanitary purposes. Chernobyl and Bhopal had exposed the appalling dangers hidden within globalization. Desertification, drought, floods, and tsunamis were slowly beginning to be understood as man-made rather than natural phenomena—and that understanding, as Naomi Klein put it, "changed everything.[1]" In Latin America, the renewed demand for minerals (especially copper), the rising price of gold, the boom in oil prices, the world demand for soy and maize for ethanol, and the exploding consumption of beef tore into the heart of the Andes mountains and the Amazon forest. Privatization drove whole populations off their lands and into the shantytowns that grew speedily around every major city in Latin America.

Mariátegui Rediscovered

Latin America has produced many original Marxist thinkers, dedicated socialists, activists, and champions of the working class. Among them are Farabundo Martí in El Salvador, Julio Antonio Mella in Cuba, Che Guevara, Luís Carlos Prestes in Brazil, and Luis Emilio Recabarren, whose suicide in 1927 robbed Chile of its leading socialist activist and organizer. Yet it is José Carlos Mariátegui whose ideas and example have survived a century of extraordinary changes and proved most meaningful for a new generation of revolutionaries.

That in itself is remarkable. Since his premature death in 1930, at the age of thiry-six, Mariátegui's political and theoretical legacies have been claimed by many, and unfortunately, they have been distorted and misrepresented in the process. The most notorious example of misuse of his work and his writing was committed by Sendero Luminoso, the Maoist Shining Path organization (also known as the Communist Party of Peru, PCP), which appropriated Mariátegui's work to justify a political movement exactly contrary to the project that Mariátegui had fought to build; its sectarianism against every other sector of the movement and its rigidly hierarchical structures flew in the face of Mariátegui's conception of a united front. Mariátegui's insistence on openness, on transparency, on a movement led from below, on the concept of a leadership following and responding to the grass roots, was caricatured in the deification of Abimael Guzmán (also known as President Gonzalo) and the ruthless internal discipline of an organization that used violence against the peasants and indigenous peoples it claimed to represent. How many times did Mariátegui rail against politicians who took power away from the people they purported to represent in the name of socialism? But there were many others who took his name, with equally little right to represent his Marxist politics. The painful end of Mariátegui's life was made more bitter and tragic by the sectarianism of the Communist International (Comintern), which mocked and parodied his Indoamerican communism, within weeks of his death, by creating a Communist Party forged in Moscow and led by the unscrupulous opportunist Eudocio Ravines. The dogmatism of the Comintern, and its "Third Period" politics of "class against class," sabotaged the united front. The predictable result was that the respect for his ideas that Mariátegui had won among indigenous people was undermined. Their resistance continued in the bitter struggles in the high Andes, though they remained largely invisible to the non-Indian world. The relationship between Marxist ideas and indigenous struggle was broken, however, and it would be decades before the resulting distrust would begin to be overcome.

Perhaps the cruelest misrepresentation was the way the American Popular Revolutionary Alliance appropriated his reputation. APRA, an opportunist formation that had once claimed Marxist credentials, attempted to build a chain of connection between Mariátegui and its populist leader Victor Raúl Haya de la Torre. It was cruel because while the two men had been friends, and for a brief period in the twenties collaborated, they represented opposing strategies. Haya's APRA looked for alliances with the bourgeoisie from an entirely electoralist perspective. By the time its then-leader Alan García ended his first presidency in the 1980s, APRA had become synonymous with betrayal, corruption, and the advocacy of neoliberal solutions. The irony of this is that Mariátegui broke with APRA definitively in 1928 on the principled basis that the movement he was dedicated to building was a class-based proletarian united front that needed to include the indigenous communities.

The Stalinist assault on his ideas, and his systematic discrediting by the Comintern, consigned Mariátegui to the shadows for a while, but in the glaring light of the collapse of "actually existing socialism," Mariátegui has reemerged. There has been an interesting tendency among his erstwhile attackers to ride the tide of approval for their own benefit. In fact, the important rediscovery was made neither by academics nor the organizations of the Left. In Seattle in 1999, the Teamsters and the Turtles confronted the WTO, a capitalist club whose existence and whose power in the global market were virtually unknown until seventy thousand demonstrators shouted them to the world. The Zapatista communities, embattled in a corner of southern Mexico, had declared their defiance on the newly formed world wide web five years earlier. The Zapatistas's eloquent spokesperson, Subcomandante Marcos, had unmasked the mechanisms of neoliberal globalization through his dispatches from the Lacandón Forest. In the period when neoliberalism was exercising its economic power to the detriment of millions across Latin America—in the form of austerity programs masked by various euphemisms—other forces were also quietly growing. The formation of the Confederation of Indigenous Nationalities of Ecuador (CONAIE), in Ecuador, in 1990, made little impact on the world's media at the time. A decade later it became part of a burgeoning movement that removed three presidents in that country. In Mexico, Zapatismo had awakened ancient memories and stories of rebellion and resistance. In Bolivia, the encroachments of multinational capital were meeting resistance too; it reached a new dimension with the victory over the Bechtel Corporation in Cochabamba during the so-called Water War of 2000.

The structural adjustment programs of the 1990s undermined the local state and created supranational organisms—the North American Free Trade Agreement (NAFTA) first among them—to assume control. The protections that the state could offer—subsidies, basic welfare, health systems, public education, jobs in the state sector—were systematically and rapidly compromised. Nineteen ninety-two may have been declared the year of indigenous peoples, and the Nobel Peace Prize awarded to the Guatemalan Maya leader Rigoberta Menchú, but for the indigenous communities of Latin America it marked the beginning of a decade of renewed oppression and impoverishment.

The multiple expressions of resistance by the First Nations of the Americas contradicted the still-dominant image of a passive and silent minority taking refuge in the remotest corners of the continent. In Mariátegui's time, an artistic current called "Indigenismo" drew attention, often controversially, to the condition of the Indian. Mariátegui's response to the advocates of Indigenismo was to insist and to demonstrate that the "Indian problem" was social and economic, that it had nothing to do with the character of the Indian people. The "new Indian," for him, was exemplified by a man he met in his home in Lima, Ezequiel Urviola, from Puno, who was a fighter for the Indian, a leader in struggle. His dialogue with Mariátegui was part of the building of a united class front in which the Indian, the peasant, and the worker would not simply fight the capitalist system for the improvement of their lives, but in doing so create a new and different world without discrimination, injustice, or exploitation—a socialist world.

Mariátegui's Marxism was heterodox, challenging, and extraordinarily creative. It is curious that the negative conditions he analyzed so insightfully in Peru—a weak and subservient bourgeoisie, a division in both economic and cultural terms that was never resolved, the consequences of an economy based wholly on the demand from the outside world—should have produced so farsighted and original a thinker. There is no single explanation. Chance and a confluence of personal circumstances—including a devastating illness—obliged him to spend his childhood and early adolescence reading. Mariátegui's answer was to describe himself as self-taught and to argue that the revolutionary intellectual—and he was most certainly that—does not develop in isolation from the movements of the class but, on the contrary, emerges from them.

Revolutionary intellectuals, like the people who struggle on the ground, derive knowledge from experience—from reality—and that experience, that knowledge, is collective—social. The myth of the solitary thinker denies a person's material existence and the history that, like it or not, he or she embodies and bears. That knowledge, that intelligence, however, is not enough to make the revolution. Something else is needed—feeling, passion. And both the vision and the passion are embodied, as Mariátegui controversially argued throughout his life, in *el mito*—the social myth.

Revolutions do not arise automatically from the battle for bread. To suggest that they might is to accept the bourgeois rationality Mariátegui contested all through his adult life: the rationality of accumulation and possession, of private property and individualism. When he arrived in

Europe in 1920, as the resonances of the Russian Revolution of 1917 were spreading across the world, Mariátegui was shocked to find the extent to which the language of socialism and revolution had become a discourse of conformity, and that revolution, under the aegis of the mechanical, evolutionary Marxism of the Second International, had ceased to be the objective. On the contrary, a mechanical interpretation of Marxism had turned that end, that would be dreamed of and fought for by human beings, into the automatic consequence of material progress. It was, of course, a falsehood, but it had undermined and caricatured Marxism, the philosophy and the method of social transformation, and save for a few revolutionary Marxists—Liebknecht, Luxemburg, Trotsky, and of course Lenin—it had robbed it of its revolutionary impulse.

In what follows, the explanation for Mariátegui's reemergence will become clear, I hope, against the background of the new questions the movement raised. Mariátegui would not have described himself as a theorist. He was always a man of action, an activist, an organizer, and a revolutionary intellectual, who thought and worked with and from the working class. His writings were responses to the issues that arose in the course of building a movement. He moves from one set of concerns to another over the course of his political life. That, as we will explore more fully, is part of the nature of his understanding of Marxism. This was how he presented his Marxism, in 1927, to the Second Workers' Congress:

> Marxism, of which all speak but few know or above all comprehend, is a fundamentally dialectical method, a method completely based in reality, on facts. It is not, as some erroneously suppose, a body of principles with rigid consequences, the same for all historical climates and all social latitudes. . . . Marx extracted his method from the guts of history.[2]

His statement contains several challenges. His Marxism was first and foremost a political method, born from a conception of Marxism as "a theory and practice of the proletarian revolution." Its insights were weapons in the class struggle: its objective was to create the workers' united front that could initiate a struggle for socialism. Mariátegui was a trade union organizer, in permanent contact with the leading militants of his day, and, by 1928, the founder of Peru's first trade union congress, the Confederación General de Trabajadores del Perú (CGTP), and the author of its manifesto (though the first conference of the organization did not take place until September 1930, six months after Mariátegui's death). He was a journalist and a teacher, an educator of the class, not in the conventional sense of providing what Paulo Freire called "banking education" (that is, the formal body of ideas that sustain the bourgeois order), but an education whose materials were the reality of working-class life and history, subjective and objective. Freire's ideas about the education of the oppressed came long after Mariátegui, of course, but Mariátegui anticipated them in his own writings on education. In his statement, Mariátegui implicitly distanced himself from the increasingly dominant dogmatism of the Stalinist orthodoxy. His was a creative, evolving, and heterodox Marxism.

His first series of lectures at the Universidad Popular, in 1923, placed Peru in a world context based on Mariátegui's recent European experience. For some writers, his detailed analysis of his own society, and in particular of the "Indian problem," makes him a "national Marxist."[3] That seems to me to misunderstand his method and his Marxism, which are internationalist in their very essence. Throughout his writing he emphasizes the dialectics of the national and the international, whose specific dimensions are interdependent. In the reality of a world dominated by imperialism—the highest stage of capitalism—of which he had a clear and profound understanding, there was no longer a national project in the sense of the construction of a bourgeois nation-state. In the specific case of Peru, for example, he demonstrated the incapacity of the bourgeoisie to realize that project and explained that its moment had passed. The tasks of development and growth would now fall to the proletariat—the tasks that the bourgeoisie had realized in the past this time would arise from the needs and priorities of the working classes. Mariátegui resisted the idea that there was a model for revolution, a formula for organization that all should follow yet that had emerged out of very different economic and social conditions. That was the core of his argument with the International and, indeed much earlier than that, of his argument with a close friend and colleague, César Falcón, with whom he had worked in Lima and traveled to Italy. Falcón was convinced by the arguments for a Leninist party defined by the Twenty-One Conditions for membership of the Comintern, while Mariátegui was not.

The international reality and the specific conditions in each country would equally affect everything about the way a revolution should and could be conducted, from the specific class formations produced by the relations of production, through culture, collective memory, and religiosity. Revolution had to be made meaningful to the different sectors of the proletariat, the universal class, in the context of their particular cultural history, embodied in the notion of myth. The general—Marxism—had to be applied in specific and real conditions—hence the considered use of the term "interpretation" in the full title of his *Seven Interpretive Essays on Peruvian Reality*, a reality in which, Mariátegui stressed, four-fifths of the population were indigenous. Their consciousness was certainly formed by their location in the economic system, but not only by that. Other elements were formative, too. The question was whether these differences would separate them from the rest of the movement, or include them, enriching and diversifying the movement. When he discusses the united front as his central organizational proposal, it is to permit difference and embrace the debate out of which unity in action could come.

Thus, in Peru, socialism would be a plural movement, just as the proletariat was a plural class. To speak of nation in that context required a sophisticated rethinking. The formation of the nation-state in Europe, for example, was built around the hegemony of a bourgeois class projecting its culture as a universal, as what Gramsci called "a secular religion," creating the "imagined community" that Benedict Anderson describes.[4] But in Peru, as Mariátegui exhaustively discusses, the nation-state had failed to emerge, and the weak and dependent bourgeoisie simply threw in its lot with foreign capital to act, effectively, as its agent on the ground. To do that, it had resisted modernization, economic development, and the creation of the strong centralist institutions of the nation-state, preferring instead to accept the continuity of "semi-feudal" economic forms that sustained slavery together with the embrace of imperialism. This analysis led to a bitter and critically important argument between Mariátegui and Haya de la Torre in 1928, as will emerge below.

The conclusion Mariátegui drew from his interpretation was that the opportunity to build a nation-state had passed, irredeemably compromised by the behavior of the Peruvian bourgeoisie. Furthermore, he reasoned that that class could never oversee a society in which the indigenous peoples were integrated. When he argued for "peruanizing Peru," it was not a call for allegiance to a bourgeois nation-state, but rather for a recognition of what Luis Vitale suggests calling a "people-nation," and the "national-popular" culture that sustained it.[5] For culture, as he understood it, was not mere reflection—as cruder Marxist interpretations argued at the time and since—but an active component of political consciousness, shaping the material as well as being shaped by it. It could be the locus of resistance and of alternative imagined communities.

Reading Mariátegui today, it is striking how close his analysis and his arguments are to the perspectives of the indigenous movements that have emerged in Latin America since the fall of Stalinism. Mariátegui argues for a concept derived from his contemporary Hildebrando Castro Pozo of *dar-recibir* (giving-receiving) which seems to parallel the idea of the *sarwak karsay*, translated as *buen vivir*, or "the good life," which has been incorporated into the plurinational state constitutions of Venezuela, Ecuador, and Bolivia. It is, in a sense, an indigenous *mito*, as Mariátegui understood the term. But he would almost certainly have disagreed with an idea of a cultural revolution disengaged from production, the economy, and the environment. That is certainly the basis of Jeffery Webber's critique of political developments in Bolivia, for example.[6] The continuity between the human community and nature is embedded in the concept of buen vivir, yet the new commitment to extractive industry in the states where that plurinational constitution prevails is a dramatic contradiction. The indigenous vocabulary has introduced into current political debate a concept that Mariátegui anticipated in his discussion of the relationship of the Indian and land—the concept of *territorio*, which is coterminous with neither land nor, indeed, with nation. This is a notion beyond geography, which embraces history, philosophy, cultural forms and practices, and the idea of enduring collective ownership. It addresses the *relationship* between humanity and nature in a way that has resonated with a slowly growing ecological movement across the world.

Mariátegui's argument, which is discussed in detail throughout this book, is that the forms of social and agrarian organization that were obtained in Inca society, and which survived the destruction of

that empire, represent a specifically Peruvian tradition that is socialist in its nature—that is, collaborative, communitarian, productive for
need, and dismissive of private property in favor of the collective. This
is his Indoamerican socialism, which has been so often misrepresented
by his detractors.

A Romantic Marxist?

Mariátegui's critics have described him, at various times, as an idealist, a
utopian, and an irrationalist. In his important writings on Mariátegui,
Michael Löwy has described him as "a romantic Marxist."[7] Approving
or disapproving, all these characterizations are responses to the significance in his work of the concept of mito, or "social myth." This will be
discussed in further detail, but it is worth addressing the general point
here: for Mariátegui, following Georges Sorel, revolution is the "myth"
of the proletariat, just as "progress" was for the bourgeoisie. It can mean
many different things, but it always represents an anticipatory vision, a
picture of an alternative future world. There are of course, reactionary
myths—images of an idealized past that is to be recreated. As Mariátegui shows in his writings on Italy, it is a feature of fascism that it produces
an idea of restoration to past grandeurs, invariably imaginary construc-
tions. But the myth of social revolution points ahead to a world without
classes and more importantly to a universe of alternative values—replac-
ing those that prevail, or are hegemonic, in a bourgeois order. They may
often be based—as they were in the work of earlier romantic artists—on
a precapitalist community, an idealized past when the commons—that
which belonged to all—prevailed over private ownership, when labor
was creative rather than mechanical and repetitive. There is, of course,
no road back, no possible unraveling of history, except perhaps in the
fevered cerebrations of a Hitler or a Mussolini. But there is, as Mariátegui insists, a way of recuperating the past for the benefit of the future.

  After the deaths of Marx and Engels, there was a battle for their
ideological inheritance. It was largely won by the Marxism of the Second International, whose interpretation was essentially determinist.
Marx's analysis of the driving forces within capitalism, the compulsion
to "[a]ccumulate! accumulate!" would, it was argued, lead necessarily to

the implosion because of its contradictions from which socialism would emerge like the phoenix. According to the Second International, the movement of history is relentless progress toward a telos that will be socialism. The philosophy associated with this notion, positivism, pursued that outcome as the necessary fulfilment of human ambition. Yet Marx himself described the world of capitalism as "a world of emptiness" as compared to an earlier time of "human fullness." The *Communist Manifesto* begins and ends with a concept of contradiction. "All that is solid melts into air" in the pursuit of bourgeois progress, of bourgeois reason, and, as we know so much more clearly now than Marx or Mariátegui could have, there is another possible outcome—as the *Communist Manifesto* put it, "the mutual ruin of the contending classes."

The current of the subjective tradition, with its emphasis on the ethical component of Marxism and the element of consciousness, was emerging in Marxism even before the First World War. The socialist tradition around William Morris, and the subsequent writings of E. P. Thompson in Britain, for example, stand in that subjective tradition. The Marxism of Ernst Bloch, and that of the Georg Lukács of *History and Class Consciousness*—as well as the work of Walter Benjamin, rest on that strong ethical and humanist foundation. The gradual recuperation of the earlier writings of Marx—*The German Ideology* and the *1844 Manuscripts* as well as the rediscovery of Benjamin's extraordinary work, have given strength to this view of Marxism. Perhaps most significantly, Gramsci, too, was won to this vision of Marx in the years before the creation of the Partito Comunista d'Italia (PCI).

As Löwy describes it, the Romantic tradition was not only literary, but more widely cultural. It included the whole range of reactions against the dehumanization that capitalism necessarily entailed, the "quantification" of everything, and the transformation of every product of human activity into commodities, measures, and prices for the market. The alternative, past or future, asserted the *quality* of all things human. And this referred not simply to what was produced—craft versus mass production, for example—but also and most importantly to the relations between human beings, the "relations of production" as Marx had called them. In the communities of the past, in rural England, or Joseph Fourier's phalansteries, exchange was not measured or priced, and production was not competitive but cooperative. It was those qualities that Mariátegui identified in the Inca commune, the *ayllu*. He was emphatic that it was not a matter of returning to but one of proceeding toward; the past would not be reproduced in the future, only the qualities and values it enshrined. It would be an imagined future.

Mariátegui identified the point of transition humanity had reached in a wonderful, brief poetic essay, "Two Conceptions of Life":

> The new humanity, in its two antithetical expressions, reveals a new intuition about life. This does not appear only in the belligerent prose of the politicians. In the words of Luis Bello, "It is time to correct Descartes to 'I fight, therefore I am.'" The correction is opportune. The philosophy for a rationalist age could not but be "I think therefore I am." But the same formula no longer serves this romantic, revolutionary, and Quixotic age. Rather than thought, life today must be action, struggle. Modern man is in need of a faith, and the only faith that can fill his deep self is a faith in struggle. Who knows when the sweet life will return? The sweet prewar life produced only skepticism and nihilism. And out of this skepticism and this nihilism was born the harsh, powerful, peremptory need for a faith and a myth that can move human beings to live dangerously.[8]

Mariátegui's most famous phrase affirmed: "Our revolution cannot be an imitation or a copy. It must be a heroic creation, *una creación heroica*, an epic struggle to create a new world."

These ideas sit firmly within the rich tradition of Marxism. After his death, the representatives of Stalinism worked hard to dismiss Mariátegui's criticisms of Eurocentrism and the Stalinist distortions of Marxism. Mariátegui's adamant refusal to prematurely found the communist party was turned on its head by Ravines and others. In the years that followed, the intellectual leadership of APRA manufactured a causal relationship between him and Haya de la Torre, as if the break between Mariátegui and Haya in 1928 had not been a fundamental parting of the ways. Others, Robert Paris in particular, have described him as a "Sorelian" as if that were a kind of anteroom to Marxism. It is the purpose of this book to show that Mariátegui was an original and creative Marxist and contributed to its enrichment.

Art and Politics

Mariátegui modestly described his own youth as his "stone age." As a prolific and perceptive young journalist, he spent the years between 1913 and 1918 living a bohemian life among the artists and writers of Lima who gathered in the cafés of the Jirón de la Unión, the emblematic boulevard of central Lima. His companions were almost entirely members of the white middle and bourgeois classes, many of them recent arrivals from the provinces. José Carlos's background was different, but nonetheless he identified with them and shared their activities and tastes. They were the literary and artistic avant-garde, who shared the bored disillusionment of the French poets, the ennui of a generation that had turned its back on a bourgeois world. The Hispanophile aristocracy of Peruvian high society seemed absurdly antiquated. For this new generation literature was withdrawal and rejection, a slap in the face of good taste. Mariátegui himself wrote poetry, a volume of which was published under the title *Tristeza* (Sadness), and two plays with his friend Abraham Valdelomar, the doyen of the group around the journal *Colónida*. They imitated the European generation that in Mariátegui's words was "sensual, elegant, and hyperaesthetic" but "affected by a strange sickness, a strange nostalgia." The deep crisis of liberal Europe, which he analyzed in his Universidad Popular lectures and in his first published book, *La escena contemporánea* (The contemporary scene) was a crisis of ideas, the aftermath of the collapse of a liberal idea of progress drowned in the mud of the First World War trenches.

Art and literature had reflected the gradual decline of that idea of progress in the tension of the prewar period, and—in the face of the devastation of war—had registered in paint and word the disintegration of prewar certainties. For Mariátegui, all art is in one form or another an engagement with history—not a History spelled with a capital "H," history as abstraction, but history as lived, experienced, and suffered in its movement. Mariátegui emphasizes movement—the process of change and of transition. In his early writings, literature absorbed much of his attention; this did not change as his interests expanded to include politics. The reality is that he was an insightful literary critic, not because of his exploration of structures and language, but because he considered texts in

their autonomy as well as in their context—their relationship with under-
lying cultural structures, or the absence thereof. His lifelong interest in
the artistic vanguard stems from a perception of the intellectual vanguard
as embracing the aesthetic, the philosophical, and the political. Spanish
does not distinguish the political vanguard from the artistic avant-garde.
Mariátegui's distaste for Émile Zola stems from Zola's "elimination of the
critical potential of artistic praxis."[9] Zola draws universal conclusions from
the present, which he treats as a single organism. For him, the dynamics and
drama of history are absent; Maxim Gorky, by contrast, does hold a place,
for Mariátegui, in the great realist tradition. Mariátegui is an admirer of
the modernist writers like John Dos Passos and Marcel Proust who represent "the disarticulation of the old conception of the human personality
and psyche," a theme he pursued in his articles on Freud. But his interest in
literature is not distinct from his wider interest in politics and ideology. In
some ways, what he seeks in myth is what he also seeks in literature—the
premonitory sense. For him "the work of art cannot inspire a heroic epoch
unless it identifies the latent possibilities that can only be realized on the
political level through the concrete transformation of reality."

Italian Futurism, which Mariátegui criticized ferociously, separated
art from politics and, in a sense, betrayed the role of an avant-garde by
turning to fascism and its restorationist myth. Surrealism, by contrast,
fulfilled the vocation of literature by responding to the social crisis and
exploring how it could be overcome both artistically and politically.

More than a century after his birth, Mariátegui's contribution, not
just to the development of Latin American Marxism but to Marxism
itself, has begun to be recognized. For some writers, it remains difficult
to locate his work within or between intellectual disciplines. He has
recently been linked to Gramsci and to Benjamin, the former for his
understanding of the philosophy of praxis, the latter for his excavations
of the potentialities for resistance and transformation buried in popular culture. Mariátegui's Marxism resisted imprisonment in dogma or
determinism and restored to its place the dialectic of the material and
the ideal, of the present and the future.

Alberto Flores Galindo, the outstanding historian of Peru's working-
class movement and of Mariátegui's critical role within it, offers this definitive assessment. According to Galindo, Mariátegui's Marxism

was not the work of a university professor, so he can't be criticized on academic grounds—for not having read everything on the subject, not quoting accurately, not having an adequate "theoretical framework." By assimilating the critical dynamic of Marxism in his concrete analyses of the Peruvian reality . . . in evaluating no more and no less than the historicity and criticality of Marxism itself . . . he expands its heuristic and epistemological possibilities and smooths the way for the unfolding of its capacity to intervene in history as a transformative social force. We ask ourselves, could the most punctilious exegesis of classic texts or the cultivation of an intellectualized Marxism, in particular in our America, demonstrate such commanding and at the same time such "Marxist" achievements?

I would like to think that this book, while it cannot aspire to imitate the breadth and passion of Mariátegui's insights and the complexity of his thought, will at least demonstrate that for him the *application* of a method, or an idea, was not about presenting Peru as simply an example of a universal paradigm. For him, application meant implication, that is, to involve the instrument of analysis in the task and involve himself in it. As he put it, "My thought and my life are one thing, a single process. And if there is anything that I hope and expect to be credited for . . . it is that I put all my blood into my ideas."[10] Or, as he declared before the International in his *Anti-imperialist Perspective*:

> We are anti-imperialists because we are Marxists, because we are revolutionaries, because we set against capitalism a socialism that is its antagonist, called upon to succeed it, because in the struggle against foreign imperialisms we fulfill our obligations of solidarity with the revolutionary masses of Europe.[11]

Chapter Two

Learning His Trade: Mariátegui's "Stone Age"

Moquegua is fifteen hundred kilometers south of Lima; the distance is not only geographical, but also social and psychological. Set among arid mountains that hide the silver, copper, and molybdenum on which the local economy has always been based, their dry brown crags are a reminder that just beyond them lies Latin America's driest desert, the Chilean Atacama. But the municipality is a historical crossroads of another order; the province of Moquegua touches the state of Puno, the heart of the ancient civilizations of Tihuanaco, of the Wari and of the Chibcha of the coast. Their historic sites attract a few tourists and some enthusiastic archaeologists, and compete with the vineyards that produce the local wine for occasional visitors.

In 1894, when Mariátegui was born there, it would have looked much the same as it does today, its slanted roofs tilted up toward the hills. José Carlos's mother, Amalia La Chira, was a seamstress of indigenous origins whose relationship with a criollo (a person of European descent). Of aristocratic lineage, Francisco Javier de Mariátegui, produced six children, three of whom died very young. The elder Mariátegui acted with the irresponsibility characteristic of liaisons between the wealthy and the poor, abandoning Amalia to care for her children after each birth. Nevertheless, Amalia's decision to break with him definitively was not the result of his behavior or his abuse of her, but rather the reaction of a deeply Catholic woman to the discovery that he was a mason and a liberal!

By 1899 the family had moved to Huacho to live with her parents. The town was just 150 kilometers or so north of Lima, and the climate was more temperate and less forbidding than that of Moquegua. His maternal grandfather worked in leather, and José Carlos spent time in his workshop, though his eventual vocation would take him in a very different direction.

It would be stretching a point too far to suggest that these early years shaped his future interest in the indigenous communities of his country. However brief his contact with that world may have been, living in Moquegua would have made him aware of it in a way that few of his contemporaries in Lima could claim, for the distances were not merely physical; the white, urban world rarely saw the Indian as anything other than an exotic primitive.

In 1902, at the age of eight, José Carlos suffered an injury in the schoolyard that dogged him his entire life and ultimately caused his death. It has been described in different ways, from tubercular arthrosis to osteomyelitis. Whatever the case, it urgently needed treatment, and Amalia was able, through a friend, to get José Carlos access to the French clinic in the capital, where he underwent an operation and stayed for four months. His recovery was slow, however, and he spent the next four years largely homebound, reading voraciously in Spanish and French. The boy never finished his primary education, and in 1909 he was taken on as a printer's apprentice at *La Prensa*, Lima's main newspaper. He graduated quickly to becoming a linotype operator, and by 1913 he was writing for the paper. Much later, when he was asked to provide a self-portrait, he proudly repeated that he was "self-taught," not a university man—in fact, if anything, he was anti-university.[1] This from someone a good part of whose brief life was dedicated to the education of working people.

His first assignment was to observe the courts and parliamentary activity. It was not necessarily the most stimulating of jobs, yet the boy's acute perceptions sought out the patterns of behavior that he saw in both. His observations of everyday life, of popular culture in its broadest sense, would remain a source of political insight throughout his life, and his reports from parliament exposed features of institutional political life of which he was deeply contemptuous. That experience would also lead him to draw far-reaching conclusions about the nature of those institutions and their distance from the experiences and concerns of the majority of the population. The elite he saw, in parliament, the state, and the universities, was feckless and corrupt to its very core.

It was not unusual for journalists to pass on information to be written up to their juniors. José Carlos appears to have been put in charge of reading the teletype, which would have kept him in touch with the headlines of international news. He wrote under several pseudonyms; the most regular was Juan Croniqueur, a reference to his advanced knowledge of French, perhaps, but also to the tradition of the feuilleton, journalism as popular narrative.

It would be wishful thinking to classify him as a fifteen-year-old prodigy, already keenly aware of the changes occurring in his own society and beyond. But there is every justification for pointing to the discontent and resistance he felt, even as a teen, for much of what he saw in the Lima on which he had been asked to observe and comment. His background would have been sufficient explanation for his scorn for the bourgeoisie, and it would also explain his sympathetic portraits of the daily lives of ordinary limeños and the popular culture that sustained them. He wrote for other newspapers and magazines; for the horse racing paper *Turf,* and for *Lulu,* a women's magazine, among others. By 1916 he had moved on from *La Prensa* to *El Tiempo,* whose position was more radical. It was later condemned and closed down by the government for supporting workers.

But while Mariátegui criticized the indolence and lack of imagination of the Peruvian bourgeoisie, other forces were beginning, slowly, to move beneath the surface.

The Guano Boom and Its Aftermath

From the 1840s onward, the guano gathered from the islands off the Pacific coast drew mainly British investors to Peru; guano, the accumulated droppings of seabirds, was an extremely rich fertilizer. At the same time, the Atacama Desert region, located partly in Chile and partly in Peru, was yielding *salitre*, or sodium nitrate. Known as "Chilean or Peruvian saltpeter," it was used both in fertilizers and in the production of explosives. The trade in both products, which were exported directly to Europe, was dominated by British capital. The profits from the guano trade, in particular, produced a wealthy Lima-based bourgeoisie that in the early 1860s founded the first banks to negotiate the transfer of the profits from the trade to England. Guano and mineral exports increased, and so did the international trade in the wool produced in the highland regions by indigenous labor. The local landowners, the *gamonales* for whom Mariátegui reserved a particular anger, appropriated indigenous lands, limiting the space available for food crops and reducing the population to virtual slavery. Ernesto Yepes explains:

> The emerging state, therefore, was the expression of the symbiosis of interests between middle and small landowners for whom institutional power fulfilled above all the role of legitimizing both the exploitation of small agricultural producers and the definition of the mass of peasants as an exploitable source of labour, taxes, and military recruits.[2]

Its political expression was the *civilista* state, which worked closely with European industrial and finance capital to the benefit of the new metropolitan bourgeoisie and its rural allies.

The economic crisis of the 1870s, however, exposed the weakness of the state and the failure of the civilistas to develop the local economy. Their European backers, concerned for their investments, backed the Chilean government, already well integrated into a world economy and more industrialized, in its declaration of war in 1879. The War of the Pacific, as it came to be called (1879–83), robbed Bolivia of its access to the sea and deprived Peru of the port of Tacna and a significant part of the nitrate-producing desert area to its south. It was a humiliating defeat for both countries, and the devastation left by the war provided an opportunity for foreign capital to assume direct control over the Peruvian economy.

Civilismo was the political expression of the new Peruvian capitalist class. The Civilista Party, founded in 1872 and led by Manuel Pardo, was to guide the country away from the successive military rulers that had dominated the country during the first half of the century and establish a functioning parliamentary system. When Mariátegui began to write his reports on the activities of the Peruvian Congress, he found an institution still dominated by what Peruvians called "the oligarchy," the network of families who had grown wealthy through the export economy and in collusion with foreign capital. In the aftermath of the Pacific War, this same network would turn again to foreign capital to restore the economy and guarantee their continuing profits. Although Pardo had founded the party on an anti-militarist platform, the civilistas did not hesitate to turn to the army whenever their regime was under threat. Indebted to Britain by the early 1870s, the war deepened the Peruvian economic crisis. The Grace Contract, negotiated in 1886 and formalized in 1890, replaced existing government debts with annual payments to British banks and corporations. The contract served to reinforce Peru's dependence on foreign capital, which was initially British and later North American.

The near collapse of Barings Bank of London in 1890 was the result of high-risk investments in Latin America. The potential crisis was averted by the intervention of other banks, but it called into question the solidity of British investment. In Peru this opened the doors to direct US and European finance in mining, rubber, export agriculture, textiles, and oil—the key sectors of the Peruvian economy that would prevail from 1900 onward. Small manufacturing grew in the last decade of the nineteenth century, but mainly in the areas of consumption, including food, drink, and tobacco, that had been recently abandoned by their European owners.

If we can speak of the post–Pacific War "recovery" of the Peruvian economy, it is only in the sense that the export sector expanded as foreign capital took on a dominant role. The discovery of copper deposits in the Central Valley led to the formation of the US-owned Cerro de Pasco Corporation in 1902. By 1914 the mines produced 35 percent of Peru's export income. In coastal agriculture, cotton and sugar displaced rice as three foreign corporations took control of production—Gildemeister (German), Larco (Peruvian but with British financial backing), and Catavia (owned by the British Grace Corporation). Their profitability rose with the introduction of advanced cultivation techniques, on the one hand, and on the other with the low wages paid to workers, who were largely recruited by force through the system of *enganche* (labor contracting). In Lima, the first factories produced textiles; the most emblematic, Vitarte, was founded in 1892 and was British-owned. The expansion of textile production was arrested after 1914 as an increasing proportion of the raw cotton produced in Peru was exported directly.

As Mariátegui would later describe it,[3] this was an economy dominated by foreign capital that benefited both from extraction of raw materials at low cost and the imports into the country that increased as production for the local market was replaced by the growing weight of exports. The state that oversaw the process, driven by civilismo, acted crudely as an agency for foreign capital and to control the capital; what lay beyond in the thousands of square kilometers of rain forest, of the high Andean sierra, remained outside their lines of sight. The regimes that prevailed there had their own dominant class, as Mariátegui would expose, although the first to criticize the inhumanity of their local systems were humanist liberals, the "friends of the Indian," to whom we shall return.

In the towns, the working populations in José Carlos's early years were almost entirely artisans. In the countryside the systems of tied labor, like the *yanaconaje*[4] or the enganche, both of which exploited indigenous peoples and communities, prevailed under the merciless hand of the *gamonales* and landowners. As the new century began, wage labor in mining was predominantly Indian, and the indigenous people continued to work their land, individually or collectively, for part of the year. The railways that Henry Meiggs had begun to construct through the Central Valley in the 1890s were largely built by Chinese and Black labor, though some small engineering workshops were beginning to appear in Lima. In the rain forest, the village of Iquitos grew from a population of two hundred in 1851 to twenty thousand in 1900 (and over a million today) as the rubber boom created its thirty-year fever, before the discovery of synthetic rubber halted it overnight.[5]

Perhaps this could be described as a beginning of modernization of Peru; but that would be a misinterpretation. Some modern technologies were introduced into some areas of export production. That is true. In Peru as elsewhere in Latin America, the railways began only to link export enclaves to ports. Lima and its neighboring port of Callao were growing—by 1910, as José Carlos was starting his first job, the capital's population of one hundred thousand represented about 5 percent of the total. Seven thousand of them could be considered workers.

Modernization as a process would imply a reordering of the relations of production, the global introduction of new and advanced technologies, the proletarianization of labor, and the emergence of a capitalist class with an economic strategy and a political plan to match. Mariátegui's key work, *Seven Interpretive Essays on Peruvian Reality*, asked: Can a modern and progressive economy rest on a combination of technological enclaves and "semi-feudal" systems of exploitation that rely on what is effectively slave labor? Even within the urban sector, the rising level of imports was in no sense reflected in a rising standard of living for the majority of the population. The imported goods were largely luxuries for the urban elite.

The changing face of Lima in the decade before José Carlos took his first job at *La Prensa* was most obvious in its working class. The early trade unions were mutualist organizations, self-help and cooperative institutions with a deeply conservative view of workers' associations; the first recognizable trade unions made their appearance in those artisan industries which were becoming industrialized and whose openness to anarcho-syndicalism was a sign of the failure of mutualism to address the new conditions of labor. The first union as such was built at the La Estrella del Peru bakery, and the bakers would continue to be a leading force well into the twenties. The shoemakers formed the first "revolutionary union" under Carlos Barba, who would figure largely in the events of 1919 and after. But it was in textiles, an industry that grew rapidly after the establishment of the Vitarte plant in 1892, that the early trade unions found their most combative base. Locally manufactured textiles went from 5 percent of the market in 1890 to 42 percent by 1905, though the recovery of the US cotton industry in the mid-1920s would dramatically reduce their share.[6]

Unlike Argentina and Brazil, where anarchism was carried over from Spain and Italy by the new immigrants, Peru did not experience mass European immigration; there was no economic expansion under way and still less any internal industrial development. And for the moment the indigenous population supplied sufficient cheap and indentured labor for the mines and the coastal haciendas.

The spread of anarchist ideas was due largely to the influence of one man—the aristocratic poet Manuel González Prada, whose seven years in Spain and Italy had won him to the anarchist cause. His fierce polemics were directed particularly at the church, and he was a sonorous voice in those liberal circles whose criticism of the treatment of the Indians was above all an attack on the landowning classes. At the turn of the century, González Prada was a powerful and authoritative presence and an inspiration to a younger generation growing restless under the domination of the unmoving civilista regime. He certainly had a major impact on the young printer's apprentice in Lima, who was also close to Prada's son with whom he worked, though Mariátegui would later temper his admiration with some criticisms, especially of the great poet's attitude to the indigenous peoples.

One commentator has made a distinction between the "brains" and the "belly" anarchists (cerebristas and pancistas); while the latter concentrated their efforts on building trade unions to address the material conditions of workers (anarcho-syndicalism), the former engaged in a cultural and ideological battle with the prevailing system to transform the consciousness of the laboring classes. It was a matter of emphasis rather than a clear alternative. González Prada's writings, and the newspaper he founded—Los Parias—belonged to the cultural and ideological project reflected in the creation of workers, cultural and educational organizations like the important Centro de Estudios Socialistas Primero de Mayo in Lima (1906–8) and the Love and Light (Amor y Luz) center in Callao (1911–19). The most influential anarchist journal, La Protesta, founded in the combative year of 1911, survived for fifteen years, despite several attempts to close it down.[7]

The presence of the pancistas, on the other hand, was marked by the publication of a series of papers written by and for workers in the different industries, like El Obrero Textil (1911),[8] founded in the year of Peru's first general strike, a high point of syndicalist mobilizations. The demands of the new unions were focused on wages, conditions, and especially on the battle for the eight-hour day (working days of twelve to sixteen hours were still commonplace). The strike was launched by a walkout of the five hundred workers of the Vitarte plant, and it was in some senses a success. The then president Augusto B. Leguía, in his first administration, passed the Law on Industrial Accidents in 1911, and two years later a law permitting strikes. The demand for the eight-hour workday would have to wait until 1919. It was these concessions to workers' demands that consolidated Leguía's reputation as a reformer and a modernizer within the Civilista Party which almost certainly won him his reelection in 1919.

By 1908, 17 percent of Lima's one hundred twenty-four thousand inhabitants were manual workers, as were a similar percentage of the fifty-two thousand inhabitants of the neighboring port of Callao.[9] But a high proportion worked in semi-artisan industries, small workplaces, or in transport and services.

The growth in the internal demand for local textiles and the consequent expansion of the industry, however, was not reflected in further industrialization. And the outbreak of the First World War reinforced Peru's position in the global economy as a supplier of minerals, raw materials, cotton, wool, and food products for export. As we have seen, these export enclaves were dominated and controlled by foreign (mainly US) capital and their local allies. Profits (and they were considerable) returned to the mother ship, and local capitalists reinvested abroad what was not spent on luxury imports.

By 1916, 48 percent of Peru's exports were the products of mining, principally copper—of which 93 percent went to the United States.[10] The world market price of the major export crops—rice, sugar, and cotton— rose, and the amount of land devoted to their cultivation expanded, at the expense of small farmers producing largely for the domestic market. The demand for labor was satisfied by the brutal enganche system, and wages reflected the intense exploitation to which the tied workers were subjected. In the cities, predictably, the scarcity of basic goods raised prices (including rents) with no corresponding increase in wages. According to Wilfredo Kapsoli, the cost of living rose from a base of

100 in 1913 to 210 in 1920—more than double.[11] The bulk of Peru's rice production, for example, was exported, and as more land was taken for export crops, land prices rose too.

In 1914 there was a tenants' strike in Lima in protest against rent hikes, and in 1916, a Committee for Lowering the Price of Basic Goods (Comité Pro-Abaratamiento de las Subsistencias), briefly formed to fight the rising cost of living for workers. These actions were expressions of the problems faced by a working class whose basic necessities were rising in price while its wages remained static.

In 1916, too, an Indian rising in Puno Province, under the leadership of a military officer who took the name of Rumi Maqui, initiated a new period of indigenous resistance against the deteriorating conditions of life in the highlands and the theft of lands and people by the war industries. As the war ended, the gravity of the postwar crisis became very quickly obvious.

Late in December 1918, twenty-nine hundred textile workers walked out in support of the campaign for the eight-hour day. In January the bakers joined them, and they were followed by most of the capital's unions. What now became a general strike was met with repression, but in the end won its demand—though the implementation of the legislation would not happen until much later in the year. But despite the repression, it had served to reawaken the trade union movement. Although Lima now had a number of factories—producing textiles, leather, tobacco, food, and drink—as well as the first railway (built by Henry Meiggs in the Central Valley) and the active docks at Callao, its industrial workforce barely reached seven thousand. It was a proletariat, but a very young one.

Faced with dramatic price increases and a fall in production, in April a meeting in the Neptune Park neighborhood of the city agreed to the formation of a new Committee for Lowering the Price of Basic Goods. A mass meeting on May 1 declared a general strike, which was violently repressed, and its leaders, three key anarchist trade unionists—Carlos Barba (of the shoemakers), Adalberto Fonkén (from Vitarte) and Nicolás Gutarra (a cabinet maker)—were arrested and jailed. But by then the movement had spread across the working class of Lima and Callao, as Ricardo Martínez de la Torre attests, and the general strike was renewed on May 27.

The city has become a barracks. The banks are under guard. The markets attempt to open under the same praetorian vigilance. The Plaza de Armas is surrounded by machine guns at every corner. President Pardo has turned his palace into a fortress. The unarmed workers have terrified him. He declares martial law.[12]

The dying government of Pardo responded with repression. But his party itself was split between the old criollo elite and a new, allegedly "modernizing," capitalist element represented by Augusto B. Leguía, the ex-president who had conceded workers' demands in 1911 and who was at that point outside the country.

César Miró, the poet, writing about another demonstration in 1923, recalls the atmosphere of those days:

> Like today, the strikes would be joined by railwaymen, printworkers, textile workers, coachmen, bakers, tram drivers. Even then, a few weeks before the fall of the last civilista government . . . there were red flags held high, but I don't recall seeing the hammer and sickle and there were no delegations there from the land. It is true that the social unrest of the May events had only very weak echoes in the rest of the country; nobody spoke for the peasants. It was the hammer without the sickle. . . . Among the crowd of students and artisans there was nothing to signal their presence. There were no communist symbols to support the protest or to give it a solid foundation. The leader of the Russian revolution would not die until the following year, yet I saw no portraits of Lenin. So, though this episode was undoubtedly part of the history of social struggles, its anarchist inspiration was unquestionable.[13]

New strikes brought further repression, but it had become "a rebellion of the masses" as César Miró put it. In a new election, early in July, Leguía, presenting himself as a defender of working-class demands and a modernizer, was elected and took power immediately by a military coup. The strike leaders were then released from prison, and Leguía granted the eight-hour day for state employees—though implementation proved to be very slow. Repression followed quickly, however.

The release of the three trade union leaders produced a massive workers' demonstration through the streets of Lima. It marched first to the offices of a small, recently established newspaper called *La Razon*, whose explicit purpose was to show solidarity and give support to the workers' movement. Its editors were José Carlos Mariátegui and his close companion César Falcón. They were carried shoulder high through the streets by the marchers.

The Political Evolution of Juan Croniqueur

Very soon after arriving at *La Prensa*, José Carlos's friend Juan Manuel Campos took him to meet Manuel González Prada, already a highly respected if slightly overpowering intellectual. He certainly read *Los Parias* and *La Protesta*, the two main anarchist newspapers, and attended sessions of the anarchist cultural circles.[14] Like most of his generation, he could not fail to be impressed by this fierce, aristocratic writer, by his wide culture, and by his high-minded rebellion. González Prada was the maestro to a generation, which was how Mariátegui addressed him in his interviews for the magazine *Mundial*.[15] A radical and a positivist, González Prada had turned against his own class in the wake of the Pacific War. He had fled to Europe and returned with an admiration for anarchist ideas. He mercilessly criticized the writers and intellectuals of his generation and his class for their elitism, and for their adherence to an empty colonial culture that could represent only their own outmoded and conservative vision of Peru, a vision sustained by the politics of civilismo (to which Prada had once belonged), a reactionary university, and a deeply conservative Catholic church.

González Prada's speech at the Politeama Theatre in 1888 was a key moment in the political crisis of civilismo, placing indigenous Peru for the first time at the heart of the national debate. The real Peru, he asserted, is not the creoles and foreigners who inhabit the strip of land between the Pacific and the Andes, but the Indian masses who live among the eastern mountains.[16] In its moment this was a radical declaration, and it echoed the liberal humanism of the Indigenistas, the group of writers and artists who for the first time acknowledged the Peru of the Indian and described their exploitation by the landowners. Its most famous expression was a novel by Clorinda Matto de Turner, *Aves sin nido* (Birds without a nest, 1887), a love story that humanized the Indians and lamented their mistreatment. González Prada echoed the denunciation, but he was not in any real sense, as Mariátegui stressed in *Seven Essays*, a political thinker; he left no political manifestos for the generation of young students he influenced, yet "he represents the first moment of lucidity of Peruvian consciousness."[17]

It is clear that González Prada had a considerable impact on this young writer; but José Carlos was also uneasy about his virulent hostility to religion. It is not that the young man was a practicing Catholic, but religiosity became a constant theme in his writings, particularly popular religion, as a vehicle for a cultural and artistic experience and as an expression of the yearnings of working people. The church had successfully absorbed many aspects of popular religion during the Colonial period;[18] it was a key to its dominion, but at the same time it conserved (and even protected) elements of popular consciousness and of what he would later describe as *mito*.[19]

Nevertheless, there was much to learn from González Prada. He was a poet in the mold of Latin American "modernismo," which found inspiration in French Romanticism and later in the schools of "art for art's sake," like Parnassianism, which emphasized the separation of art and life. Hence the reference in the name of this movement initiated by the French poet Théophile Gautier to classical perfection. González Prada was a writer of ferocious political polemics that sometimes, according to José Carlos, strayed into excessive rhetoric. The younger man's writing, by contrast, would carefully avoid bombast, therefore following Prada's advice, rather than his practice, that the greatest masterpieces were democratic and accessible to the masses (he mentions Homer and Cervantes). Perhaps another influence on Mariátegui's lucid and clear style was his experience as a proofreader on *La Prensa*.[20]

The same disenchantment informed his accounts of the Peruvian parliament and of the *behavior* of politicians. He had learned from Prada to be suspicious of academics who represented the conservative neocolonial culture that Prada had attacked so mercilessly. That is why, much later, Mariátegui would describe himself not just as "self-taught" but as "anti-academic."

But Juan Croniqueur, as his biographer Guillermo Rouillon describes the young Mariátegui's alter ego, led a kind of double life.[21] At

La Prensa he met Abraham Valdelomar, the leading avant-garde poet of Lima at the time, and became part of his *Colónida* circle. As a group they took their lead from the decadents, the European poets of the fin de siècle whose defining tone was a weariness, an ennui that was not simply fatigue but a disenchantment with the world. Its leading poet was Baudelaire, though the world in reverse created by Huysmans in his novel *A rebours* (Against nature, 1884), was a powerful metaphor for the rejection of a bourgeois universe. The poets' world was bounded by the Jirón de la Unión that linked Lima's Plaza San Marcos to the Plaza de Armas. Valdelomar had famously quipped, "Lima is the Jirón de la Unión and the Jirón de la Unión is the Palais Concert." The Palais Concert was a famous café where the Bohemians and artists gathered, Juan Croniqueur among them. José Carlos recalled one afternoon in particular:

> One afternoon in the Palais Concert, Valdelomar said to me "the light fine glowworm is here referred to as a needle pusher." I was as decadent as he was in those days, and I pressed him to defend the noble and disregarded rights of the glowworm. He asked the waiter for paper and he wrote one of his "maximal dialogues" amid the mellifluous noise of the café. His humour was like that—innocent, childlike, lyrical.[22]

The *Colónida* rebellion, of which Mariátegui was part, revealed the existence of

> a group of intellectuals who from a literary point of view, amid the frivolity and posing and the seriousness of their aesthetic proposals, was questioning the established order. For the first time there was a group of artists and writers who were political within their own sphere, legitimizing the specificity of their spaces and from there challenging the politicians and the state. And all this without ever leaving the mirrored walls of the Palais Concert.[23]

These were the years of formation of the new avant-garde—José María Eguren would publish his *Simbólicas* in 1911, and César Vallejo his *Trilce*, a signpost of Modernism in Peru, in 1922.

Today Jirón de la Unión is a rather-shabby pedestrianized street for tourists, but it still bears the marks of its turn-of-the-century elegance (if you look up). It was a symbolic space as well as a physical one, in whose cafés the bored young scions of Lima's aristocracy would meet to write and talk. José Carlos, of course, came from a very different background; he had been brought up in poverty, and his accident had in some senses robbed him of his childhood.

As a young man, Juan Croniqueur, aka José Carlos, wrote poetry full of melancholy; his first volume of poetry was called *Tristeza* (Sadness). But his sadness had a deeper root than the stylish tedium of his avant-garde circle. He had missed an education (though he had almost certainly a much richer and more extensive culture than his upper-class companions who had attended university), and he would have found difficulty financing his studies on an apprentice's salary. He had a permanent limp and was almost certainly in pain for much of the time. He wrote at least two plays with Valdelomar,[24] though neither seems to have been performed. And he was a participant in one of Peru's most notorious avant-garde scandals, when his group of Bohemians organized a performance by the Swiss ballerina Norka Rouskaya in the main cemetery of Lima, where she interpreted Chopin's "Danse Funebre" at midnight.[25] The horrified traditionalists demanded, and received, an explanation of the event from Mariátegui. Looking back, he analyzed the significance of the group. The oddness, the aggressiveness, the injustice, and even the extravagance of the Colónidos (the members of the group) were useful. They played a renovating role. They shook up the national literary world, which they denounced as vulgar rhapsody to the most mediocre Spanish literature. They proposed new and better models, new and better directions. They attacked their fetishes, their icons. They set in motion what some writers have described as "a revision of our literary values." *Colónida* was a negative, dissolving, belligerent force, a spiritual gesture by a group of writers who opposed the dominant national celebrity of an "outmoded and pretentious official art."[26]

This assessment, written nine years after Valdelomar's accidental death and twelve years after the famous funeral dance, underlines a key element of Mariátegui's thinking about the relationship between an artistic and a political vanguard; we will return to it in the chapter on art and politics. The iconoclasm of these young bohemians anticipated the more self-conscious avant-garde movements; *Colónida* did not offer a manifesto, as the surrealists did, nor did they see their work as in any sense "political." Yet they were, for Mariátegui, rebellious iconoclasts, dissident members of their class, anti-bourgeois pursuing new artistic directions, new imaginative expressions that would be, perhaps, artistic anticipations of a new reality. And in that sense, these bohemians and their literature form part of a continuity, a body of critical responses, albeit individualistic, negative, and belligerent. They might well have been influenced more by Schopenhauer than by Marx or even Bakunin, but they were signs of the dismantling of bourgeois culture.

Juan Croniqueur, however, was still young and impressionable. After all, he was a boy from a poor home moving around the edges of aristocratic social and artistic circles. Rouillon and others attest that he dressed with careful elegance, as befitted someone who wrote for (and edited) the horse racing journal *Turf* and wrote *crónicas* for the fashionable *Lulu*. At the same time, however, his participation in anarchist cultural and political circles brought him into direct contact with the trade unions, dominated as they were by anarcho-syndicalism, and his political education began there.[27] In 1918, he founded the newspaper *Nuestra Epoca* (Our times) together with his close friend and collaborator César Falcón. Two years earlier, after *La Prensa* changed its editor, he left and moved to *El Tiempo,* a newspaper that supported Leguía's criticisms of Pardo. José Carlos was its parliamentary correspondent, and he wrote the column "Voces" (Voices), which offered direct political commentary.

Mariátegui's writings at this stage show a young man drawn in several directions; he described himself then as "a young man, part mystic part sensual." His poetry expressed the sensual side, his articles the acute cultural observer. In political terms his future direction was not yet clear, which may be why his early writings have been largely ignored by those mainly concerned with his Marxism.[28] Yet without exploring the ideas and attitudes that shaped this early part of his life, it is far harder to understand his complex and creative interpretation of Marxism. Although the search for "epistemological breaks" is something of a hobby for many writers, the reality is that there is continuity throughout his body of work—as he put it, "I did not change, I matured." Anarchism was a major influence, in particular in its attitude to education, to morality, and in its consistent discussion of the role of women—all of which is reflected in José Carlos's work. But the issue that had separated him from both González Prada and the anarchist tradition was religion, or more precisely *religiosity*. In 1917 Mariátegui withdrew to a retreat, where he wrote "Elogio," which addressed "the weariness that prevented him from acting" that he had complained of in an earlier poem:

> *A disdain for life, a vague unease*
> *Facing the certainty that I must die*
> *And although my youth has borne no fruit*
> *Great sorrow, deep sorrow, at the thought that I must leave*[29]

We will return to his understanding of religion, and specifically to popular religion as embodying the mito, the premonitory vision embedded in popular culture, in looking at his Marxism, but it is clear that he still considered himself a Catholic, albeit one critical of the institution of the church. He identified more with the popular Catholicism he described in his article on the procession of "El señor de los Milagros"; in these cultural rituals he found expressions of the yearning for another world and the critique of the dominant reason, which in a different form he had identified in the work of his comrades in *Colónida*. But where one was the product of an individual imagination, the other expressed a collective imagination and a shared history.

There is some dispute as to whether José Carlos already considered himself a socialist.[30] He certainly attended a socialist discussion circle at *El Tiempo*, until the editors objected and closed it down. In 1918, a colleague named Bianchi gave him books by Sorel and Labriola—both had a significant influence on his work. On the other hand, it is also the case that there was no socialist tradition in Peru, as there clearly was in Argentina by then. As he puts it in his lecture *History of the World Crisis*:

> It is rather outdated socialist, syndicalist, and libertarian books that circulate amongst us. We know a little of the classic literature of socialism and syndicalism, but the new revolutionary literature is not known here.[31]

Nuestra Época, which Mariátegui and Falcón began to publish in 1918, "did not carry a socialist program, but ideologically and propagandistically it pointed in that direction."[32] It reflected José Carlos's commitment to a kind of journalism he had discussed with González Prada (who died in 1918) and presumably with González Prada's son Alfredo, who was a close friend and a fellow member of *Colónida*. Journalism should be more than simply information, he would later argue; it should also offer analysis and direction. *Nuestra Época* emerged at a time of increasing working-class activity and of a deepening discontent with Pardo's civilista regime; the crisis that developed with the end of the First World War had intensified both. But *Nuestra Época* was not destined to last. Mariátegui's anti-militarist article entitled "Negative Tendencies: The Duty of the Army and the Duty of the State" infuriated the military, who attacked the paper's offices. One officer challenged Mariátegui to a duel. José Carlos was briefly detained, and *El Tiempo*, on whose presses the paper had been printed, locked them out. Early the following year, and in the context of the rising confrontations of early 1919, the two editors founded another paper, *La Razón*, this time explicitly socialist and committed to supporting the working-class movement.

The march of workers through Lima's streets, carrying Mariátegui shoulder high, was evidence enough of the impact of *La Razón* and of the reputation that the young journalist and activist had earned for himself. Juan Croniqueur was a persona created by José Carlos to win himself a place in the artistic and literary circles of Lima, but something changed in this transition year. His own writing about art had led him inexorably to a conclusion about the limitations of the bohemian protest against the poverty of bourgeois intellectual life, its "elitism and aristocratic spirit." For a while Juan Croniqueur joined the group of dandies at the Palais Concert, but he was also part of a more political circle, the anarchist centers, which were by and large hostile to the clientele of the Palais Concert, most of whom were members of the criollo upper class. They would have seemed frivolous and superficial, and despite Mariátegui's conviction that they were rebels with a cause, remote and uninterested in the activities of the workers.

The Russian Revolution posed an unavoidable challenge to a young man whose background and developing political views drove him to question the limitations of the Bohemian circles, though he never abandoned the idea that their challenge to the values of the old order was both legitimate and significant. *Nuestra Época* and *La Razón* marked an important crossroads in his life, stimulated by critical external events. At the newspaper, news began to arrive in late October 1917 of the Russian Revolution and its enormous significance. His anarchist comrades would have celebrated the fall of tsarism but were, from the outset, suspicious of and hostile to the Bolsheviks who were leading the revolution. One writer dismissed Marxism in the anarchist press as "a false redemptive theory," and as it did everywhere, the October Revolution sparked often-bitter controversy within the Left. But the fact that Mariátegui placed his socialist credentials on the masthead of *La Razón* was a signal of his evolving ideas.

The second major event of the times beyond Peru was the university reform movement, La Reforma, which began in 1918 at the University of Córdoba in Argentina. The development of a modern capitalist economy in Argentina had produced a new middle class not linked to the old ruling groups, and a working class that had begun to organize and agitate for improvements. The election of Hipólito Yrigoyen and his radical party to power in 1916 marked a historic crossroads, and the entry of new social forces on to the historical stage. La Reforma was the expression of demands from the same forces for access to the universities but also for their transformation. It was not only a matter of their mode of governance, which was to include teachers, students, and workers; it was also, critically, a matter of the *content* of higher education, which the movement argued should reflect the modern world and the experience of these new layers of the population. It was to be modern, national, and democratic.

In the radical environment of the early 1920s, people's universities, run by students and radical intellectuals, mounted their challenge to the old intellectual order. It was significant, for example, as César Miró had noted, that workers' protests were now joined by students. In Peru, the new student movement found its first base in Cuzco before joining the postwar agitation and founding the first workers' university in Lima as an expression of a new concept of popular education. It was called the Universidad Popular Manuel González Prada, and Mariátegui would deliver a series of lectures there in 1923.

The impact of La Reforma was immediate and dramatic, spreading its demands across the region and sending delegates from Argentina to encourage the formation of a new democratic university. The mass universities of Latin America—the National Autonomous University of Mexico and the Central University of Caracas in Venezuela, for example—are products of that movement. The University of San Marcos in Lima today has a student population that is clearly of working- and lower-middle-class origins; its original campus in the city center bears all the hallmarks of the elite institution it once was.

On July 4, 1919, Augusto B. Leguía was elected to the presidency, but decided not to wait for the diplomatic niceties, and took power in a military coup. It was the end of Pardo and civilismo. Leguía was still seen as a modernizer, and he immediately conceded the key demand of an eight-hour day. Its implementation, however, took far longer than its announcement. In September *La Prensa* was closed; more significantly, *La Razón*, like its predecessors, only reached its second edition. It was printed at the presses of the Archbishopric of Lima, which refused to allow it to continue.

Yet, in 1920, Leguía still claimed a modernizing role and raised no objection when the Universidad Popular Manuel González Prada was set up by radical students to offer an alternative education for workers. Its organizer was Victor Raúl Haya de la Torre, a radical student leader from Cuzco who would become a key figure in Peruvian politics; he represented, through much of the twenties at least, a rival point of reference to Mariátegui.

In October of 1919, Mariátegui and Falcón left for their "fact finding mission" in Europe.

It would be a journey both physical and ideological, from which Mariátegui would return, in his own words, a convinced and committed Marxist—*un marxista convicto y confeso.*

Chapter Three

The Discovery of Marxism: Mariátegui in Europe

Mariátegui had left Peru with an established reputation within the country's working-class movement, an important body of journalistic work, and some knowledge of Marxism. His trip to Europe clearly had one purpose: the development and deepening of his understanding of Marxism. Having spent a little time in France, he went on to Italy where, as he later put it, he "acquired a wife and some ideas." He was present at the founding conference of the Italian Communist Party at Livorno in 1921 and learned much of his Marxism during this period. Through the prism of the Italy of the factory occupations as well as of Benedetto Croce and Piero Gobetti, Mariátegui participated in the great debates that absorbed the socialist movement in the wake of 1917. In that debate, Marxism was first and foremost the ideology of the Bolshevik Revolution and its application to other processes.

Mariátegui arrived in Italy just after after the Turin factory occupations; his articles and essays reflect his immersion in the debates around hegemony that arose in their wake. In Italy, he saw firsthand how the political weakness of the bourgeoisie and the vacillations of reformism could permit the emergence of fascism. And while he followed closely the debates among Marxists of the early 1920s, he insisted that these must be interpreted in the context of the specific conditions of Peru and Latin America. That interpretation in its turn would add new dimensions to Marxism itself.

His articles from Europe were published regularly in *El Tiempo* and the magazine *Mundial,* and later republished as *Letters from Italy.* As always, he covered a range of issues in Italian literature, art, architecture, and history in his articles, thereby illustrating a common thread in his discussions of art and politics—and particularly the question of the artistic avant-garde. His brush with Italian Futurism, and his criticism of it, connected back to his discussions about the *Colónida* group and forward to the ongoing debate on art and politics in *Amauta.*

The European years were an intense Marxist apprenticeship for José Carlos, both as a revolutionary politics and as a revolutionary theory. Though the early writings of Korsch, Lukács, and Gramsci only became available later, we know that Mariátegui was reading Marx, Lenin, and Sorel, and that he was influenced by what Michael Löwy describes as "revolutionary romanticism," the conviction that the transformation of human beings occurs through an engagement with the real, informed by a vision of the future. This controversial idea, derived from Sorel, of "the revolutionary myth," will be discussed in this chapter. These were the central themes in the lectures and classes on the world situation that Mariátegui gave at the Universidad Popular after his return to Peru and in a subsequent series of articles in various newspapers in 1923–4. They were published later under the titles *History of the World Crisis* and *Figures and Aspects of International Life.*

A great deal has been written about the various influences on Mariátegui's Marxism, and his voracious reading and reviewing of a wide range of European writers has encouraged that. The key point is that his contemporary writings show a clear recognition of the world-historical significance of the 1917 Bolshevik Revolution and an admiration for Lenin; a dedicated reading of current Marxist debates; and, simultaneously, a consistent reflection on his own reality from the perspective of the international situation. That internationalism is a defining feature of his thought despite the regular accusations leveled against him of evolving a "national Marxism."

He returned from Europe in 1923 a "convinced and committed Marxist" with a developed critique of the Second International's version of Marxism. He demonstrated what this meant in the activities that absorbed the remaining six and half years of his life. It meant, firstly, an active role in the building of a nascent working-class movement; secondly, the publication of *Amauta*, a magazine that would provide a platform for political debate between all the currents of thought within the socialist movement in Peru and beyond; and thirdly, the working out of the key ideas that would inform his work as a trade union and party organizer in the late 1920s and bring him into conflict with the Comintern.

Mariátegui and Falcón boarded ship for New York on October 11, 1919. It was a dramatic year for them. The experience of *La Razón* had brought them directly into the orbit of socialist ideas, possibly with the significant influence of the "Bolshevik" minister Victor Maúrtua, who owned the paper. The two young men had formed a Committee for Socialist Propaganda, which supported the paper, and they had moved from commenting on the working-class movement to becoming participants and activists within it. They were meeting regularly with the anarchist union leaders Adalberto Fonkén, Nicolás Gutarra, and Carlos Barba, all of whom were jailed at the beginning of the May general strike. Their release in July by the newly installed government of Leguía motivated the march through the streets on July 7. Although Leguía initially granted some of the workers' demands, creating an impression among some of the anarchist leaders that he might prove to be a friend of the workers, within weeks he was arresting and jailing strikers. His 1920 constitution showed the direction his government was taking, with its imposition of compulsory arbitration and a generally corporate vision of the role of the state.

And there was a decline in trade union militancy, but not because of any improvement in living standards or the availability of jobs; in fact, the postwar crisis deepened quickly. Perhaps the reasons were ideological rather than economic, in that Leguía had successfully sown confusion in the ranks of the militants. The debate within the incipient workers' movement about the Russian Revolution created further divisions. As articles in anarchist newspaper *La Protesta* made clear, the anarchists favored the overthrow of tsarism but were extremely hostile to the Bolsheviks and the new Soviet regime. The regular order of *La Protesta* at the key Vitarte plant, for example, was canceled in 1918 at the suggestion of Haya de la Torre, whose influence had spread from the student movement in Cuzco to the workers' movement in Lima, where he had enrolled in the University of San Marcos. The dominant current in the trade union movement was anarchism. Haya de la Torre represented the ideas of the university reform movement that had begun in 1918, whose Argentine founder Alfredo Palacios, a socialist, had visited Peru. The reform movement emphasized that it was a political movement in which the alliance of students and workers was a central concept. Haya won a hearing in the workers' movement by mobilizing students in support of the strikes of 1919.

While information from Russia was generally slow to reach Peru, part of Mariátegui's job at *El Tiempo* had been to read the foreign cables, and he was certainly aware of the impact of the revolution and enthused by it. By the same token, the consequences of war must have seemed remote until he reached Europe.

It was José Carlos Mariátegui, journalist, socialist, agitator, who boarded the ship. Juan Croniqueur disappeared, together with what José Carlos had described, unfairly to himself, as his stone age. He would later resist republication of the eight hundred or so pieces he had written in his hyperactive years.[1] Yet they contain not just the record of a young man's personal transformation, but also a range of thematic lines that would recur and evolve in his equally prolific last decade. His involvement in the workers' movement in Lima-Callao involved broader forces than the trade unions, which remained very small, though they were very active. The Committee for Lowering the Price of Basic Goods, for example, drew in the poor communities of the city and some of the recent indigenous immigrants too. The Rumi Maqui revolt in the remote Andean province of Puno reminded some of the long and courageous history of indigenous resistance, and although he was only able to travel once to the conflictive Mantaro Valley near Jauja, in 1918 with Martínez de la Torre, the role of indigenous communities in the socialist movement became central to his thinking from that point on.

In 1919, in New York, Mariátegui and Falcón met and spoke with striking dockers and experienced "a boundless sense of liberty." From there they sailed to Paris and to a meeting with Henri Barbusse and some surrealist poets, among others. They also found a socialist movement divided by the repercussions of 1917, locked in the debate about affiliation to the Third International that was taking place throughout Europe. With the victory of the October Revolution in 1917, the nature of Marxism as a revolutionary idea became the central debate among socialists. October was both the proof that workers' revolution was possible and a model of how to achieve it. The Comintern called for the creation of communist parties that would break with the old, gradualist socialism of the Second International and, in turn, create a network of support for the besieged new Soviet state. In France, the debate produced a majority for the Communist International, and the Communist Party was formed with one hundred thirty thousand original members. It was in Paris that news reached Mariátegui of the birth of his daughter, Gloria, mothered by Victoria Ferrer, the daughter of a typographer whom José Carlos met in 1918. By early 1919 they were living together in the La Victoria area of the city. She was eight months pregnant when he was sent out of the country. He and Victoria remained in contact throughout his life, and he supported her financially; his daughter became a regular visitor at the house in Washington Izquierda.

In December 1919, José Carlos moved on to Italy, while Falcón went his own way to Spain. In Italy José Carlos found a society in a state of high agitation and a Left that was repeating the great debates he had heard in France. As Rouillon says, "Mariátegui was experiencing an extraordinary and accelerated evolution of his socialist ideas."[2] In the following two years, Mariátegui spent the majority of his time in Italy where he was correspondent for the new *El Tiempo*. In a brief autobiography sent in response to a press inquiry in 1927, he explained, "For more than two years I lived in Italy where I found a wife (Ana Chiappe) and some ideas." At the beginning of 1923, he traveled to Germany, to Belgium, and to France en route to Peru; the illness of his wife and his newborn son prevented him from going to Moscow.

In Revolutionary Italy

It was Italy that provided the intense course in Marxism and socialist politics that would shape him definitively. Mariátegui arrived in Genoa in December 1919. It was the end of the first of Italy's Two Red Years or *Biennio Rosso*, when Italy, and in particular the industrial north of the country, lived through its most intense revolutionary moment.[3] The industrial triangle that embraced Turin, Milan, and Genoa was home to its engineering and automotive industry. The First World War had transformed the area into an engine of dramatic capitalist growth, dominated by the Fiat factories in Turin. Half a million workers lived and worked in the city, many of them recent immigrants from a very different rural Italy.

Italy entered the war in 1915. The importance of the war industries meant that many workers were exempted from military service; its soldiers were overwhelmingly recruited from the peasant population. This reflected the reality of a country whose advanced capitalist sector contrasted dramatically with a rural society where the peasantry (still the majority population) lived in dire poverty, in conditions that were often described as semi-feudal, dependent on local landholders, and where landless laborers still survived outside the wages system. In 1916, levels of protest were rising in the countryside, as food prices rose and poverty deepened. In 1917, the opposition to war was growing as the wounded returned to find their families suffering and bereft. In the industrial north, news of the October Revolution was received with excitement; a meeting addressed by delegates from the Petrograd Soviet turned into an anti-war protest numbering forty thousand. In August of that year, a general strike was met with brute force; fifty thousand troops put down the strike, leaving one hundred dead and eight hundred injured. The government then placed the whole of the northern region under military control, ensuring the hostility of both rural and urban populations whose protests against rising prices and shortages had spread from Genoa. The end of the war, in November 1918, produced new protests as the weary and disillusioned troops returned to scarcity, hunger, and the ravages of Spanish flu, which had first arisen in the German prisoner-of-war camps. There was rioting in Genoa, and land seizures throughout the country; both were severely repressed. Then in April 1919, five hundred thousand people joined a general strike called by the official internal commissions within the factories, which were under pressure from their own rank and file.

In the following month, two young leaders of the Socialist Party, Angelo Tasca and Antonio Gramsci, began the publication of the newspaper *Ordine Nuovo* (New order). The paper campaigned for the internal factory commissions to be replaced by factory councils elected directly by workers; they were modeled on the Russian soviets and on the new shop stewards' movement that had emerged in Britain during the course of the war. The newspaper was well received in the working class of Turin. The national General Confederation of Labour, CGL, had grown to a membership of two million. The metalworkers' union, Metallurgical Workers Employees Federation (Federazione Impiegati Operai Metallurgici, FIOM), had one hundred thirty-six thousand members. These central events formed the background to Mariátegui's intense political learning experience, and *Ordine Nuovo* would later provide a precedent for his influential journal *Amauta*.

Confindustria, the bosses' organization, reduced the levels of production when the war ended in order to divert their huge wartime profits into financial speculation, but it also watched and waited as the level of grassroots agitation grew in numbers and intensity. They even accepted the eight-hour day. But the immediate beneficiary was the Italian Socialist Party (PSI), which in the elections in November of that year won 32 percent of the popular vote and 156 parliamentary seats. The Popular Party, a social-christian organization silently backed by the Vatican, whose base was predominantly rural, won 20 percent and 100 seats.

Yet when the factory occupations began again in Genoa, Naples, and Turin, the PSI did not react. *Ordine Nuovo*, by contrast, hailed the occupations as a new and potentially revolutionary moment in the class struggle. The factory councils that ran them were indeed the most advanced expression of socialist democracy in Europe at that moment. And their actions coincided with increasingly militant protests outside the cities. But they only *coincided*; they were not linked organizationally or politically, for the potential political leadership of the PSI, which contained reformist and revolutionary wings, denied them its support or direction. In March 1920, Edoardo Agnelli, the owner of Fiat, picked a fight over a trivial issue (to do with the method of clocking in) and then locked out his workers. The factory was occupied; after two weeks the occupation was resolved by a series of concessions, but when the employers demanded the dismantling of the factory councils, a general strike was called in their defense. The Fiat tactic was repeated by Alfa Romeo in Rome, with the same response. It felt very much as if two kinds of power were confronting each other in Italy. In that situation Gramsci called for the formation of a communist party. Within the PSI there had been support for Gramsci's position, but it was rejected, resulting in a victory for the reformists and a defeat for the young revolutionaries who were successfully isolated by the party leadership.

The reality is that the PSI's refusal to act, and the marginalization of *Ordine Nuovo*, ensured that the revolutionary opportunity of April and May would be lost. It was an extraordinary moment, or it could have been. But instead of building a politics combining the demands of peasants and workers, as the Bolsheviks had successfully done in Russia, the PSI chose to treat the division between country and city as "natural" and structural. In September five hundred thousand workers occupied their factories, led by the rank-and-file factory commissions now under almost entirely anarchist leadership, whose scorn for the socialists' parliamentary cretinism had presumably gained them a great deal of credibility and enabled them to "scoop up popular disappointment and frustration."[4] This prompted Lenin's famous, but rather unfair question, "Was there not a single communist in the occupations?" The reaction, of the PSI and the CGL confirmed their prejudices; the official organizations were more frightened by this mass militancy and the emergence of a new kind of power from below than by the actions of the state. Their concerns above all were control and the assurance of the 156 parliamentary seats they had won in the previous year.

Against that background, the factories returned to work in September 1920. *Ordine Nuovo* had fallen apart, as both Palmiro Togliatti and Tasca had broken away to form a left wing within the maximalists and to devote their energies to a workers' campaign against sending troops to Albania.

In January of 1921, the PSI congress met at the Tuscan port of Livorno. Mariátegui was in attendance as a correspondent for *El Tiempo*. The conference was historic. Its various factions ranged between right-wing reformists, centrists, and the so-called "maximalists," led by Bordiga, who, in response to the pressure from the Comintern, were arguing for the creation of a communist party. Gramsci had advocated its creation a year earlier, but in the very different circumstances of the factory occupations, when *Ordine Nuovo* enjoyed real authority among the revolutionary workers. The group had never had the support of either wing of the PSI, however. The reformist leadership was more concerned, as Mariátegui would later put it, with the restoration of "normality," while Bordiga, the leader of the "maximalists," took an abstentionist position. In reality both were standing back from the struggle. By the time of Livorno, Gramsci was "an isolated and marginal figure."[5] The maximalists split from the party to form the PCI (Communist Party of Italy). Gramsci had little role to play, and he did not speak at the conference, much to Mariátegui's surprise.

Mariátegui's time in Italy was seminal in his development as a socialist and a Marxist. Yet curiously there was little in his early writing as Juan Croniqueur to suggest any specific interest in Italy. The exception was a fascination with the Romantic reactionary Gabriele D'Annunzio. He was probably introduced to the poet by his friend and colleague at *Colónida*, Abraham Valdelomar, who had spent a year in Italy and met D'Annunzio there. While the extravagance of D'Annunzio did not connect very directly with a Mariátegui still locked in his melancholy, decadent moment, he did resonate later with the Peruvian's increasing fascination with "men of action." This vision of D'Annunzio corresponded to the image of a soldier of fortune, a *condottiero*, seizing Fiume in the name of the Italian nation. It would make him a hero of the fascist movement, but it would seem that it was only in Italy that José Carlos understood the connection and changed his views. What might have seemed at a distance like epic adventurism looked very different in the face of the realities of the First World War.

> D'Annunzio's adventure, for example, stripped of its lyrical qualities, is clearly the adventure of a reactionary and militarist mentality. It amounts to a rebellion of the military power against the civil power."[6]

Mariátegui was clearly surprised by what he encountered in Italy, politically and culturally. The *Letters from Italy* (Cartas de Italia), a collection of his brief dispatches to Lima, are descriptive yet restrained. The real analysis of his trip and its implications came later, in his lectures to the Universidad Popular and the articles in *The contemporary scene* (*La escena contemporánea*). He was an avid reader of the Italian press, and especially the official paper of the PSI *Avanti!* and of Gramsci's *Ordine Nuovo*. Rouillon and others stress that he was writing less because he was reading and studying—and there is no doubt about the intensity of his learning process.

He arrived in a Europe still dealing with the ravages of war and the repercussions of the first socialist revolution. For Mariátegui it was a logical decision to go to Italy, the European country that was experiencing a revolutionary upsurge and in which the social and economic conditions bore some close resemblance to Russia—a modern and burgeoning capitalist sector with large concentrations of workers coexisting with a rural world where precapitalist relations still prevailed. A year earlier he might perhaps have gone to Germany.

There is a very moving article in *Letters from Italy* that powerfully expresses his response to the impact of war in Italy. "The House of the War Blind" describes a grand house near where he was living in Rome that was a center for the war blind:

> People will generally only know the optimistic version of the tragedy of these blind men, a version created for universal consumption. . . . This version says that the war blind are a legion of glorious invalids, proud of their medals, ribbons and decorations, at ease with their sacrifice, proud of their victories and resigned to their unfortunate fate. . . . But they surely will not even remember that they are heroic sons of their country and of civilisation. And just as they don't care about the view over Rome, or the spring or the Tusculum or Cicero they're not interested in their glory or its merits. No literature can console them. The scenario painted for the tourists doesn't exist for them. The vision that they retain in their useless eyes is the vision of the terrible trenches.[7]

In political terms he describes, very acutely, the situation of an Italian socialism that summarized many of the contradictions of Second International Marxism. If he expected to find a postwar return to Marxism there, he was deeply disappointed. It was, in a real sense, the first casualty. Its mechanical interpretation of Marx, and the assurance that socialism would emerge from the process of capitalist development itself, lay under the ruins of Ypres and Paeschendale. Italy showed very clearly that war was a time of bonanza for the wealthy, as the Italian engineering industry multiplied its profits ten times over. At the same time, news must have reached him as soon as he arrived in Genoa of the food riots and violent confrontations on the land in northern Italy. From Genoa he moved straight to Turin to meet with the PSI. What he found must have generated further confusion. The PSI had adopted an ambivalent position at the start of the war, neither collaborationist nor abstentionist. Benito Mussolini, one of its leaders and the editor of its newspaper, had pressed for involvement, arguing that intervention in the war would "accelerate the revolutionary process." The end of the war "was a revolutionary and socialist moment," reflected in the high level of support in the first postwar election for the PSI. The petty bourgeoisie enraged by the outcome of the war for Italy and bitterly hostile to the working class found an echo in fascism. Mussolini was able to "offer an organization that responded to their state of mind and their fears." But Mariátegui is adamant: Mussolini was the creation of fascism, not its ideologue.[8]

In Italy he was struck, as he could not fail to be in that dramatic year of the Biennio Rosso, by the weight of the working-class movement in Italian politics. But the political party that claimed to represent that working class, the PSI, had displayed a permanent ambivalence in the course of the war. Internally divided between interventionists and abstentionists, the party (like the Vatican) preferred to maintain a discreet silence once Italy entered the war in 1915. But both wings maintained a presence within the party—the war faction led by the ex-editor of their newspaper *Avanti*, Benito Mussolini, until he left the PSI and founded his own newspaper *Il Popolo d'Italia*, the mouthpiece of fascism, the other faction led by a group of liberal intellectuals represented by Francesco Nitti. The disagreement over the war produced a split, essentially between the politics of the Second International, whose member organizations supported the war; and the main leadership group who, in 1917, supported the Third International in support of the Russian Revolution and indeed affiliated the party to it. It was curious, if not contradictory, that a party that had formally maintained neutrality in the war should now support revolution. It was above all a response to the enormous popularity of the Russian Revolution among the workers who were the mainstay of the party, and a recognition of the deep anti-war feeling that the reality of war at home as well as in the trenches had generated within the working class. But it remained a formal support—at least until 1921, when the Comintern's Twenty-One Conditions set out the criteria for remaining within the International. The PSI formally agreed to the conditions, but laid down its own caveats and reservations, which the International did not accept. The maximalist current, uncompromising supporters of the International, called for abstention from the electoral process and the immediate creation of a separate communist party.

In his early writings on the Italian political process, Mariátegui resists generalities and, characteristically, carefully analyzes the specifics of the Italian situation.[9] As we shall see, however, he certainly found important parallels to develop between Italy and elements of the Peruvian situation. Both Nitti and Giolitti, liberal leaders of the PSI, attempted to hold to an ambiguous neutrality. In the conflictive and tense conditions of the Biennio, they tried to hold a fine line between the nationalists in their ranks and the socialists, satisfying neither. The rising clamor from an emerging fascist movement, many of whose members were returning ex-soldiers, was matched by the extraordinary levels of working-class militancy and resistance in 1920. In early 1921, Mariátegui still argued that the essential antipathy to war of the Italian people would stop fascism in its tracks. His optimism soon changed to alarm, and in a series of perceptive pieces later published in *The contemporary scene* he provided a profound and comprehensive analysis of the fascist phenomenon, together with a withering critique of the failure of reformism, and indeed of Italian socialism in general, to recognize its impact in time:

> Fascism arose at a moment when revolution seemed imminent, in an atmosphere of agitation, violence, demagogy, and delirium created by the war, intensified by the postwar crisis, excited by the Russian Revolution. In this tempestuous moment, charged with electricity and tragedy, their nerves and weapons were steeled,

and they absorbed the energy, the exhilaration and the spirit of the moment. Fascism, drawing together these elements, is a movement, a proseletysing current.[10]

By June he was clear as to what was involved, as the PSI remained in government and supported its initiatives. "Fascism (he says) represents an offensive by the bourgeois classes against the rise of the working class."[11] The source of the weakness of the state is the nature of Italy itself. Its unification, less than a century old, was no guarantee of unity. The city-states of history still remained, in many cases, virtually autonomous, and regional differences remained huge—politically, socially, and economically. Italy was still, in a real sense, a federal state.

But the rise of fascism in Italy was a manifestation for Mariátegui of a much deeper crisis that was not restricted to Italy. The liberal intellectuals of Italy, like those who supported the Wilsonian outcome to war, imagined a return to a bourgeois normality. But the war was not a mere interruption in the course of capitalism's inexorable progress from which socialism would emerge like a phoenix from the ashes. The very notion of progress, what he called the "myth of progress," lay in ruins, scattered around the trenches of Europe. As an ideology it could not respond to or explain the industrialization of war, the scale of death and destruction, nor the contradiction at its very heart illustrated by the rocketing profits of the Italian war industry. Italy was erupting in class conflict in the factories and on the land; the state had no means of resolving the class struggle, and worst of all, the politicians who enjoyed the mass support of workers withdrew from leadership. This crisis, this decadence of the bourgeois order, would be the subject of Mariátegui's lectures at the Universidad Popular and of his first published work, the articles collected in *The contemporary scene*.

Ordine Nuovo was an inspiration for Mariátegui during his European trip and later. In his article on the Italian press, he develops a theme he drew from his conversations with González Prada, who had argued that a press that simply provides information, in a context of intensifying class struggle, is playing a reactionary role; its impartiality is a fraud.[12] Here he brought to bear the experience of *La Razón*, where information gave way to agitation and solidarity. In his trips to

Rome, starting in early 1920, Mariátegui met regularly with members of Gramsci's group.[13] After falling ill in Rome for four months, he and his group of friends (Falcón, Roe, Maquiavelo) returned to Turin and met with Togliatti, Umberto Terracini, and Tasca, all three still members of the *Ordine Nuovo* group, and went in to some of the occupied factories. By this time the abstention of the PSI had produced divisions within the occupations and a shift in the leadership of the trade unions toward anarchism.[14] There was also an internal debate among the PSI Left, with Gramsci arguing for maintaining a current within the PSI and others, including Togliatti and the others, pressing toward Bordiga's demand for the immediate creation of a separate communist party. As we know, this finally happened at Livorno in January 1921, but in circumstances in which the *Ordine Nuevo* group had split and Gramsci was marginalized. The *Ordine Nuovo* that reemerged later that year as the party's organ was not the paper it had once been. The emphasis on the factory councils as the engines of revolution diminished, and the paper became much closer to an organ of the Comintern, a line that Gramsci approved, though he was opposed to downgrading the councils.

By now the role played by both the PSI leadership and the CGL was becoming clear. Fascism was becoming stronger and more visible as it pulled in frustrated ex-soldiers around an ideology of reactionary nationalism. For José Carlos, the weakness of the Communist Party was a pressing and obvious problem. Where *Ordine Nuovo* had spoken with the voice of the militant minority, its weakness in terms of party politics had undermined that connection, and José Carlos commented on the absence within the group of a rooted and experienced leadership. By now Togliatti and the others had moved to a different arena too. In April 1922, the four Peruvian friends formed the first cell of the Peruvian Communist Party. There is no evidence that it led to setting up any organizational forms; it would seem more probable that it was a symbolic gesture of support for *Ordine Nuovo*. It was also a sign of the political distance that Mariátegui, in particular, had traveled in Europe. But others in the group may have seen it as a more serious commitment to creating a party. In the following year, after their return to Peru, César Falcón entered into a very angry correspondence with his old friend. Falcón was adamant that it was the right time to found the party; Mariátegui disagreed and continued to resist any premature formation of a communist party that would distance committed socialists from the wider movement.[15] In May 1922, José Carlos decided to return to Peru, though he would do so over seven months, visiting a number of European cities en route, except, to his regret, Moscow.

Consequences

There is general agreement that Europe changed Mariátegui permanently, and that his intense Italian experience laid the foundations of his Marxism. But, despite his famously modest appraisal of his time there, when he had acquired "a few ideas" the reality is that he had embarked on a creative journey. Learning from Europe, he saw at a very early stage, did not mean reproducing the European experience. There were general lessons about organization—and a number of warnings; there was the great debate that divided the Left and the workers' movement internationally—between reform and revolution—which, in the absence of socialist organization had not arisen within Peru; there was the matter of the role of intellectuals and of the press; there was the issue of the political role of culture; there was the question of the party. And central to them all was his understanding of Marxism.

In Italy he had seen the potential power of an organized and militant working-class movement, and the contribution of a revolutionary newspaper to its development. Yet in three years or less the counter-revolution had taken the central role on the historical stage. It was critical to understand how that had been possible, what forces or failures had undermined the factory council movement and allowed the bombastic, strutting Mussolini to steal leadership of a mass movement. Mariátegui's analysis is subtle and profound; his method undoubtedly learned from Gramsci's *Ordine Nuovo*. He would elaborate the lessons learned in Italy throughout the rest of his short life, but he would present them first in his lectures at the Universidad Popular.

The bankruptcy of reform in the wake of war became clear as he observed the conduct of the PSI, which was, as he put it, "theoretically revolutionary but reformist in practice." The party had enjoyed the support of a significant part of the Italian working class; at the time of the

November 1919 elections, it had over two hundred thousand members. The main trade union federation, which it dominated, had two million members. Yet it had seen them only as voters, and the leadership's role was to represent them at the highest levels of the state—to negotiate with the state on their behalf. Their revolutionary credentials went no further than a cautious socialist language and a wholly abstract support for the Russian Revolution. This had a great deal to do with the internal life of the party, and the maintenance of a balance between internal factions covering the spectrum from left to right. It had very little to do with understanding the implications of 1917. And it certainly had nothing to do with the concept of workers' power enshrined in the soviets and the factory councils. Thus, when in 1921 the Comintern insisted on the Twenty-One Conditions for membership to become a communist party, the PSI leadership hesitated and tried to insist on its reservations, specifically on the question of a new party. The refusal of the Comintern to consider their objections, and Lenin's controversial recognition of the Turin group, made the Livorno split inevitable.

There was no doubt that the occupation of the factories represented a revolutionary moment; Mariátegui reaffirms that a number of times. Nor was there any question in his mind of the crisis of democracy—that is liberal democracy—itself. Yet he appears to retain a degree of confidence that the Italian working class, despite the betrayal by its leadership and the paralyzing uncertainty of the Communists, still had the capacity and the will to resist fascism. That stemmed in part from his understanding of fascism itself, and in part from the conviction that the crisis of liberal democracy leaves socialism as the only alternative.

What constitutes the moment or the impulse that transforms economic struggles into a movement for a new and different future? And who is the historic subject of that transitional moment? At an early stage Mariátegui defined that new subject as the "multitude." Given the resurgence of the term in the writings of Hardt and Negri, as a shifting and inchoate force defined by its diversity and its restless shifts in space, it is important to distinguish Mariátegui's use of the term, and to recognize that it proposed a different or an alternative subject to the "proletariat" that was the subject of European Marxism's understanding of revolution. In Italy, Gramsci's response in *Ordine Nuovo* to the failures of the August 1919 mobilizations was to argue that the key was "a lack of preparation." Mariátegui repeats that conclusion in regard to Italy, but he addresses the problem more generally. "Preparation," in the case of Peru, specifically involved creating an organ of information between the Peruvian working class and the international proletariat, developing the organic intellectuals that Gramsci also discussed at length, and creating "the instruments of popular culture."[16] But what did Mariátegui mean by these "instruments"? It is much more than a vanguard party. In fact, he returned again and again to the affirmation that the vanguard of the movement must arise from within it, that thought emerges from practice, from life, and not the reverse. This idea was elaborated by the Italian Marxist Antonio Labriola, who was not only a key figure in Gramsci's development but also coined the notion of Marxism as *the philosophy of praxis,* which was fundamental for both Mariátegui and Gramsci.[17]

It seems likely, on reflection, that two things had had a major impact on the Peruvian. The first was the abject failure of the reformists to *lead* their working-class supporters. On the contrary, they had allowed themselves to be led by bourgeois ideology and the rules of bourgeois state institutions, while using the language of socialism. Exposed in their ineptitude, it was urgent that the Communists, the radicals, assume the leadership of the whole movement remembering as José Carlos said, that "a variety of tendencies and a range of ideological nuances are inevitable in that great human legion called the proletariat."[18]

But within what he called the multitude, or sometimes the masses, there was a recognition of the enormous diversity of the non-bourgeoisie, which in the Peruvian case must embrace peasants, artisans, agricultural workers not yet involved in the wages system, and indigenous communities. They were the collective subject of revolution. In the Italian case it didn't escape Mariátegui's notice that while the revolutionary crisis and the instances of insurrection involved peasants and agricultural workers, the PSI and the Left generally had neglected and ignored them, essentially leaving them to the Popular Party. Gramsci's background (as a Sardinian) as well as his political sensibilities (formed at an earlier stage by an anarchism that did address rural struggles) gave him the perspective to see that a revolution that involved only the urban proletariat would be stillborn. In the Two Red Years the struggles of city and countryside often coincided in their content and in their common enemy. Yet the PSI did not look for ways to link, let alone coordinate those struggles, to provide shared demands, in the way Lenin and the Bolsheviks had. The parallels between what Gramsci described as "the southern question" and the necessity that a revolutionary movement everywhere, including Peru, must embrace and include those in struggle against the capitalist system outside the factories—on the land, in the communities and neighborhoods, among women, among the oppressed generally, and in the case of Peru, the indigenous communities—could not be clearer.

At the heart of Mariátegui's analysis was the notion of crisis. The economic consequences of the end of war, from the point of view of the masses, were catastrophic. The decline in industrial production meant a sharp rise in unemployment and a battle over wages, now that the necessity for full production was less pressing than the reestablishment of control over the the labor process. In Italy, as in Britain, war production had paradoxically produced new forms of rank-and-file organization in the factories. In the countryside, war reduced the numbers of workers and redirected production toward sustaining the armies in the field— although the Italian government had refused to send food to prisoners of war on the curious grounds that it would make them more likely to desert. But the rising price of food had also encouraged the large landowners to grab peasant land to extend production, which led to violent confrontations throughout the country. As Mariátegui later argued, the crisis was not simply economic, but social and ideological; and the main casualty was the bourgeois myth of progress. That central ideological column that had bound together liberals and social democrats in the prewar years now lay in ruins. The letters to and from the front told the same story—of the wealthy bourgeoisie living well and continuing their lives,[19] while at home and at the front the soldiers and their families experienced pain, hunger, and a deepening disillusionment.

What he had seen in Europe made very clear that liberal democracy was in its death throes. Its promise, its myth of the relentless development of productive forces, had been exposed in the first great industrial war. Social democracy and the politics of reform had exposed their complicity in the lie and revealed as they did so that capitalism had no inherent commitment to the full development of humankind. As Mariátegui writes:

The defenders of democracy do not want to recognize that it is outdated and exhausted as an idea but only as an organism. What these politicians are defending is the transient form rather than the enduring principle. The word democracy no longer serves to designate an abstract idea of pure democracy, but rather to refer to the liberal democratic bourgeois state. The democracy of today's democrats is capitalist democracy. It is democracy as form not democracy as idea.

And that democracy is in decline and decay. Parliament is the organ, and democracy is the heart. And parliament has ceased to respond to its objectives and has lost its authority and its democratic function. Democracy is dying of heart failure.[20]

In the same essay he suggests that the alternatives that both reaction and revolution offer are "dictatorial." In the essay itself, it is not clear whether he uses the term in a critical sense. But in his discussion more generally of the Italian experience, he emphasized the democratic organization of workers' power, with the soviet and the factory councils as examples.

In the fervid atmosphere of Europe after 1917, the Russian example—unsurprisingly—became the reference point, and the Bolshevik party the model of political organization. But Germany had shown that even in the most advanced industrial democracy, with its mass socialist party, its proliferation of trade unions and workers' cultural associations, socialist ideas had been captured by the Second International, and the extraordinary leaders of the Bavarian Soviet had not developed their project to the point where the German working class could be moved to take power. The internal divisions were too deep, the weight of social democracy and the fear of a workers' insurrection too great. He wrote in "Ebert and Social Democracy"

> Ebert represents a whole epoch in German social democracy, the epoch of the development and decline of the Second International. In a capitalist regime reaching its fulfillment, the workers' organizations solely concerned themselves with material gains. The proletariat used the power of its unions and its votes to win immediate benefits from the bourgeoisie. In France and elsewhere there emerged a revolutionary trade unionism in a reaction against this tame, parliamentary socialism. The social movement

in Germany has placed itself firmly within the bourgeois state in a bourgeois order.[21]

The opportunism of social democracy had "made the bureaucracy spiritually and intellectually incapable of fulfilling the tasks of revolution."

The failure of the socialist offensive in Italy and Germany, therefore, was due in large part to the absence of a solid revolutionary elite. The leading cadres of Italian socialism were neither revolutionary nor reformist, like those of German social democracy. The communist nucleus consisted of young people with very little influence among the masses. The quantity required by the revolution was there; the quality was not, as yet. The new elites had to emerge from the socialist ranks.

Mariátegui's use of the term "elite" grates with a twenty-first century audience; but it was also used by Gramsci to refer to the revolutionary vanguard—the leadership of the revolution that is yet to be "prepared."

In Italy, Mariátegui encountered Marxism made flesh, as an idea and a practice informing living processes. Gramsci, especially in his understanding of the relationship between an industrial working class and a poor peasantry, enriched the idea of the revolutionary subject. The vacillations of the Socialist Party were a reminder of the persistence of "the muck of ages" and its capacity to undermine the revolutionary impulse. During his lengthy journey home, José Carlos must have sensed the urgency of the revolutionary moment; he had, after all, glimpsed the alternative in an emerging fascism that was menacing in its intent.

Chapter Four

The World Crisis

José Carlos's dispatches from Europe were acute and insightful. But because they were destined for a public newspaper, they gave only a limited sense of the personal transformation he underwent while he was there. The reflection and deeper political analysis, and the political conclusions to which they led, would begin on his return.

The crisis that Mariátegui chose to address in his lectures was above all political. The First World War had left much of Europe in ruins, but more importantly it had destroyed the notion that capitalism was an instrument of human progress. European social democracy had interpreted Marx's writings as evidence of the inevitable collapse of capitalism under its own weight; socialism, in this view, would be the logical outcome of its material development. In the Europe Mariátegui discovered on his journey there, however, the crisis of the liberal idea of democracy could equally result in the emergence of a reactionary utopia, fascism, which would turn back the historical clock. Yet at the same time, and on the same journey, José Carlos had seen the potential of a working class to create a new future through its actions. It was, however, disunited, led by cowards, and most importantly, unclear as to the future it was fighting for. The crisis of liberal capitalism, therefore, confronted two possible outcomes—and in determining which would prevail, the role of revolutionaries was indispensable, but only to the extent that they were deeply rooted in the mass movement.

Mariátegui and his family reached Guayaquil, Ecuador, in March 1923 and traveled from there to Lima. He was returning to a Peru during the fourth year of Augusto Leguía's regime, and to a Lima much less agitated than the city he had left in 1919. Leguía had by then consolidated a more repressive regime, with his brother Germán gaining a reputation as a brutal manager of state repression.

While Mariátegui was away, the profile of Víctor Raúl Haya de la Torre, the student leader who had supported the 1919 strikes, had grown, and Haya de la Torre had persuaded Leguía at meetings in 1921 to allow the formation of the Manuel González Prada Universidad Popular, directed specifically at worker education. Haya de la Torre's family had come down in the world, but he nevertheless had direct family connections to Leguía. They might explain Leguía's willingness to allow an institution to be established bearing the name of the fiery aristocratic anarchist González Prada, but he clearly saw the project as less political than educational—and one that allowed him to appear as a liberal and a benefactor.

On his return Haya invited Mariátegui to offer a lecture series titled the *History of the World Crisis*, starting in June 1923. The series provided the opportunity for Mariátegui to process the experience of Europe but also to explore, with a mainly working-class audience, Peru's place in the world. Because Mariátegui's internationalism was clear and insistent from the outset in every sense, the economic realities of the country, however remote much of it may have seemed from the wider world, were conditioned historically and currently by the relationship between Peru and international capitalism. Politically, Marxism defined the capitalist system as global in its reach.

Between June and November 1923, Mariátegui delivered seventeen lectures at the Universidad Popular. He was not immediately well received, despite the high level of respect in which he was held. Mentions of socialism or references to the leaders of the Russian Revolution provoked some boos and whistling from anarchists in attendance. Yet the audience for the lectures increased with each one, because the topic he addressed had never been shared with working-class people until then, still less in the context of what Mariátegui insisted should be seen as a "conversation," an opportunity for mutual learning.

To a twenty-first-century audience, the lectures could easily seem elementary; yet they describe the immensely complex situation of post-war Europe accessibly and clearly. The question really is why Mariátegui chose to speak on the topic to a working-class audience from a Marxist point of view. The key is in one phrase: "The working class is not a spectator to these events; it is an actor in them." For the small and relatively isolated Peruvian working-class movement, this might have come as a surprise, but Mariátegui was emphasizing that they formed part of a worldwide working class whose experiences were often very similar to theirs, but more importantly whose interests and whose future were shared across the planet. It is to misunderstand what he was doing to describe him as someone developing a "national" variant of socialism. After all, the crisis he was describing was a *world* crisis, and he took pains to show that the behavior of the bourgeoisie at a global level emphasized that reality. Capitalism, as he points out, functions economically on a world scale, but it deploys the instrument of nationalism to divide the international working class against itself and to forge a spurious unity between bourgeoisie and proletariat. The First World War, as he shows, had underlined that tendency—but in the case of Italy, the message had failed in the course of the war, at least until the Caporetto defeat of September 1917.[1] The profiteering of big capital would become clear after the war's end; but in the course of the war, for a while, capital won over sections of the working class with high wages and subsidies in exchange for full production. When the war ended, however, it went on the attack again, driving down wages, sacking thousands of workers, and refusing to return the land taken by the big landowners to the peasantry.

The problem was not just that the capitalist class acted as it did, but that the spurious commonality of nation broke down. The postwar crisis was not simply economic; it was also ideological. The consensus could not be rebuilt after the horrors of war, and the myth of a capitalism bent on an inexorable road to progress could not overcome the memory of the material and human waste of those four years. In the ideological vacuum that ensued, the urgency now was that the leadership of the working class, its vanguard, should arm itself with the new understanding that had emerged from war and its aftermath.

Mariátegui insisted that the old socialist and anarchist literature was no longer enough; it belonged to another time. The situation had reached a point where capitalism could not continue, but the socialist movement was not yet ready to go forward. That equilibrium, however, could not last; the crisis would seek out its resolution. "Out of that crisis will emerge the proletarian civilization, the socialist civilization that is destined to succeed the declining, decadent, dying capitalist civilization, individualistic and bourgeois."

In his lectures he discussed the Russian Revolution, the rise of fascism in Italy, the failure of the German Revolution, and the Treaty of Versailles among other topics. But the core of his argument is that the crisis he describes is not a *European* crisis, but a crisis of Western civilization itself, of its ideas and its values. And Latin America, in that sense, is part of that civilizational model because it has absorbed those values and ideas, the idea of democracy, of progress, and so on. As a statement this is neither Eurocentric nor anti-European. It is a historical observation. And it does not imply, he is quick to add, a rejection of the scientific and technological advances that have occurred in the course of its development—the airplane, the radio, Einstein's advances in physics.

Writing in 1923, Mariátegui saw the crisis as the death of bourgeois reason, but also as the birth pangs of a new, revolutionary future which was close at hand. That optimism led him to underestimate the impact of fascism in Italy, for example, and to assert that the working class would turn against Mussolini as soon as he was exposed. He had seen in Italy an expression of an advanced workers' democracy, a counter to the bourgeois democracy whose forms persisted, and indeed had been exported to Latin America, but which were empty of content. In every revolutionary experience he described in these lectures, the reformists, the Second International Marxists, had defended bourgeois democracy and acted not as leaders of a combative working class, but as their representatives in parliament, the single most significant organ of bourgeois democracy.

When the working class was challenging for power—in Italy, in Germany, in Hungary—the reformists drew back and tried to reconcile the opposites. The mobilized working class, building its own organs of power, frightened them as much as it did the liberal democrats. Yet we are left with a key question: Why in such circumstances, did the working class not act, sweeping aside the bureaucrats and the bourgeois socialists?

Mariátegui wrote in a letter to Samuel Glusberg much later:

> I am a revolutionary. But I think that between people with clear ideas and a defined position it is possible to respect and understand one another, even while we're fighting. But above all, fighting. The political sector that I will never be able to reach an understanding with is another—the mediocre reformists, the tame socialists, the democracy of the Pharisees.[2]

Mariátegui's contempt for the social democrats is withering and repeated. He wrote, "the democracy of today's democrats is capitalist democracy, the form of democracy rather than the idea. And that democracy is falling apart.... dying of a heart attack."[3]

In May 1923, Leguía decided to dedicate the city of Lima to the Heart of Jesus. The result was a protest movement involving students and workers and led by Haya de la Torre. The protest was repressed, and Haya was imprisoned and then exiled to Panama. Mariátegui, although he was present in the city, took no part in the protests, for which Haya criticized him publicly. Mariátegui claimed it was of no interest to him, but his sympathy for religion is well known, and he may well have decided not to participate in solidarity with popular religion. It must have also seemed contradictory to mount a protest at a popular ritual, albeit one that was being cynically used by church and state. In any event, Mariátegui later acknowledged that he should have taken part in the protests, and the result was that Haya was no longer able to continue running the Universidad Popular nor edit its newspaper *Claridad* (modeled on Romain Rolland's *Clarté*). Mariátegui took over the directorship, but he was ill, and the two tasks proved to be overwhelming, though he continued his course of lectures until January 1924. Almost immediately afterward he was hospitalized, and his leg, which had developed gangrene, was amputated. He was sent from Lima to Chosica in the Central Valley to rest and recover, but he continued his relentless activity from his sickbed, writing and receiving visitors.

The Universidad Popular lectures were supplemented and developed in his first published collection, *The contemporary scene* published in 1925. But a year earlier he had published what is certainly one of his most important documents, at once a key document for the organization of the Peruvian working-class movement and a theoretical statement, "The First of May and the United Front" was published in *El Obrero Textil*, one of Lima's longest-standing workers' papers. An excerpt reads:

> This international day invites many thoughts. But for the workers of Peru the most immediate, the most opportune concerns the necessity and the possibility of a united front. There have recently been some attempts to set up sectional ones. It's urgent that we understand and take concrete action to prevent these attempts from prospering because they would sabotage and undermine the nascent proletarian vanguard in Peru. . . . I have always been a fervent advocate of the united front. I remember saying . . . in response to some expressions of resistance and concern from some old and hieratical libertarians more concerned with the rigidity of dogma than the effectiveness and fruitfulness of action. . . . 'We are too few to divide. Let's not make an issue of labels and titles.'
>
> We have more urgent tasks. The working-class movement is still incipient and our job is to raise class consciousness and class feeling there. Our duty is to resist reactionary attacks, and repression, to defend workers' organization and the workers' press, and to support the demands of the oppressed and enslaved indigenous people. And in doing that we will come together, whatever the final objective.
>
> To argue for the united front is not to encourage ideological confusion. Within the united front each will conserve their own allegiance and their own ideas. Each will fight for his own beliefs. But all should feel united by class solidarity, linked by a common enemy, connected by the same revolutionary will and the same passion for renewal.
>
> The privilege of incomprehension and sectarian egotism belongs to those mean spirits, bereft of horizons and of wings to fly, to those dogmatic minds who want to freeze and immobilize life in a formula.
>
> The workers' united front, is what the masses want. Unity and faith.[4]

The manifesto is seminal in Mariátegui's development. It was an assertion that political practice arises in and is shaped by specific social and historical conditions. His repeated warnings against dogma and sectarianism, and his reminder that the movement is still small and young, are both statements of principle and tactical recommendations. "Until the time comes for division, as it inevitably will, we have much common work to do and solidarity to build. We have a lengthy task ahead of us to undertake together. It is down to us to awaken in the majority of the Peruvian proletariat class consciousness and class feeling. And that falls equally to socialists and syndicalists, communists and libertarians."[5] The united front concept remained central to his thinking, and we shall return to it, specifically in the context of the debate about the nature of the party in which Mariátegui confronted the full authority of the Comintern.

As we shall see below,[6] for Mariátegui, Marxism was a philosophy of praxis, a concept articulated by Antonio Labriola and later taken up by Gramsci. There has been discussion among interpreters of Gramsci as to whether Gramsci, then in prison, used the concept to veil the fact that he was discussing Marxism rather than to define his specific understanding of it. I have set out my own views on this in the final chapter of this book. Mariátegui had returned from Europe inspired by "the action of the multitudes." But where he differed from anarchism was on the role of ideas; he laid great emphasis, even in his introductory lecture, on the role of intellectuals, praising those who had resisted the blandishments of the official culture like Romain Rolland or the four German scientists, one of whom was Einstein, who publicly repudiated the so-called "Manifesto of the Ninety-Three" of their colleagues who supported the war.

The revolutionary intellectual was not necessarily a product of the universities or the official culture, however. Mariátegui was self-taught and hostile to the academic milieu. The new intellectuals would emerge out of the movement of the masses, and their ideas would reflect and elaborate the lessons of practice. This would be the vanguard to whom he addressed his lectures. And one of the key components of this new consciousness would be the understanding of the dialectics of the global and the local, the international and the national. Proletarian consciousness was not the automatic outcome of selling your labor or experiencing exploitation; it was the understanding of that shared reality as a value. "It was not simply a matter of 'informing themselves' about world events; the proletariat should feel itself an active component of that totality."[7]

The "multitude" or the "masses" (he uses both terms) are not a dispersed and accidental meeting of individuals, but a united force, a community or a totality of different experiences forged into a common understanding. It was, as he elaborated, close to Gramsci's notion of the "historic bloc." This is an idea that has been much discussed and disputed. At one level, it has been defined as an argument for an alliance of forces;[8] Gramsci ascribes the notion (in his *Prison Notebooks*) to Georges Sorel. But it is not a notion that Sorel uses; it seems more probable that what Gramsci was referring to was Sorel's notion of "myth," an absolutely central concept in Mariátegui's thinking too.

Perhaps the Italian experience had reinforced for him the dangers and consequences of division and of rigidity of thought. In his discussions of the role of the vanguard (and indeed in his final lecture, of which only a short newspaper report survives, which was "An Elegy to Lenin"), Russia and the Bolsheviks are clearly his reference point. But the manner and timing of the split in the PSI that led to the formation of the Communist Party had far-reaching consequences—and there is a particular and tragic irony in his concern about an early sectarian division within the movement, given the way in which the representatives of the Comintern later forced a Communist Party on Peru in the face of Mariátegui's wishes—with the dire consequences he feared.

"The First of May and the United Front" is a more complex document than it may appear to be at first glance. The united front concept itself would develop and expand in the course of what remained of Mariátegui's life. But it is the first step in the creation of a working-class organization that would later find expression in the Confederación General de Trabajadores Peruanos (CGTP), which Mariátegui founded and whose manifesto was another major step in his political journey. But at this stage, the call for a united front is a challenge to the sectarian anarchists who have prevailed in the Peruvian working-class movement; they are mentioned explicitly as "the old hieratical libertarians" whose dogmatism is a barrier to the building of a new working-class culture and consciousness. The old craft traditions must now be superseded, and the limitations of syndicalism overcome. It is significant, too, that the call for solidarity in the manifesto embraces the peasantry and the indigenous communities. Only a broad concept like the united front could meaningfully include them—but it could only function on such a broad basis if it could contain ideological diversity. At one level Mariátegui argues that position tactically, in view of the small numbers of workers and their lack of experience. At another his concept of the united front is strategic, one that can be the foundation of a revolutionary transformation. But of his areas of concern, the united front responds only to one—the creation of expressions of working-class culture and class consciousness.

Is there a contradiction here between the united front and the vanguard whom he specifically addresses at the beginning of his university lectures? He refers often and critically to the notion of a vanguard entering the class from the outside, as a separate body. Time and again he repeats that the vanguard must emerge *from* the class itself, in the sense that Gramsci refers to "organic" intellectuals. Mariátegui's work was in considerable part devoted to the "preparation" (a word he takes from Gramsci) of that layer of intellectuals whose ideas are generalizations from practice; in the philosophy of praxis, practice precedes thought, and the body (as Mariátegui puts it) prevails over the mind, where the body is the multitude in action and the mind the vanguard.

At the same time, the united front is a response to the specificity of the Peruvian and the Latin American experience. European rationalism, or the positivism that was so enthusiastically adopted by the emerging Latin American bourgeoisie, delineated a process of positive development, which would be achieved by deepening the exploitation of the peripheral economies. Thus, in Peru, the most advanced sectors of the global economy could coexist with forms that, in the historical evolution of Europe, belong to the past. The exploitation of the colonial world as a necessary component of the development and progress of European capitalism makes it impossible to simply reproduce the European experience in Latin America. The call in his manifesto for a united front of industrial workers, miners, peasants, and indigenous communities makes that very clear: "Our landowners, our miners are vassals to the European capitalist trusts. One of our workers in the cotton fields, for example, is in reality simply a yanacon (an indentured laborer) for one of the major English or US industries who dominate and control the global market in cotton."[9]

The Third International, Mariátegui argued, had itself recognized that on a world scale the revolution could assume many forms. In Europe it may be led by socialist ideas and organization; elsewhere it might take the form of national liberation. In the early twenties, Lenin had no difficulty acknowledging that fact, though he was emphatic that "national liberation struggle should not be given communist coloration." It would become socialist in the course of what was a struggle against global capitalism.

The third component of his socialist project was the growth of a working-class press, above all (and his lectures were in some sense a model of the task) to establish the connections between the national and the international, between workers through the international capitalist system. In that sense, solidarity, another key term in the Mariátegui vocabulary, was more than empathy or sympathy, more than fellow feeling. It applied both within each instance of struggle and between them, an active instrument with which to forge a common purpose—a working-class community defined as a moral and ethical universe.

In his analysis of European events in the lectures, Mariátegui looks at each revolution—Italy, Germany, Hungary—as the result of a conjuncture of circumstances; that is what he means when he insists on its "concrete" character. If the "abstract" is the realization of the idea, the "concrete" is the concatenation of circumstances that produces the revolution. There are of course general features that link them—the role of the trade union bureaucracies and the reformist organizations (whose behavior does follow a pattern), the moral collapse of the bourgeois order and the consequent discrediting of its concept of progress, the failure of the institution of consensus, the crisis of hegemony, and the destructive impact of capitalist competition expressed in war. But the way in which these events are received and understood, "localized" as it were, will shape the unfolding of the response. And that is not just an organizational question, but also an ideological one.

"As I said when I was discussing the German Revolution, a revolution is not a coup d'etat, nor yet an insurrection; it is not any of those things which we arbitrarily sometimes describe as revolution. A revolution is only realized over many years. And often there will be periods in which revolutionary and counter-revolutionary forces prevail at different times."[10] The revolution cannot, by definition, be the act of individuals or small groups, though their actions might precipitate it. Thus, it cannot be a coup or an insurrection. Revolution is the act of "the multitude," driven by a myth. At that point the old reformism, incapable of imagining a working class actually assuming power, becomes an enemy of revolution.

In his discussions of these experiences, on the other hand, Mariátegui expresses a profound optimism about the outcome of the crisis, which, in Diego Messeguer Ilhan's view, lasted for too long and prevented him from seeing that fascism in Italy and Germany could survive and take power.[11] In some ways, at this point, he seemed convinced of the inevitability of socialist revolution. He would later recognize his error.

The manifesto ends unexpectedly on the word "faith." Elsewhere he speaks of "an ideal," and specifically in relation to internationalism.

> A great idea does not emerge from . . . the imagination of a genius [but] from life itself, from the present historical reality. . . . A capricious, impossible utopia, however beautiful, never moves masses. The masses are moved and inspired by that theory which offers an imminent objective, a credible end . . . a new reality in process of becoming.[12]

This returns once again to the concept of myth, which Oshiro Higa's brilliant study defines as "the anticipatory consciousness of a class, or properly speaking of its most advanced sector, at a given moment in time and which glimpses or senses on the horizon a new reality and struggles for its realization."[13]

"Mariátegui," he writes, "introduces for the first time in his country and in Latin America the multitude as the real protagonist of history."[14] The multitude, in Mariátegui's definition, is "the social location of political action, the sense of community in part derived from the labor discipline imposed by capital in the factory, in part the result of a long peasant tradition of communal living, later absorbed into the proletariat." Yet for that multitude to fulfill its historic mission, it needs to develop and articulate its moments of praxis. That is the role of the vanguard, "but not so much to lead it from outside—because the vanguard is part of the multitude, the most conscious and combative part—as to make it aware, conscious of its own potential."

And to fulfill that task the vanguard must integrate the particular totality of the multitude (in one country) with the general totality (the global). This internationalism is the only consistent way to respond adequately to the advances of capital in its imperialist phase.[15] But the struggle in one country could not be imported into another: "The search for the universal for him began always with the specific and the first task of the movement was precisely to find its own cultural identity, its singularity and autonomy in feeling, doing, being."[16]

The significance of this argument is better understood in the specific context of Peru in 1924. Haya de la Torre, then in exile outside the country, was having some impact in the working-class movement, particularly in the textile industry (though its influence beyond that is a matter of some dispute)[17] and in competition with the anarchists. Leguía, having brutally repressed strikes and jailed and tortured many of their leaders, had incorporated some anarchist leaders into his compulsory arbitration regime. The new leader of the anarchists, Arturo Sabroso, was less committed to anarchist ideas and was more pragmatic. In fact, he later joined Haya's organization, APRA, in the early thirties. Certainly, Haya's role in the Sacred Heart protests had raised his profile, and for a time he became a very prominent figure in Peruvian politics. At this point he described himself as a Marxist, or at least employed Marxist discourse, and flirted with the International. But his vision of working-class politics was very different. As the brilliant historian Alberto Flores Galindo related in a letter to Esteban Pavletich in 1926, Haya said: "Don't lose heart. Five Russians have shaken the earth. There are twenty of us, so we can make Latin America tremble."[18] It is just an anecdote of course, but it reveals Haya's vision of politics as a combination of a disciplined party and a messianic leader. He stood in the classic mold of the *caudillo*, the individual leader moving his troops in the assault on power, the only objective such an authoritarian method proposes.

Myth

> *Mariátegui counterposes the concept of myth; against science and*
> *organization, faith and the collective will . . . The myth is synony-*
> *mous with the collective alternative to the established order and for*
> *him revolution and truth, politics and morality are indivisible."*
>
> **—Alberto Flores Galindo**[19]

It is the concept of myth that has excited most controversy and debate around Mariátegui's Marxism. His First of May manifesto makes oblique reference to the idea that "[m]an, as philosophy defines him, is a metaphysical animal. He does not live productively without a metaphysical conception of life. Myth moves man in history."

Georges Sorel was much admired in syndicalist circles and almost certainly introduced to Mariátegui by his anarchist connections in 1918 or 1919. It is interesting to note that Sorel also enjoyed a high reputation among revolutionaries in Europe especially, though not as Mariátegui mistakenly asserts, with Lenin, who was fiercely critical of him in his *Materialism and Empirio-criticism*. Sorel was also an influential writer among the Italian Left in the war years, particularly on Gramsci.

Sorel's immensely contradictory body of work has allowed him to be all things to all people; a Marxist in the 1890s, at different points he forged alliances with monarchists, fascists, and anarchists, for whom he is an architect of the notion of revolutionary syndicalism. But it would be extremely unfair to charge Mariátegui with a defense of Sorel's body of work or his very diverse career. The issue here is what he took from Sorel: what it was about the concept of myth that he found relevant to his Marxism.

Among other things, Sorel was extremely critical of dogmatism, of versions of Marxism that presented Marx's ideas as truths. For Mariátegui, Marxism was a philosophy of praxis, the theory and practice of proletarian revolution. And Marxist politics were a method for developing the capacity and understanding among the working class to enable it to realize its historic mission to end capitalism on behalf of the whole of humanity. The myth as he saw it was the vision that could impel the movement, an anticipatory sense of the alternative future, a premonitory sense born out of collective experience. That myth, in his view, is the social revolution—the definitive overcoming of the class struggles that capitalism inescapably generates. It has other names. In Latin America the term that Mariátegui also uses—*mística*—is widely used among the Left, particularly among those organizations born out of the theology of liberation in the 1980s (for example the Landless Workers' Movement in Brazil) but also among the Bolivarian Left emerging at the turn of the twenty-first century. It is a difficult term to translate—but perhaps "myth" is the most appropriate rendering of it.

In another essay, "Materialist Idealism," his analysis of the proliferation of quasi-mystical doctrines adopted by the bourgeoisie in the aftermath of war is withering: "[T]he best sign of the health and power of socialism as the source of a new civilization is . . . its resistance to all these spiritualist ecstasies." His concept of myth, in contrast, derived from the writings of Georges Sorel, whom he admired throughout his life. For Robert Paris, a pioneering Mariátegui scholar, the Peruvian was "an ambiguous Sorelian." Mariátegui found in Sorel's writing a critical account of bourgeois rationalism, an anti-reformist skepticism about the state, and an emphasis on the significance of workers' self-activity. But he did not accept Sorel's world view entirely; indeed, he clashed with the anarchist supporters of Sorel at the Universidad Popular and afterward, especially around the Second Workers' Congress in 1927.

What he took from Sorel was a concept that allowed him to address the significance of ideas and cultural and historical memory in shaping the consciousness of "the multitude," the protagonist of the social revolution.[20] He meant something far broader than theory, or faith—elsewhere he calls it a passion—forged in struggle but directed at a future society. Yet he does say that "the exigencies of revolution impose the theoretical autonomy of the proletariat," a point he had made forcefully in the first of his lectures at the Universidad Popular.[21] For the proletariat, socialist revolution is the myth. And the myth, in its turn, is the understanding born of collective experience. It is sometimes expressed symbolically, sometimes by images or rituals, ceremonials or parodies. They are an expression of class, but they may not always be recognized as such. One memorable example was Mariátegui's youthful essay on "El Señor de los Milagros."[22] For beyond the struggle to improve the material conditions of life is what Oshiro Higa describes as "anticipatory consciousness," a category sometimes interchangeable with "imagination." Despite his earlier formulation, this is not actually metaphysical or religious, for "it has moved from heaven to earth." The difference between the idealists he had earlier criticized and the idealism of the present is that "idealism can only prosper when a social class becomes the instrument of its realisation."

This was not an abstraction. The Latin American reality, and the Peruvian in particular, demanded a Marxism able to respond to very different externalities from Europe. Mariátegui did not propose a different revolutionary subject, but rather a broader perception of that subject in which other social layers and classes could identify with and participate in the social revolution impelled by the laboring classes, the proletariat. The bourgeoisie had abandoned its own myth of progress in theory and in practice. The First World War had left it in ruins, and the confusion and decadence of the ruling class in both Europe and Latin America made a mockery of all bourgeois utopians. To the extent that they existed, they were rebels against bourgeois optimism itself—the surrealists, the bohemians like Chaplin, the poets, and especially the great César Vallejo, for whom God was an old man throwing dice and the future an unanswered question.

Yet as he analyzes at length in *The contemporary scene*, the bourgeoisie is less than willing to renounce hegemony. Paradoxically, the most enthusiastic defenders of the forms of bourgeois democracy and the content of bourgeois rationalism are the reformists, the Marxists of the Second International whose authority derives from their function as mediators and attenuators of class struggle, representing the working class to and for the capitalist class. The 1925 collection offers examples from a number of countries, reinforcing the general themes presented in his lectures. In the crisis that follows, a revolutionary myth will not simply offer the vision of an alternative future; it will also serve to encourage and strengthen the abilities and capacities that will enable the oppressed and the exploited to envisage an end to exploitation and see themselves as capable of administering a new society.

Marx said "men make history but not in circumstances of their own choosing"; the circumstances may well obscure the fact that they are making history at all. The occupations of the Turin factories, for example, were launched in a dispute with the Fiat company over wage rises, and later in defense of the internal organization of the workforce. Seen in retrospect, they took an enormous leap beyond the negotiation of the conditions of labor into a contest for power over production itself. There were certainly many among the workforce—those influenced by *Ordine Nuovo* among them—who recognized the depth of the challenge they were mounting. But one of the leaders of the movement, Angelo Tasca, noted that the majority of workers in the plant were probably Wilsonian democrats by instinct, and accepted the new order of global capitalism that Woodrow Wilson proposed, even though it represented an attempt to restore a prewar world at the expense of the class who had fought and died in the war. And there were those among the ruling class (Agnelli, the head of Fiat, almost certainly among them) who understood what was embedded, *in practice*, in the occupations—a challenge to capitalism itself. It was, beyond any doubt, a class confrontation, but it may not have been perceived as such by the working-class participants. The class response was not, and is not, automatic.

In his elaboration of hegemony, Gramsci described the complex machinery through which the bourgeoisie maintains and defends its economic power, mechanisms that include religion, ideology, culture, and common sense. Interestingly, he describes it as "a secular religion." When Mariátegui discusses religiosity, it is, in a similar sense, a concept of the cultural milieu in which we live, but it carries for him a critical component, an element of resistance, however muted or oblique. Throughout the history of Latin America, popular religion has survived in a syncretic relationship with the official religion of empire. It is there in the eighteenth-century Cuzco school of painting, with their dark-skinned saints and virgins and their proliferation of indigenous images in the undergrowth or the frame. It is there in the parallel universes of Catholicism and Black religion in Cuba, where saints double as Yoruba deities. In that sense, the clandestine religions also function as myths. In his analysis of the rise of fascism in Italy, Mariátegui described the confrontation in a different way—as between two myths, the reactionary and the revolutionary.

Sorel was a harsh critic of economism in Marxism, and an enemy of bureaucracy. Both limited humanity to an economic status, and its choices to those measured and calculated to be available within a prevailing system. However ambivalent and contradictory his insights, Sorel saw human beings as more than their material circumstances. And so, of course, did Marx. The strike, or other more limited actions, has clear but limited objectives. The general strike, which for Sorel was the proletarian myth, represented an assumption of power by the proletariat on the basis of new values and a new, proletarian, reason. For Mariátegui that is the consequence of the socialist revolution, which extends its framework into every aspect of culture and daily life to become hegemonic. The socialist bureaucracy—for whom Mariátegui reserved such venom—reinforced the bourgeois definition of the human, and in doing so corroborated that "natural" existence of working people within capitalism, where for both bourgeois and proletarian, all was calculation and measurement. In the context of a Peru, where only the bourgeoisie had access to luxury goods and the appurtenances of a good (material) life, the promise of future consumption could lead the working class not toward a transformation of the world toward other and superior human values, but toward integration into a bourgeois order. That is where bourgeois rationalism inevitably led.

But Marxism had far-greater ambitions for humankind. The development of the fully human, the "fullest development of each in the fullest development of all" is not an economic statement, but a political and philosophical affirmation of how limited and restrictive, how repressive, is capitalism's vision of what it means to be human. For Mariátegui, that is the intimate connection between imagination and revolution. Bourgeois society has physically separated creative from mechanical labor;[23] the artist is isolated and marginalized, and his imaginative activity consigned to a realm somewhere between self-indulgence and madness. Yet as a young man Mariátegui had found among artists, or among radical artists at least, an intimation of the future and a critique of the past. For the avant-garde of the Palais Concert, it was an individual rebellion, a neurotic sense of exclusion, but its expression was innovative and challenging—a remaking of the language that is our social being.[24]

In his transition to socialism, Mariátegui conceived his project as collective. But it was in Turin, or rather after Turin, that he began to develop the sense of the totality, of the integration of the economic, the creative, the social, and the political, that Marxism could and did provide. But, like Gramsci, he had first to rediscover Marx the revolutionary, and disengage him from Marx the academic and Marx the economic analyst. His political economy, after all, was much more than a historical description of the structures of production. It was concerned centrally with the *relations* of production *and their transformation*. To know capitalism was to understand its rhythms and cycles, to identify its points of weakness, and to discern its contradictions, the most important of all: the difference between two conceptions of the social and the human.

Against this background, the encounter with Sorel was Mariátegui's indirect route to Marx. He had moved *away* from syndicalism by the time he returned to Peru, and the critique of mechanical interpretations of Marxism was now filtered through his European, and especially his Italian, experience. He would not have known the early writings of Marx—the *1844 Manuscripts* nor, more significantly, *The German ideology*. But he had read the *The Communist Manifesto*, whose lyricism and passion were anything but turgid and mechanical. And although he continued to give Sorel credit for part of his thinking for the rest of his life, he had had the opportunity in Europe to read Lenin and absorb the Soviet experience (or, more precisely, the experience of the soviets) through Gramsci and the Italian events. His final lecture at the Universidad Popular, after all, was a homage to Lenin, though sadly we have only a very brief report[25] of what he said, rather than his own notes.

Mariátegui took from Sorel those elements of his writing that illuminated his own thinking. It would be stretching a point to argue that Sorel had an alternative theory; his work was in many senses a collection of idiosyncratic individual insights. So, there was no overarching theory for Mariátegui to adopt. Had he lived longer, he might have found many of his ideas and concepts extensively developed in Marx and in Trotsky. But he did not have the opportunity to read the *1844 Manuscripts*, *The German Ideology*, nor the work of Walter Benjamin, which mirrored his own in many ways.

With this in mind, the concept of myth should be addressed in direct relationship to the united front. What at first sight may seem to be little more than a tactical mechanism goes far beyond that limited application. The social myth, after all, does not propagate itself; the collective through which it emerges and develops must exist objectively. The united front is an expression of a conscious community, or at least it is intended to become that. But sectarian divisions and discussions disengaged from practice serve to hold back the growth of the collective actor, what Mariátegui calls the multitude. His objections to the sectarianism of the Left, as well as to the bureaucrats and reformist ideologues, is that both delay the formation of the united front and divide it.

This interpretation of the united front brings it closer to another, less often mentioned, concept developed by Sorel and picked up by Gramsci—the concept of the historic bloc. Again, this is more than another name for political alliances; it is a way of addressing the collective actor reflected in myth. What is important for Mariátegui is that the united front, or the historic bloc, consists of a range of different forces and actors, each of whom may come with their distinct "credo," their own traditions, their own histories (in the double sense of their body of experiences and of the narrative that retells them for their own use). In his *Prison Notebooks* (which were published after Mariátegui's death), Gramsci described the "historical bloc of purely individual and subjective elements and of mass and objective or material elements" (Book 10); "in other words, a crystallisation of structure and superstructures."[26] Taken together with the concept of hegemony, this is clearly a dynamic relationship, not static but in process.

How far can the united front be seen in the same framework? Mariátegui speaks of passion and the revolutionary will, of an ideological diversity within the movement of "unity and faith." These final words, and their conjunction, are not accidental. It is worth recalling Gramsci's ideas in this respect:

> The fundamental problem facing any conception of the world, any philosophy which has become a cultural movement, a "religion," a "faith," any that has produced a form of practical activity or will . . . is that of preserving the ideological unity of the entire social bloc which the ideology serves to cement and unify.[27]

The closeness or otherwise of Mariátegui to Gramsci, either personally or theoretically, is a theme to which most writers on Mariátegui have returned. My intention here is not to argue that they collaborated, nor that Mariátegui took his ideas from Gramsci. But it would be hard to deny the coincidence in their thinking at this stage of their lives. Of course, Mariátegui could not have known or read the *Prison Notebooks* from which I have quoted, but Gramsci was a central figure in the Italian events that Mariátegui observed and that had such a powerful influence on his thinking. There is a good reason for that. Both had worked in a milieu dominated by anarcho-syndicalism and with activists who were heavily influenced by its ideas. Sorel was a respected and influential thinker in these circles, especially because of his emphasis on trade union organization, his focus on the working class, and his skepticism about the self-appointed leadership of the trade unions, which the activists shared. He had welcomed the Bolshevik Revolution with fulsome praise of Lenin,[28] and he identified in the soviet the form of organization that most closely corresponded to his vision of a class organization. For Gramsci, clearly, the factory council was an Italian version of the soviet.

Mariátegui was very clear that the Peruvian working class was not in a position to create soviets—it was too small and, at this point, in a phase of disorganization and demoralization. Yet the general conclusion he did draw was that a socialist revolution, however far into the future it may occur, must at all costs avoid the emergence of a bureaucratic layer acting on behalf of and against the general interests of the class. The possibility of a socialist transformation would hang on the existence of a driving narrative with the emotional power to bind together the collective will—in other words, a myth.

Chapter Five

Building
the Movement

Mariátegui spent most of the second half of 1924 convalescing in the pleasant climate of Chosica, in the Central Valley above Lima, in a house owned by Dr. Hugo Pesce, who would go on to be a key figure in the life and political development of Che Guevara.[1] The amputation of his gangrenous right leg (not the left, which had been affected by his childhood injury) had almost certainly saved his life, but recovery was slow and difficult. The family was also in severe economic straits, but his friend and critic Luis Alberto Sánchez organized a benefit concert in Lima for him, which paid the medical bills. Undaunted, José Carlos continued his writing and his work with the trade unions, together with his correspondence with activists in the indigenous movement.

The Manifesto for the First of May (1924) called for a united front, a tactic that has come to mean several very different kinds of alliance. The position adopted by Haya de la Torre a few years later argued for a coalition of the working class with elements of the bourgeoisie; the popular front imposed by the Stalinism in Spain in 1936 was essentially an electoral pact between the communists and a wide spectrum of reformist organizations, based on a minimal program acceptable to all. It immediately succeeded the period in which the Comintern had pressed for a complete break with all non-communist parties on the basis that the collapse of capitalism was imminent—the so-called "third period" policy. The disastrous effects of both are now all too well known.

Trotsky posed the question of the united front in a famous speech in February 1922, a year and a half before Mariátegui. It is not known whether the Peruvian was familiar with the speech, but his argument on the first of May 1924 is very similar:

> Should the struggle of the proletariat for its daily bread stop until the moment when the communist party, supported by the entire working class, is in a position to seize the power? No, this struggle does not stop, it continues. The workers who belong to our party and those who do not join it, like the members of the social-democratic party and others, all of them—depending on the stage and the character of the working class in question—are disposed and able to fight for their immediate interests; and the struggle for their immediate interests is always, in our epoch of great imperialist crisis, the beginning of a revolutionary struggle.[2]

The circumstances of the two proposals were, of course, very different. Trotsky was speaking directly to the communist parties in the context of the revolutionary upheaval in Europe. Mariátegui was writing at a time when the Peruvian working-class movement was at an ebb, in a period of flux after the peaks of 1919.

Peru's principal industries in the mid-twenties were mining, oil, export agriculture concentrated in sugar and cotton, and wool produced in the Andean highlands. The paradox of the Peruvian economy, as Mariátegui would analyze it in his *Seven Essays*, was the conjunction on the one hand, of a modern, industrial, principally extractive sector with access to the most recent technology, and an export agriculture sector dominated by two companies, the Gildemeisters and the Larcos. And on the other was a majority sector of the economy, located in the Andes, characterized by what he called "semi-feudal" relations that had barely entered the wages system, though it was the location of the expanding export-based wool-producing industry.

The conditions of labor in each sector were vastly different. While each part of the population was subject to exploitation in a capitalist economy, the intermediate network of social relations veiled that reality. The highland peasant, in thrall to structures of power and control dating from previous centuries, perceived the gamonal as the exploiter and beneficiary of his labor. The Huaylas rebellion led by Pablo Pedro Atusparia in 1885, for example, began as a rebellion against the Indian impost, the special tax on indigenous communities. The protest was sparked by worsening conditions on the land, due in large part to the expansion of the latifundia into community lands. The 1916 rebellion of Rumi Maqui, in Puno, was a reaction against the enganche system through which labor contractors forced indigenous people into working outside the communities, either on the land or in the mining areas.

The world of the urban worker, recently emerging from a craft system and employed mainly in small plants, on the docks, or in transport and distribution industries, was culturally and socially distant from the life of the Andean highlands on the one hand, and the brutal conditions of work in the coastal estates producing sugar and cotton on the other. Yet each of these social groups were selling their labor, or in some cases giving it away, for the benefit of a foreign capitalism to which their visible exploiters were subordinate.

In some senses, it was in the mining sector where that was most tangible. Yet the mines were mainly in a Central Valley still almost inaccessible from Lima, with which there was little or no physical or cultural communication. If there was a vanguard of the working class, then it was the workers in mining and on the oil fields, which only began operation in a major sense in the mid-1920s. The key foundry at La Oroya, for example, only started to function in 1923. And the most combative section of the small working class of Lima and Callao, the protagonists of the 1919 events, possibly amounted to seven thousand people by 1930.[3]

It is in this context that Mariátegui addressed the question of building the *proletarian* united front whose features he had set out in "First of May and the United Front." "Let's not make an issue of labels and titles," he argued there.

It is the task of every socialist, syndicalist, and activist to fight against their common enemies—the "yellow unions," the self-styled representatives, and the reactionaries and their repressive machinery. It is a common responsibility to defend working-class organization, the working-class press, *and to support the demands of the enslaved and oppressed indigenous race.*

The proletariat whose organization he was committed to building included both these sections of the population, without distinction. The united front starts with solidarity, a central concept in all of Mariátegui's writings; its significance is that it is applied equally to the mutual support of workers in struggle, as in 1919, and to the practices of indigenous communities—the *dar-recibir* described by his contemporary Castro Pozo, which has recurred in the indigenous movements of the twenty-first century as *buen vivir*. It refers to a harmonious and mutually respectful relationship between human communities and nature, and to a respect for and commitment to the collective. But in both cases the obstacle to solidarity is the capitalist system itself. It is not a moral question to be cured by debate or re-education; morality is rooted in the material, and there can be no moral order in a system whose motor impulse is exploitation and oppression.

The First Workers' Congress, to which the manifesto was addressed, met in Lima in 1921 for the first time. It was attended by around sixty delegates representing twenty-three organizations. The Second Congress, meeting in 1927, assembled just twenty-seven unions. Both were dominated by a still-influential anarcho-syndicalist current that had led the 1919 movements, but they now faced two rivals. Mariátegui had used the opportunity of his lectures at the Universidad Popular to set out a Marxist position on the national and international situation and to develop a Marxist analysis of Peruvian economy and society. He followed this immediately with the first steps toward building a class-based organization, but one that was open both to anarcho-syndicalists and to the growing layer of the middle class, many of them products of the student movements of 1918–20 whose leading voice was Haya de la Torre. Haya had won himself a reputation and some authority with the workers of Lima during and after 1919, while Mariátegui was absent in Europe. He had won influence in the textile plants of the city, especially the emblematic Vitarte plant, and he had persuaded the workers there to stop subscribing to the main anarchist paper, *La Protesta*. As Leguía's promises of modernization proved hollow, and as his "new" Peru rapidly entered an alliance with foreign capital, whatever opportunities for national economic growth the new middle class had hoped for turned to sand. The state sector did grow, and there was some infrastructural investment, but this hardly amounted to the full-scale modernization Leguía had promised. This discontented middle class was now open to an anti-imperialist discourse, and Haya tailored his to this sector with what would become his proposal for the creation of a Peruvian state capitalism in an alliance with imperialism that the new state would control. His model was the Mexican Revolution; in fact, he lived there for two years working for José Vasconcelos, the Mexican writer, philosopher, and politician who has been called the "cultural caudillo" of the Mexican Revolution. Mariátegui's analysis of the the Mexican Revolution of 1910–17, where the struggle for land was articulated with a bourgeois revolution, was a direct response to the strategic view that APRA represented, and through his critique, a proposal for a revolutionary proletarian alternative.

The Mexican Revolution

José Carlos had expressed an early fascination with the charismatic, if contradictory, figure José Vasconcelos, minister of education in the post-revolutionary government of Álvaro Obregón (1921–24) and a writer and philosopher of Nietszchean dimensions. His article "Pessimism of the real, optimism of the ideal" attributes the epigram to Vasconcelos, though it was also used by Gramsci, who rendered it as "optimism of the will, pessimism of the intellect" and attributed it to Romain Rolland.

Mariátegui sees in many intellectuals a convenient nihilism that veils "a refusal to participate in any great effort of renewal, or to explain away their disdain for the actions of the multitude. Yet they will happily support some limited campaign, some small ideal, but turn away from grand schemes."[4] Instead he points to the validity of a philosophy of skepticism. In recognizing the relativity of human affairs, it refuses to accept absolutes, recognizing the power of myth and faith.

The two concerns were linked. Mariátegui used the interpretation of the Mexican Revolution to revisit the question of the peasantry. It was part of the common sense of the Left in the early 1920s that the peasantry was by nature reactionary, individualistic, and traditionalist; more prone to ally with the landowners than with a working class of whom it knew little and for whom it cared less. Yet Lenin had fought for the idea of a revolutionary organization that would defend both workers' and peasants' rights, for soviets and a redistribution of land to individual peasants as well as the collectives, assuming that winning the individual peasant to the collective interest was a question of politics and education in consciousness. But the central political link was the core slogan of the Bolsheviks: Bread, Peace, and Land. The demand for land was the defining element for the peasantry, and its association with the core demands of the working class was a stroke of genius by Lenin.

The Mexican Revolution was not a single process, but several. Beginning in 1910, Emiliano Zapata led a peasant revolution under the slogan Land and Liberty from his home state of Morelos. Zapata's was undoubtedly a social revolution, striking directly at the system of land ownership and calling for collectivization of land under the ancient indigenous *ejido* form. Pancho Villa, a fugitive from the law, led a revolution against the landowners who dominated the states of northern Mexico. At the same time, Francisco Madero initiated a political opposition to the dictatorship of Porfirio Díaz under the slogan No Re-election, Effective Suffrage. But Madero's revolution was exclusively concerned with institutional political changes, and once in the presidency he was easily persuaded to send troops to disarm the Zapatistas. He was then killed in a counter-revolutionary coup under Victoriano Huerta, who in his turn was replaced by Venustiano Carranza, a powerful landowner who was nevertheless supported by Villa and Zapata's forces in the battle against Huerta. It was Carranza who issued the first decrees of a new revolutionary government in 1915 and who oversaw the new constitution of 1917. This new charter laid the foundations of a bourgeois revolution, though one that undertook to carry out an agrarian reform and whose constitution nationalized the country's natural resources and set down, in article 123 of the charter, a basic guarantee of workers' rights. Carranza had succeeded in separating the working class from the peasantry, sending "Workers' Battalions" against Zapata under the command of Álvaro Obregón, who was later elected president, in 1920. It is true that Mexico's was Latin America's first revolution, but it is also true that it was a bourgeois revolution whose revolutionary rhetoric concealed a reactionary drift. Plutarco Elías Calles, who dominated the state through the twenties, formed the first state party.[5] The historic significance of the Mexican Revolution is beyond question:

> But the character and objectives of the revolution, according to its leaders, the economic factors that shaped it and the nature of its process are those of a bourgeois-democratic revolution. Socialism cannot be achieved except by a class party; it can only be the result of a socialist theory and a socialist practice.
>
> The new state . . . claims to be the absolute and infallible repository of the ideals of the Revolution. Yet it has set itself against the proletariat, whose historic role it is to achieve socialism whenever it exercises its right to fight for it, independently of any bourgeois or petty bourgeois influence.[6]

This analysis of the Mexican Revolution was quite clearly a veiled intervention in the argument with Haya and APRA, which would reach its dramatic division of the waters in 1928.

Shaping the Trade Unions

Mariátegui's proposal for a united front was directed at anarcho-syndicalist workers and the indigenous and peasant organizations. It was, nevertheless, an early objective to win the dissident middle class and the anarcho-syndicalist militants to a socialist and Marxist perspective—and in the case of the anarchists, to win them away from an abstentionist political position. At the Second Workers' Congress of 1927, and despite his appeals, there was an atmosphere of sectarian confrontation, which made the Congress less productive than it might have been. At the same time, Leguía's repression of the middle-class radicals was deepening; many of them were expelled, beginning with Haya himself, in 1923, when he was jailed and then exiled as a result of his leadership of the movement against Leguía's decision to dedicate the country to the Sacred Heart, in a theatrical gesture to the most conservative sectors of society.

Martin Bergel suggests that the Universidad Popular, which was based in the Vitarte district, "produced the workers' leaders that would later form the Aprista and the communist trade union congresses."[7] He is repeating an assertion that is often made by Apristas. It refers to those who, like Fonkén, Barba, and others, were already established leaders of the emerging trade union movement and had come from an anarchist tradition. But Haya had succeeded in winning over some leaders of the textile unions through the Textile Unions Federation he had formed in the early 1920s.

Several leading anarchists had also been drawn in to Leguía's corporate plan, which absorbed the trade union leaders into the state while intensifying repression against the rank-and-file activists. Presumably, they were among the "self-styled workers' representatives" that Mariátegui referred to in his First of May manifesto. Leguía's 1925 vagrancy law (Ley de Vagancia) marked a new stage in the evolution of a repressive regime, and of its increasing subordination to US interests. Those not expelled were subjected to imprisonment and torture, which became a regular feature of the treatment of dissidents and protesters. Delfino Lévano was left an invalid as the result of his treatment in prison, and Mariátegui campaigned actively on behalf of Lévano and other imprisoned workers, seeking the support of intellectuals and artists.

The Peruvian economy under Leguía was now wholly reliant on the export sector, dominated and controlled by foreign capital, and a pliant Peruvian bourgeoisie collaborated and imported its consumer goods while investing, if it did, abroad. In fact, in Flores Galindo's view, the state was too weak to intervene in anything other than a repressive way.[8]

Mariátegui devoted himself in this period to political education through his own work and the publications of his family firm, Minerva. But the key political instrument in this respect would be *Amauta*, first published early in 1926. The magazine, at least in its first phase, was an open platform for the discussion of socialist ideas and the debate between socialism and the arguments of Haya de la Torre and the APRA current. Though Haya and the Apristas on the one hand, and Mariátegui and the members of his socialist Lima Group on the other, contributed to *Amauta* in a fraternal spirit, they were competing for the audience of workers and intellectuals. Their disagreements were clear—Mariátegui's position was socialist, in sympathy with the Communist International, and argued for a movement built from below by a united front of workers, peasants, and indigenous people. Capitalism already existed in Peru, he argued, in a particularly brutal and supine form. The only possible future was socialist. Haya, on the other hand, while using an anti-imperialist rhetoric and often claiming Marxist credentials, proposed a capitalist solution, in collaboration with imperialism, to Peru's underdevelopment. Until 1928, and the irreparable split between them, it still seemed possible for the two currents to coexist in a broad united front—which APRA also argued for, though, as would become very clear, a front dominated by the middle class. It was a formation that was closer to the popular fronts of the mid-1930s, in which communists formed alliances with bourgeois parties (for example in Spain in 1936,) as opposed to Mariátegui's proletarian united front where the interests and objectives of the working class prevailed. And central to his project was the integration of indigenous Peru, to which Haya referred only with vague rhetoric about Indoamericanism. The difference was that for Mariátegui the united front of workers and indigenous peasants was fundamental to his understanding of what a revolutionary workers' movement must look like in Latin America in general, and in Peru in particular.

Mining

What that meant in reality is best illustrated by the evolution of the mining industry. Mariátegui had been slowly and patiently building a network of contacts across the country through *Amauta* and *Labor* on the basis of gathering reports from local worker and indigenous correspondents, rather as the Bolsheviks had done through *Iskra* in prerevolutionary Russia. He had successfully built this group of contributors to the journals who also distributed the papers—*Labor* in particular—in their own areas.

José Carlos himself was not able to travel far from Lima since the amputation of his leg, so his comrades and collaborators would often come to his home in Washington Izquierda to debate, discuss organization, write, and determine the distribution of the journals. At the same time, partly to earn a sparse living, he wrote prolifically for local journals and newspapers.

The Indigenous Congress, which had taken place in 1924, had not been a great success, but the fact that it had taken place at all was, as Mariátegui pointed out, a success in itself, and it provided some of the contacts who would later contribute to the Indigenous Bulletin inside *Amauta*. Mariátegui's work had not gone unnoticed, and in 1927 the journal was closed and Mariátegui arrested—not for the last time—accused of conspiracy against the state. He had the grace not to deny it. It would begin publication again after a six-month silence.

The most dynamic sector of the Peruvian economy in the 1920s was certainly the copper mining industry; it represented about 35 percent of the economy. The industry was dominated by the Cerro del Pasco Corporation, formed in 1901 by a group of US investors.[9] It was based in the Central Valley, an area of peasant cultivation by indigenous communities, from which the first miners came. Both Flores Galindo and Flores Bordans use the songs and stories of these communities as their primary research material. Here is one ballad from 1908 that says a great deal about the impact of the mine on the local communities.

> *Poor mineral of the Mountain*
> *The foreigners are everywhere*
> *They claim to be protecting us*
> *With our own money*
> *Now everything is joyful and glorious*
> *For this incomparable mineral*
> *But it will be deadly, a hell on earth*
> *When it's exhausted*

The poorest and the landless were the first to work the "incomparable mineral," copper. The working conditions were appalling. But worse than that, the mine workings contaminated the land and affected the crops and the animals, forcing the locals to sell the land to the company at rock bottom prices and then seek work in the mine. Later, the Cerro del Pasco Corporation installed filters and brought cattle to the region, thereby becoming a major beef producer. The company also opened the highly profitable truck shop, La Mercantile, where miners were forced to buy their necessities, most of which were imported. There were reactions to the conditions, though these mainly took the form of riots or machine wrecking. The first actual strike was over the provision of lamp oil, in 1912.

The miners were drawn from the surrounding area, which was dominated by small-scale peasant production. The indigenous communities supplied these first laborers, though there was significant resistance; conditions in the company enclave were brutal.[10] According to one report, one thousand workers died in the mine between 1902 and 1911.[11] The company then turned to the system of contracting labor through the enganche system, which sent contractors to indigenous communities and villages to, essentially, force local men into the mines, where they were held by a system of debt peonage. As the mining labor force grew, some of the richer peasants sought work there too, employing poor peasants to work their land. Nevertheless, the miners maintained strong roots in the countryside, to which they returned at first seasonally and later after a period spent in the mines. But whether they were poor peasants or members of a community, they brought with them traditions of organization with deep historical roots. The peasant resistance to the encroachments of the company was expressed in rural banditry; what peasant organizations there were tended to be conservative and were often controlled by landowners.

Their situation was contradictory—selling their labor power, but maintaining their cultivation through family labor and still seeing themselves as members of the rural community to which they would return. They constituted what Flores Galindo describes as an unstable, semi-proletarian labor force, with divided loyalties and a resistance to proletarianization reflected in their songs and stories.[12]

In January 1919, the miners launched a strike on the question of the cost of living. The company's monopoly of essential provisions through its truck store not only put local commerce out of business, it also meant that the cost of living in the mining regions was higher than Lima's, where a protest movement for lowering the prices of basic goods was simultaneously underway, though there was no organic connection between the two. There was no support for the strike from the conservative peasant organizations; indigenous discontent still expressed itself in community risings like the Rumi Maqui rebellion, though these were largely brought under control by government and the military in the early 1920s. By then, mining was the most profitable sector of the export economy, especially after the opening of La Oroya. Cerro del Pasco Corporation expanded to absorb some of the smaller mines in the area, one of which was Morococha. *Labor* had drawn in a network of individual contacts who sold and distributed the paper. One of them, who would later play a key role, was Gamaniel Blanco, a teacher in Morococha who had set up a reading circle among workers.[13] He was in regular contact with Mariátegui, and his reports appeared in both *Amauta* and *Labor* together with contributions from the Peralta brothers in Puno, among others. Jorge del Prado, a young militant in Arequipa—who would later grow very close to Mariátegui, and who then became general secretary of the Peruvian Communist Party—described his first contact with *Amauta* when he joined a group called Revolución in his home city of Arequipa. He describes, in his long interview recorded with Denis Sulmont over the course of 1976 and 1977, how both APRA and the *Amauta* made strenuous efforts to win his allegiance. The Venezuelan novelist Rómulo Gallegos, visiting the country, told them there was no difference between Aprismo and communism. But Del Prado was unimpressed by APRA because, he says, they couldn't produce any workers, and his Revolución group joined Mariátegui. Del Prado's first contact with him was on a visit to the organizing committee in Lima:

> It was on the basis of attention to concrete problems, through the correspondents, the discussion of these problems and the interest in addressing them that trade union and political organization was developed. Almost all Mariátegui's agents—the representatives of *Amauta* in the provinces—were organizers, even those who weren't workers."[14]

Given the physical difficulties of contacting them from Lima, Mariátegui communicated with them through the network of correspondents for *Amauta* and *Labor*. Del Prado provides evidence that the contact group was growing by 1928. The economic crisis that culminated in the October Crash of 1929 was already felt by Peruvian workers as their foreign employers began to cut back on wages and bonuses, before cutting wages a year later, and by beginning to dismiss workers in growing numbers. The result was a new level of militancy in Lima, with Vitarte's textile workers once again playing a leading role, but also involving urban transport and railway workers. In the mines, Cerro del Pasco began to attack wages and conditions, and organizing began for a Miners Congress in October 1928. By then, the majority of miners were full-time wage earners, though with contacts in the communities from which they came and very recent memories of their experiences there. Flores Galindo argues that they were still in "a state of transition." Del Prado would later be sent to find work in Morococha.

On December 5, 1928, a long history of neglect of safety resulted in a huge mine collapse that left twenty-eight dead and dozens of miners injured. Cerro del Pasco, unsurprisingly, denied all responsibility. Mariátegui moved very quickly. *Labor* dedicated three whole issues to the disaster, giving a detailed analysis of the responsibility of the company. *Amauta*, too, carried lengthy and detailed reports, including correspondence from Gamaniel Blanco.[15]

Flores Galindo demonstrates that 1928 was the year in which the largest number of periodicals and journals were published—some 473 in all, of which seventy-two were new. It was a sign of the growing audience for ideas, especially among the student population, now numbering nearly two thousand, and for radical ideas in particular. The growth was reflected in Mariátegui's work. The Manifesto for the General Confederation of Peruvian Workers (CGTP), written by Mariátegui, was launched that year—though its first congress would not take place until 1932, and under very different conditions. And there was an emerging working-class Marxist leadership around him, including Julio Portocarrero—who would become the first general secretary of the CGTP—and del Prado himself. The emergence of that leadership explains Mariátegui's anxiety to have a voice at the Conference of the Red International of Trade Unions in Moscow in 1927, to which Portocarrero and Armando Bazán were his delegates.

For Mariátegui, the Morococha events and the workers' organization that led to the Morococha strike in October 1929 had a special significance. They were in some senses a test both of his level of influence among the key sector of workers and of the validity of the united front strategy. Flores Galindo described the miners as a semi-proletariat, referring to their still-strong connections to their peasant background and their indigenous communities. But they were a proletariat nonetheless, and in the key, imperialist-run sector of the economy. They were moved both by their experience as workers and by the oppression and exploitation to which they and their families were subjected. When the price of copper fell in 1929, a Morococha committee was formed. It launched a strike over wages and in protest at sackings in October of that year. The mining labor force was reduced from its high point in 1929 of thirty-two thousand to twelve thousand by 1932, as the impact of the crash spread.

For Mariátegui, Morococha represented the beginning of a period of political radicalization and trade union militancy, and also the proof of the validity of his analysis of the movement and the relevance of indigenous traditions of struggle. But Mariátegui was faced with serious obstacles to his work. One was his own failing health; another, the direct repression to which he was subjected by the state. In November of that year, he was again arrested and detained, this time for an alleged Jewish plot!

There is a very well-known photograph of Mariátegui taken close to the end of his life. It is taken in the open air. José Carlos is in a wheelchair looking very frail; he is surrounded by a group of men. It includes del Prado and Martínez de la Torre, but also Gamaniel Blanco and other delegates from the mining areas. It demonstrates the growth of the influence of both Mariátegui and *Amauta*, but also his frailty.

What is not visible in the photograph, though perhaps it had contributed to José Carlos's weakness, is the rising level of hostility directed at him by the Comintern, which began at the Moscow conference of 1927, continued at the Montevideo trade union conference, and culminated in a ferocious attack on him by the Comintern delegate, Victorio Codovilla, at the Buenos Aires Communist Conference.

To fully appreciate the importance of Mariátegui's work, it is crucial to see the multiple activities in which he was involved, at the center of which were *Amauta* and the united front. He was a revolutionary intellectual, but also—and fundamentally—an organizer. He built a network of solidarity in support of the Morococha strikers, which in turn opened the possibility of direct contact with the peasants of the Central Valley. And the journal had provided a vehicle of communication with activists among the indigenous communities, especially after the first Indigenous Congress of 1924.

When the 1920s began, the working class was fragmented, as Flores Galindo points out;[16] there was limited contact between different sections of workers, or between Lima and the rest of the country. There was still no highway linking Lima to the Central Valley or the further regions of the country, and the railway built by the American engineer Henry Meiggs linked the mining region to the port directly. By 1924 (when "The First of May and the United Front" was published), there was still no sign of the promised development or industrialization that Leguía had undertaken to set in motion. His commitment to progressive legislation, like the eight-hour day, proved short-lived, and his new constitution, passed in 1920, created a corporate state model based on repression rather than social progress.

Mariátegui was always clear that the organization of the working class must spread beyond Lima-Callao and into the mines and coastal haciendas. Flores Galindo estimates that there were probably around seven thousand industrial workers in the capital in 1930, among the nearly forty thousand designated urban workers in the 1931 census. But the peasantry and the indigenous population remained the overwhelming majority of the population. For Mariátegui, the united front he proposed in his "First of May" article would draw together workers and the indigenous peasantry with the radicalizing sections of intellectuals and students. Haya de la Torre, by contrast, envisaged a coalition of workers with the middle classes. On the surface the two projects seemed close, but within four years, with the formation of his Aprista Party, it would become clear that Haya de la Torre was committed to forging an instrument to bring the middle class to power, with popular support. The model here was the Mexican Revolution.

This was very different from Mariátegui's socialist vision, whose critical distinguishing feature was the central role reserved for indigenous people and their communities. And in terms of political method, too, these were different and opposed projects. It would soon emerge that Haya's vision was fundamentally elitist and populist. Even a sympathetic analyst like Bergel had to acknowledge that he was an "egomaniac" (*ególatra*). Julio Portocarrero, the workers' leader who went on to represent Mariátegui at a number of international congresses, remembered that while José Carlos "was obviously a man ready to share his ideas, in his desire to build something," Haya "was self-important and arrogant." "I never saw Mariátegui put himself above other people," he said. The main task was to establish organizational links between them. The difficulty was that many urban workers still retained a craft consciousness; among the miners the links to the peasantry and the rural communities were still strong, and the same was true in the coastal haciendas where a significant part of the workforce was effectively forced labor. The petty bourgeoisie's growing frustration with the broken promises of Leguía was producing a radicalization reflected, in *Amauta*.[17]

The difference between the two uses is reflected in Portocarrero's comment quoted above. The "front" to which Haya referred was a broad multiclass alliance, a "popular front" as it would later be called. Haya was clear in stating that "APRA cannot be the exclusive party of one class."[18] Its working-class base was concentrated in the Lima textile factories, and among the newly unionized labor force on the sugar plantations. It claimed also to have some support among the miners of the Central Valley, but APRA had no organized presence in the Peruvian trade unions at this point, as del Prado had noted.

There was, of course, a sense of urgency in Mariátegui's activity as 1929 ended. His correspondence with Samuel Glusberg and his declared intention to move to Buenos Aires suggest that a combination of ill health and persecution were having powerful effects, and these must have been greatly deepened by the responses to the carefully argued position papers he sent to the Montevideo and Buenos Aires conferences.

The launch of *Amauta*, in September 1926, represented much more than the publication of a new journal. Mariátegui saw it, as discussed below, as an organizer. It addressed the groups of radical intellectuals, workers' leaders, and, centrally, the indigenous movement—as its title and front covers made very clear. In general, building grassroots organization was difficult in these years. Repression became progressively more intense. On June 5, 1927, an editorial meeting at Mariátegui's publishing house, Minerva, was raided and all its participants arrested for their involvement in a "communist conspiracy." Mariátegui was among those detained, though he was transferred to the military hospital, where he was briefly interned. The others fared less well. Some were sent into exile in the north or outside the country; others, including two indigenous leaders, were jailed in the notorious San Lorenzo facility. *Amauta* was closed down. *Amauta*'s account of the so-called communist conspiracy was a model of cold irony and ridicule.

It was a central role of *Amauta* to deepen and extend the links between indigenous mobilization and the workers' movement. The Morococha mine had a central place in the strategy. As Julian Laite puts it, "In the mines, the decade of the 1920s was a period of underground organisation as Mariátegui circulated his periodical *Labor* and organised a cultural circle in Morococha."[19]

The networks of contacts spread through Peru and beyond. A stream of visitors attended the regular meetings at Washington Izquierda, including activists from the indigenous communities of the Andes. Through its *Boletín Indígena*, *Amauta* served to inform and connect indigenous and pro-indigenous groupings. The turning point in this respect was the Indigenous Congress that had taken place in 1924, where 150 communities were represented.

A year earlier Mariátegui had offered a harsh assessment of the state of the workers' movement:

> This year, the actions of unions and federations have produced a series of ill conceived and badly led movements.... [I]n the majority of them workers have been robbed by the employers of their most hard-won advances and with their unheard-of insolence have refused to recognize the organization."[20]

In 1928, he analyzed the situation in the document titled "Antecedents and Development of Class Action," which he sent to the Montevideo conference the following year, elaborating on his earlier comments:

> The June repression among its other effects impelled a revision of methods and concepts and the elimination of weaker and confused elements in the social movement. On the one hand the cur-

rent favouring organization grew stronger, having rid itself of the remnants of anarcho-syndicalism, purged of a "subversive Bohemia"; on the other the Aprista deviation became clearer with the proposal to set up a National Liberation Party."[21]

The document in which this comment appears uses a more dogmatic tone than was typical of Mariátegui; it may well have reflected a concession to the discourse of the Comintern.

At the same time, he was developing the network of connections with indigenous organizations across the country. The Morococha tragedy very directly affected the communities from which the miners came, and the intense organizing work among the miners using both *Amauta* and *Labor* resonated with other sections of workers.

The Lima Group, meanwhile, largely meeting in the Red Corner, brought together a range of people to discuss socialism, some of whom were members of APRA and contributed to *Amauta*.

In the polemics and debates around Mariátegui's thinking on the Indian question, his contribution to Marxism, and his views on political organization, what tends to be left aside is that his Marxism was a *politics*, a guide to action and organization, as well as a materialist method and a philosophy of history. From the moment of his return to Peru in 1923, he was dedicated to building a broad and inclusive working-class movement. He did work with a concept of the vanguard, made explicit both in the statutes of the CGTP and in the program of the Socialist Party. But it was a vanguard conceived as a "tribune of the people," whose status as such had been recognized by the class and won in the course of a growing struggle. The vanguard was *of*, not *for*, the movement. In this sense, Mariátegui's tactical and strategic thinking and his writing are consistent and coherent.

In 1928 and 1929, there were a series of employers' attacks on the working-class movement; the repression of an oil workers' strike in Talara, attacks on miners' wages and conditions, and confrontations on the coastal estates, among others. Faced with this employers' offensive, the imperative for Mariátegui was a unification of workers' struggles through a national trade union congress. On May 1, 1929, the congress was proposed and its general principles—written by Mariátegui—presented. Among its arguments was the urgent necessity for a working-class newspaper—and *Labor*, a companion publication to *Amauta* directed at the working class, was born. Its pages contained detailed studies of the movement and regular news from correspondents in different unions and workplaces. But it also included some of the more general articles from *Amauta*—on Mexico by Martí Casanovas, on Bolivia by Tristán Marof, on women workers and on the ayllu. *Labor* 9 (August 1929) contained the statutes of the General Congress of Peruvian Workers (CGTP). Significantly, the document broke definitively with the craft or guild union principle, arguing that the new form of class organization must be the industrial union and the factory committees, which should include all workers, whether trade union members or not (echoing Gramsci's arguments in Italy).[22]

But perhaps the key clause of his message is this:

> The working class of the city must set the example, by organizing. But it will not be able to maintain its struggles alone. It is important that we help others to organize—the peasants, the thousands of wage labourers who have no eight-hour day nor laws on industrial accidents; we have to encourage and help the miners, the oil workers to organize, for until now the only "right" they enjoyed was the right to hunger and poverty; we have to arouse the mariners and the exploited agricultural workers from their lethargy. In short, we have to unite the proletariat of the Republic in the struggle for our victories.

It was a critical moment. The formations of both the Socialist Party and the CGTP were impelled by the split from Haya de la Torre and APRA.[23] Not only had APRA taken an electoralist and popular front position, breaking definitively with what Mariátegui believed up to that point to be a residual anti-imperialist and united front position; it had also won over some workers' leaders, particularly ex-anarchists. It thus became urgent to establish a coordinated working-class organization based on socialist principles. The task was made more pressing by the internal crisis of Leguía's regime, but more importantly by the existence of political alternatives: APRA's insurrectionary strategy, which expressed itself and failed in the Trujillo rising of 1932; and its electoral organization, which presented the candidacy of Haya in 1932, but failed to win. The strategy of APRA in any event would have placed the workers' movement under a petty bourgeois leadership; as became very clear in their 1928 polemic, Mariátegui's vision was for a socialist leadership and a proletarian movement. On the other side, the sectarian view of the vanguard had already been clearly expressed in a letter to Mariátegui from the Comintern leadership.

Mariátegui had been consistently clear that while the *tasks* of a bourgeois revolution would have to be carried through in Peru, the bourgeoisie had demonstrated its incapacity to carry it through—and the petty bourgeoisie would certainly bend to the ruling classes sooner or later. APRA had seen itself as a kind of Peruvian Kuomintang, the same party that had turned upon its erstwhile communist allies and slaughtered them in Canton in December 1927. Until that moment, the Comintern had continued to argue for the incorporation of APRA. The subsequent turn threatened, in Mariátegui's view, to deliver the working-class movement into their hands in Peru by undermining the united front and imposing an ultraleft and sectarian model that could not embrace the plurality of Peru's working classes.

It would be little more than guesswork to try to imagine a movement still led by Mariátegui. He had held off the pressure of both the International and APRA by his sheer political authority. It is not surprising, then, that both his detractors immediately devoted their energies to trying to destroy his reputation. The immediate beneficiary was APRA. The Communist Party of Peru could not survive the twists and turns of Stalinist policy. As Sulmont suggests, APRA did occupy a central role in mass politics for several decades, but at the expense of the socialist perspective that would have placed the proletariat at the heart of the construction of a new order and a new nation, which was Mariátegui's legacy.[24]

The First of May Manifesto of 1929 clearly set out the urgency of the creation of a national trade union congress in the wake of the Morococha tragedy:

> When we study the day to day struggle of the workers, the balance shows an enormous deficit. Why do we say that? Because this year

has seen the actions of trade unions and federations badly organized and badly led. There has been a marked regression across all
the unions and federations, the majority of whose members have
been robbed of their most precious conquests by the employers;
we have seen how the employers in their arrogance have refused
the recognize their organization . . . refusing to recognize the
demands of commissions of workers who have had to tolerate
the abuses and iniquities of the bosses with resignation. Yet the
proletariat has not lost its thirst for justice, nor abandoned its
demands, but they have lacked leadership and their organizations
have not developed.

In the urban sector, from factories to the railways and the merchant
marine, it was "rationalization" that prevailed, intensifying the rate and
manner of exploitation. Women workers were underpaid (averaging 40
to 60 percent of the male wage in factories) and doubly exploited; young
workers were used for tasks for which they were paid an absolute min-
imum. Agricultural workers on the large estates worked long hours for
paltry wages. In every case, the situation was made possible by the absence
of collective organization. In the case of the peasants and the indigenous
peoples, Mariátegui placed an emphasis on political education:

The unions, particularly the agricultural workers and miners face
an extra burden with the seasonal influx of indigenous laborers,
and their education by the union will be more difficult if class
consciousness is lower. There has to be a major effort in the communities and the ayllus to set up libraries and education committees to fight against illiteracy.

In other words, the workers' movement had an organizational task at
the same time as a political responsibility: pressing for social legislation
on the one hand, but developing the class consciousness of its members
at the same time. And as the crisis deepened, the task became all the
more urgent because 90 percent of Peruvian labor faced a situation of
intensifying exploitation.

Despite his deteriorating health, or perhaps because of it, Mariátegui was intensifying his activity on several fronts at once—in the trade
unions, in the work with the indigenous communities, and in editing

both *Amauta* and *Labor*. The Leguía regime managed to invent a Jewish plot as a pretext for once again closing *Amauta* and detaining its editor. And politically, both APRA and the Comintern were pressing in on him with their very different projects.

Chapter Six

Amauta

This magazine ... does not represent a group. It represents, rather, a movement, a spirit. In Peru there has emerged a current, more rigorous and defined by the day, in favour of renewal. The people behind it are called the vanguard-socialists, revolutionaries. History has still not given them their final name. There are formal discrepancies between them, and some psychological differences. But above all that divides them these spirits are all close to one another, and what unites and links them is the will to create a new Peru in a new world...

Amauta *has gone through the normal process of gestation. It did not emerge suddenly from some personal decision of mine. I came back from Europe with the project of setting up a journal. Painful setbacks prevented me from doing it then. But the time has not passed in vain. My efforts have been coordinated with other intellectuals and artists who think and feel as I do. Two years ago, this magazine would have had a very personal voice. Now it speaks for a movement and a generation.*

The first objective of those of us writing in Amauta *is to get to know one another and find points of agreement. The work on the journal will help us to do that, at the same time as attracting good people it will also serve to distance from us some floating and indolent people who for the moment identify with the avant-garde, but who will rush to abandon it as soon as some effort is required of them. Amauta will filter the vanguard, its militants and sympathisers, to separate the wheat from the chaff. It will produce or precipitate both polarization and concentration. . . .*

Those of us who have set up the magazine are not agnostic about art or culture. We see ourselves as belligerent, polemical. We will make no concession to a generally false criterion of tolerance of the ideas of others. For us there are good ideas and bad ones. In the prologue to "The contemporary scene" [La Escena Contemporánea] I described myself as a man with a commitment and a faith. I can say the same about this journal, which rejects everything that contradicts its ideology, as well as everything that is lacking in ideology.

. . . Amauta has no need of a programme, only of a destiny, a purpose.

The purpose of our journal is to pose, clarify, and understand the problems of Peru from a doctrinaire and scientific point of view, but always seeing Peru within a world scene. We will study all the great movements of political, philosophical, artistic, literary, and scientific renewal. This magazine will link the new men of Peru first with others in Latin America, and then with the peoples of the world.

Introduction to *Amauta*, September 1926[1]

It would be very short-sighted, Mariátegui concludes, not to recognize that "today a historic journal is born."[2] And he was right. It has often been suggested that *Amauta* was the realization of the kind of magazine that Gramsci had proposed to publish, before his imprisonment. Two years earlier, in *Claridad*, Mariátegui had announced the imminent publication of a similar journal entitled *Vanguardia*. The change of name was clearly significant. As he would later explain:

> We began by looking for a title in the Peruvian tradition. *Amauta* could not be a plagiarism nor a translation. We took an Inca word to recreate it. So that Indian Peru, indigenous America, should feel this journal was their own.[3]

There was no clear indication, in 1926, that Mariátegui was committed to the idea of a vanguard party. His notion of the avant-garde, as the introduction to the text suggests, was artistic and literary as well as philosophical, a reflection of his preoccupation with forging the body of intellectuals who, to use Gramsci's term, would be "organic" to the movement he was building. And just like the united front he had proposed for the working class, this "front" would also be inclusive and contain difference and argument. The debates would be a mark of the health of a growing movement rather than the reverse. In a sense, therefore, *Amauta* was the logical next step in the formation of the united front first proposed in his 1924 manifesto.

The title *Amauta*, the Quechua term for the wise men of Tawantinsuyu, marked a change of emphasis from the plan for the original journal. It announced the centrality of the indigenous question, the intended role of the magazine in developing the analysis of Indian Peru, and the nature of the "integral Peruvian nation."

Others have suggested that the magazine was a "prologue to the party"; that, in my view, is much more questionable and forms part of the retrospective rewriting of Mariátegui's history from the perspective of the Comintern. It is true that he formed the Peruvian Socialist Party in 1928, but that was after the split with APRA. The long-term objective was always to form a revolutionary nucleus within the united front. But it will be obvious from the introduction that the central objective of the magazine was to create a ferment of ideas and a debate out of which a leadership for the movement could emerge. There is nothing in the content of the magazine that points to the creation of a party; in fact, it is clear that Mariátegui was already resisting pressures to set up a communist party—as in his polemical correspondence with his friend César Falcón. His outrage at APRA's decision to form a party to contest elections clearly arose from a sense of betrayal. If he had hoped that the united intellectual front formed around *Amauta* would eventually become a political front including many of APRA's members, then the announcement of the formation of the PAP (Partido Aprista Peruano) ended that hope. But it was much more than a competition between them to be the first to create a party. Mariátegui was quite right to accuse Haya de la Torre of being motivated entirely by an overwhelming personal ambition. But more than that it was the *nature* of the party that angered Mariátegui, who could never be accused of similar ambitions, and never was, even by his enemies. The organization he envisaged would be broad, inclusive, and built and controlled from the grass roots. The leadership he envisaged was a political leadership, but not a controlling bureaucracy. Nonetheless it is described as "the vanguard of the Peruvian working class and its leadership in the struggles of the class."

In his youthful writings, Mariátegui had identified among the artists of the avant-garde, the majority of them from bourgeois origins, a critical spirit, a withdrawal from the conservative cultural universe of Lima at the beginning of the twentieth century. The exercise of the imagination was itself an act of rebellion, but a rebellion of an exclusively aesthetic kind. Yet any project for social transformation must include a leap of the imagination, a future project enshrined in social myth that could generate the passion and commitment that was an indispensable component of the revolutionary spirit. In the creation of that project, "intelligence," intellectuals, would have a key role to play in elaborating on and expanding the project and winning the subject of revolution—the masses or the multitude—to its potentiality. But these intellectuals would not be the academics and cultural icons recognized by the existing society; they would arise in and with the movement, interpreting and giving expression to its aspirations and purposes.

Writing in *The contemporary scene,* Mariátegui discussed the role of politics in the "quiet" times, when it is essentially "administrative and bureaucratic." His points of reference were the trade union bureaucrats and reformers he had watched in Italy. But in revolutionary periods, like the 1920s,

> politics ceases to be the province of a routinized bureaucratic caste. In such times, politics overflows the limits of the ordinary and invades and dominates every area of human life.... The revolutionary idea must drive out the conservative ideas not only from the institutions but also from the mind and spirit of humanity. At the same time as conquering power, the Revolution conquers in the realm of ideas.[4]

It is this concept of ideas as active and revolutionary to which *Amauta* is dedicated. Not all intellectuals will be open to the project, of course. There are the avant-garde artists who will melt away as soon as they are asked to act;[5] and there are the "anarchoids and individualists" to whom he referred in his opening lecture at the Universidad Popular, who reject the idea of intellectual commitment or who suspect the involvement of anyone other than workers in the building of a socialist movement.

The new myth, the new revolutionary idea, will emerge from a process of argument and debate. In the process, a new proletarian culture will emerge. But by "proletarian culture" he does not mean the kind of art that Proletkult had commended in Russia. The idea of an artistic expression rooted solely in the experience of workers under capitalism would reproduce the alienation that is the characteristic of labor under the rule of capital. It was an argument vehemently addressed in Russia, with both Lenin and Trotsky arguing that the proletariat as the "universal class" must absorb and appropriate every element of culture.[6] Beethoven and Bach, after all, were the cultural inheritance of the whole of humanity, appropriated by the bourgeoisie for itself. "For the poor the revolution will not only be the battle for bread, but the conquest of beauty, art, thought, and every attribute of the spirit."[7]

Who were these new intellectuals, and where would they come from? When *Amauta* began publication in 1926, Lima's middle class was growing; the generation of students who had attended the University of San Marcos in the iconic year of 1919 and joined the demonstrations in support of the university reform movement were now themselves professionals in their mid- to late twenties. A new generation of middle-class students was now attending university and benefiting from some of the public works inaugurated by Leguía. But they would find no work in Leguía's Patria Nueva, and they would not be won ideologically by a bourgeoisie that was stagnating and without a project for national development. *Amauta* would appeal to those new middle-class elements who were developing an interest in the popular classes and, slowly, in indigenous Peru. The increase in the number of magazines and newspapers in circulation in 1928, noted by Flores Galindo, was evidence of this wider reading public in Lima as well as Cuzco, Arequipa, and some other cities.[8]

As Mariátegui's introduction makes clear, *Amauta* is not to be the journal of an organization, but an open forum for a debate from which would emerge a group of intellectuals capable of representing the spirit of change and of contributing to the creation of an organization. This "preparation" of a vanguard, however, would not occur independently of the political movement, but as its reflection. The new vanguard, drawing together the artistic and the political, would help to generate the passion and understanding that would produce a revolutionary impulse.

Mariátegui no longer saw the anarchists as part of the debate, and they do not figure in *Amauta*. The central ideological debate would be between the anti-imperialism of APRA and the Marxism of Mariátegui. Although Leguía had sent a number of intellectuals, including Haya, into exile, there was a new emerging student generation that *Amauta* could and did attract.

Amauta therefore had an audience.[9] Its sales were remarkably high—according to David Wise they floated around four thousand, a very creditable readership. Its range of articles was wide enough to draw in the artistic and the political community, but it also informed them about the situation of Indian Peru as well as international developments. The "Libros y Revistas" (Books and journals) supplement, which had been a separate publication until it was incorporated in the sixth issue of *Amauta*, offered reviews and comments on recent publications from across Latin America. In January 1927, (number 6) a regular section called "El Proceso al Gamonalismo" (Landowners on trial) appeared, exposing the social and economic regime that prevailed in the indigenous areas and that very few urban readers would have known. In issue number 5, a separate section, "Defensa Indígena," began to mobilize opinion in support of indigenous resistance, and the section later appeared as a separate bulletin.

The early issues (numbers 1–9) were as inclusive as the introduction suggested. Despite a clear avoidance of direct comment on the Leguía regime, it was still enough of an irritant for the government to close down the journal for six months and to briefly arrest its editor on the basis of a spurious communist plot.

Mariátegui was ecumenical in his Marxism, and his commitment to an open forum of debate was authentic, as the magazine's contents demonstrate. In fact, he clearly saw it at this point as something close to a joint enterprise. Haya had visited Russia, and in his public statements he used Marxist discourse. It seemed, therefore, that a discussion around Marxist method was plausible, especially since APRA had also adopted the commitment to a united front of manual and intellectual workers.

The specific project to which *Amauta* was dedicated, however, concerned the development of intellectuals who could participate in and reflect that. The participation was fundamental. Mariátegui's suspicion of "professional intellectuals," be they bureaucrats or academics, was well known. They were the functionaries of an existing order; the revolutionary intellectual, by contrast, would serve the cause of the future:

> In history's tempestuous moments, no spirit sensitive to life can stand outside politics. In periods like this, politics is not a minor bureaucratic activity, but the gestation and birth of a new social order.[10]

For the revolutionary intellectual, "revolution is more than an idea, it is a feeling. More than a concept, it is a passion." He was a great admirer of Romain Rolland's newspaper *Clarté*, which was "dedicated to the preparation of a proletarian culture." Of course, it would contradict every perception of a historical subject to suggest that its consciousness would have to be imported. Instead, it represented "an effort by intellectuals to give themselves to the revolution and an effort by the revolution to draw in the intellectuals," because the battle of ideas does not take place in the institutions. While preparing the conquest of power, the revolution seeks to win the battle for the mind. At times like these, "politics goes beyond the basic levels to enter every area of human life."

Marxism, therefore, was a politics, a means of transforming social life, human relationships, and aspirations, as well as changing the relations of production. In that spirit, *Amauta* reached into the range of political and artistic activity. But it followed certain key thematic threads throughout its existence. The "problem of the Indian," for Mariátegui, was central to the possibility of building a united proletarian front. It is not accidental that the first article of issue number 1 (September 1926) is an extract from Luis Valcárcel's *Storm over the Andes*. There is some controversy as to whether Valcárcel, whose entire life was devoted to the indigenous cause, was a restorationist who argued for the return of the Inca Empire. He emphatically denied it. What his famous work certainly *does* do is present the central contradiction as between whites (*mistis*) and Indians. His portrait of a noble indigenous people, inheritors of the grandeur of the Inca past, is contrasted in the book with the miserable, morally corrupt milieu of the mestizo and white community. And as Mariátegui points out in his prologue to Valcárcel's extraordinary book (which was published by Mariátegui's family press), its tone is millenarian and evangelical, a contribution to the creation of an indigenous "mito." *Amauta* develops the discussion of the Indian question through articles by Dora Mayer de Zulen (founder of the Asociación Pro-Indígena) and Enrique López Albújar, a writer whose work represented the Indian as passive, a stereotype reinforced by a clear biological determinism. The writing of Indian artists like the Puno poet Alejandro Peralta and his brother Gamaliel Churata appeared regularly in the journal.

Mariátegui's own contributions to the debate in the magazine include the writings that would later appear in *Seven Essays*. And in keeping with his own assertion that the revolution embraces every area of human activity, and in particular the artistic activities that can explore the as yet unrealized potential of the community, the journal reproduced the work of contemporary artists and carried photographs and images of popular and folk art together with articles on Indian music and culture. The emphasis was on the reality of indigenous life, rather than on its historical roots.

The key, for Mariátegui, was that the indigenista movement, for all its positive and humane instincts, must move from a philanthropic and charitable perspective to a vision of the Indian as the *subject* of revolution. And that required an acknowledgment of the history of Indian struggles and resistance, and an understanding of the material causes for the condition of the indigenous communities. It was Mariátegui's major contribution to the debate to understand that the oppression of the Indian had its source in an economic system that dominated and exploited them. And that the central issue for the Indian was land—not in the sense in which APRA discussed it, however, as individual ownership, but in a much more profound sense that today's indigenous organizations have defined by making a distinction between "land" and "territory" (*territorio*). Territorio includes the physical land, but also the collective relationship between community and nature, and the history embedded in place through popular memory. Territory cannot be parceled out, individualized, or privatized; it is, as the great English revolutionary Gerrard Winstanley put it in the seventeenth century, "a common treasury for all." Its alienation or appropriation negated past and future, and the fragile network of relationships that is subsumed in the concept of community.[11]

The land is intimately interwoven with the social myth of the community, of the collective being. The bourgeois order fragments and individualizes; socialism restores what is common to all. Mariátegui found the confirmation of the concept in the ayllu as a model of socialist organization. It was indigenous to Peru, yet it shared the values and practices represented in the contemporary world by the notion of participatory democracy. Of course, the Inca Empire was a theocracy, in which a governing class appropriated part of the product of the labor of the grass roots. But the destruction of the Inca ruling class by the Spanish conquerors left intact the base social organization, which survived the conquest. Issue 5 of the magazine (January 1927) included the first issue of the *Boletín de Protesta Indígena*, which carried reports and information for and from indigenous communities in struggle. We know that the daily gatherings around the red sofa at Washington Izquierda now included regular visitors from the sierra, many of them indigenous teachers as well as writers and artists. The network of correspondents on which the project was to grow was forming and extending into the indigenous community.

The second thread of debate in the journal was undeclared at first. Many of the leading intellectuals of APRA, formed by Haya de la Torre in 1924, were in exile. It was, in reality, more influential outside Peru in the mid-twenties than within. But it was in a sense competing for the allegiance of the same audience, or the petty bourgeois intellectual part of it, with Mariátegui, though the politics of APRA remained largely at the level of rhetoric, and the formation of the Aprista Party was mainly stimulated by Haya de la Torre's electoral ambitions. A number of prominent Aprista writers contributed from the outset—among them Antenor Orrego, a poet and philosopher who edited the influential Trujillo newspaper *El Norte*, Carlos Cox, Manuel Seoane, and Luis Alberto

Sánchez, whom Mariátegui would debate directly the following year. Haya, too, contributed several articles from exile.

Amauta resumed publication six months after its closure, in December 1927. The first issue of the new phase (number 10) was introduced with a new editorial, called "Second Act":

> This is not a resurrection. *Amauta* could never die. It would always have risen again on the third day. It has never been so alive, inside and outside Peru, as during these months of silence. We have felt defended by the best spirits of Latin America.[12]

The second series continued the policy of an open forum. David Wise suggests it is cautiously less anti-imperialist than in the first, having in mind Ricardo Martínez de la Torre's major article "Them and Us," on US imperialism. Juan Andrade, the Spanish revolutionary socialist, has a major piece on imperialism in number 15. But, in fact, the second act, which lasted until issue 17, published in September 1928, includes articles by Haya and Orrego, as well as the separate appearance of the seven essays published later that year.

The editorial for number 17, in September 1928, however, marks a significant ideological break—with APRA. "An anniversary and a balance sheet" (Aniversario y balance) marked a parting of the ways. And it is a key document in Mariátegui's political journey. The journal had reached a point of ideological definition. To be faithful to the revolution, it was enough to be a *socialist* magazine:

> We have to restore to the word revolution its true, strict meaning. The Latin American revolution will be nothing more and nothing less than a stage in the world revolution. You may add to the word any adjective you wish: "anti-imperialist," "agrarian," "national-revolutionary." Socialism presumes, precedes, and includes them all.

American Popular Revolutionary Alliance (APRA)

Víctor Raúl Haya de la Torre could not have come from a background more different from Mariátegui's. He was the son of a very well-connected family from the northern city of Trujillo, which had fallen on hard times.

He had emerged as a student leader in Lima in 1919 and had become a mediator between the government and the workers' movement in the city in negotiations over the eight-hour day. He was a confident and charismatic orator, and was elected president of the Peruvian Student Federation later that year. In 1920, he attended the first Student Congress in Cuzco, which made the decision to establish the Popular Universities, in the spirit of the University Reform Movement. It was Haya who invited Mariátegui to give a series of lectures there. When Leguía decided to dedicate Peru to the Sacred Heart, Haya led the protests and was first jailed and then expelled from the country to Panama. From there he traveled to Mexico, where he founded the organization APRA, the American Popular Revolutionary Alliance. Haya was relentlessly active, traveling through Latin America and Europe. He visited Russia in 1924 and for the next two years lived in London, where he published his first manifesto "What Is the APRA" in the journal *Labour Monthly*. He attended the Anti-Imperialist Congress in Brussels in 1927, after which he publicly distanced himself from socialism, having declared himself a Marxist some time earlier.

In fact, Haya only returned to Peru for the presidential elections of 1931, in which he was a candidate, and spent many of the following years in a continuing exile. Haya was a flamboyant and skillful self-publicist. Part of his irritation with the Anti-Imperialist Congress stemmed from the fact that APRA had not been invited, suggesting that his conception of its importance as an organization may not have been shared universally. The ideology of APRA was presented in two books, *For the emancipation of Latin America* (1927) and *APRA and anti-imperialism* (1935). Its five-point program is simply summarized: For the political unity of Latin America; against Yankee imperialism; for the nationalization of land and industry; for the internationalization of the Panama Canal; and for the solidarity of oppressed peoples and classes across the world. It was an abstract program and not sustained by any form of organization; there were groups in a number of places, including Paris. In 1929, the Cuban communist leader Julio Antonio Mella wrote a particularly ferocious pamphlet denouncing APRA called *Qué es el Arpa?* (turning APRA's name into the word for a harp), which was later published in *Amauta* (numbers 31 and 32). Mella was enraged that the manifesto mentioned only US imperialism and not British or French. In fact, in his 1935 book,

Haya would explain that contrary to Lenin's definition of imperialism as capitalism's final stage, APRA saw it as the initial launchpad for a modern Latin American state capitalism. Hiding behind its ambiguous language was a program for a broad alliance of the middle and lower-middle classes—a popular front, as opposed to the united front of the working classes that Mariátegui was advocating. Its methods, while equally undefined, were demonstrated in practice within a very few years, as APRA built support among the younger army officers after the Sánchez Cerro military coup of 1930. At one level it was a cross-class populist alliance, but at another it organized among a layer of the military preparing direct seizures of power.

Mariátegui and Haya were friends during the twenties, and Mariátegui actively contemplated joining APRA, though on the basis of forming a critical left current within it. Ideologically the two men were very different, although this may not have been immediately clear during Haya's "marxisant" phase. But what was clear was that through the Popular Universities, and his participation in the workers' struggles of 1919, Haya had earned a reputation as a radical. He certainly brought a number of the key workers' leaders to the Universidad Popular, and *Claridad*, the newspaper he edited until his exile and then left in Mariátegui's hands, was a radical journal with a readership among the workers' organizations.

The founding statement of the Popular Universities had been unequivocally progressive:

> The Popular Universities are dedicated to the formation of a proletarian culture, free of the superstitions and limitations of bourgeois culture. . . . The Popular University proposes to connect the Peruvian people to the great currents of renewal that are transforming the world in our time.[13]

The university opened in the district of Vitarte, site of the largest textile plant and the heart of the new trade union movement. Bergel suggests that the Universidad Popular "produced the workers' leaders that would later form the Aprista and the communist trade union congresses." This repeats an assertion that appears in other Aprista texts, but it is problematic. The workers' leaders to which he refers, like Fonkén, Barba, and others, were already established leaders of the emerging trade union movement. Among those offering classes were a new layer of young university students, many of whom would become Aprista leaders under Haya—Luis Heysen, Carlos Cox, and many others. They would become familiar names in the pages of *Amauta*. But whatever its subsequent claims, APRA was at this stage a network of individuals, largely emerging from the student movement, who now found themselves dispersed around the world after following Haya into exile.[14] José Carlos remained in Lima, building a working-class organization. As we have seen, Julio Portocarrero considered Haya to be "self-important and arrogant," and even a sympathetic analyst like Bergel had to acknowledge that he was an "egomaniac" (*ególatra*). Nonetheless, APRA had won some support in the trade unions, and that would increase toward the end of the decade.

APRA commentators regularly claim that Mariátegui was a member of the group in the mid-twenties. There is no clear evidence for this. Luis Heysen claimed at the time, for example, that "[t]here are no Marxists in Latin America. Marxism in Latin America is Aprismo." What is clear, and *Amauta* testifies to it, is that Mariátegui was anxious to develop a united front among intellectuals, many of whom—because of their university origins—followed Haya. There are common elements in the discourse of APRA and Mariátegui in 1924 and 1925. Both speak of the United Front and a number of group members, like the philosopher Antenor Orrego, echo the notion of popular religiosity. But the "front" to which Haya referred was a broad multiclass alliance, a "popular front" of the kind later advocated by the Comintern in the mid-1930s. Haya was clear on that; "APRA cannot be the exclusive party of one class," he argued.[15] Its working-class base was concentrated in the Lima textile factories, and among the newly unionizing labor force on the sugar plantations. They claimed also to have some support among the miners of the Central Valley. But until the late twenties, APRA had only a limited organized presence within Peru. Haya himself said that theory preceded practice, and the five points of the APRA program[16] were statements of principle at a high level of generality. Haya's argument was that economic development in Latin America had been the direct consequence of foreign investment, which had financed the growth of the industrial and agricultural export sectors. It was logical, then, that he should find support among miners and sugar workers (of whom there were one hundred thousand by 1930). But the political conclusion was that since it was not possible to jump stages, and the proletariat would only grow on the basis of capitalist development, socialism would come after a bourgeois capitalist phase preceded by the phase of imperialist exploitation.

Perhaps the very ambiguity of most of Haya's pronouncements at the time encouraged the hope that APRA could be drawn into the kind of united front that Mariátegui was proposing. Yet the meeting in Paris in 1927, presided over by Haya, included representatives from the Kuomintang, with whom Haya had already compared APRA. He was clearly seeking international recognition for his project and had distanced himself from the Communist International, which was the major influence in these initiatives. A year later he claimed a "huge" membership in Peru, but, as with most of his claims, it was probably untrue. In fact, speaking to Luis Alberto Sánchez on his return to Peru after the fall of Leguía, he laughingly suggested that the party could probably fit on a sofa.[17]

Mariátegui agreed with part of the economic analysis, in relation to imperialism—in fact, he quotes Haya on it in *Seven Essays*; the political conclusions he drew, however, were diametrically opposed to Haya's. But whatever continuing hope he had of winning, if not Haya then key elements of APRA to the socialist project, ended abruptly and definitively with the news that the Paris meeting had formed a National Liberation Party to back Haya's presidential candidacy in the next elections. Two years later the Peruvian Aprista Party (PAP) was declared in Peru. It exposed very clearly where Haya's ambitions were directed and that his strategy was electoral. He said clearly, "[I]t is power we are interested in."[18]

In summary, the argument with Mariátegui centered on three issues.[19] First, the APRA project was a cross-class initiative, as opposed to the proletarian party to which Mariátegui was committed. Second, would capitalist development in Peru take place in conjunction with imperialism,[20] or would development occur through a confrontation with imperialism? The implication for Mariátegui was that the tasks of the bourgeois revolution could only be realized by the proletariat. And third, the revolution must be socialist. Haya's proposal was the creation of "an anti-imperialist State," state capitalist in nature.

The exchange of letters between the two men is revealing. Mariátegui writes to the Aprista cell in Mexico on April 16, 1928:

> I have read the "Second manifesto of the central committee of the
> Peruvian Nationalist party"; with great sadness. First, because as
> a piece of political writing it belongs to the most detestable kind
> of political propaganda of the old regime; and secondly because it
> reveals an intention to build a movement—whose strength until
> now had been its honesty—on a foundation of bluff and lies. If
> this had been produced by some irresponsible group, its demagogy
> would not concern me. . . . This document is signed by a central
> committee that doesn't exist, though a naïve people will believe it
> is real. . . . The word socialism does not appear at all. It is all the
> noisy, empty rhetoric of liberals in the old mould. . . .
>
> I will have nothing to do with this nationalist Peruvian party
> that in my judgment has no authority to assume the historic task
> on whose preparation we were, until yesterday, agreed. I think our
> movement has no need of measuring its success in tricks and false-
> hoods. Its strength is the truth. I don't agree with you that you
> have to use "all the old tricks" to win. . . . The means, even in well
> prepared movements, end up substituting for the ends. . . ."
>
> In these years of illness and suffering, of struggle, I have
> always found strength in my optimism and hope in that youth
> that rejected the old politics, that repudiated "the old criollo
> tricks"—caudillismo and windy empty rhetoric. . . . I write with
> a high fever and in despair. All those who have seen your propa-
> ganda, who know you, know that it will fail.
>
> My best wishes,
> JCM[21]

Haya replied on May 20

> I received your letter, but I didn't reply because it seemed to me
> infected with tropical demagogy and a lamentable sentimentality.
> You are full of Eurocentrism. How different the effect of Europe
> on you and on me.
>
> You should calm down. It's important for your health. Deep
> down—as Freud would say, subconsciously, you're reacting against
> me. Haya is the target of your hidden suspicions. But Haya is more
> revolutionary than ever, which is to say, more realist than ever. . . .

> APRA is a party, an alliance, and a front. . . . Just because there's
> nothing like it in Europe doesn't mean it can't happen in Latin
> America. There aren't skyscrapers or cannibals in Europe either. . . .
> You demand the word socialism. . . . Words, words, words! . . . Let's
> get rid of the contagion of Europe. Don't fall into the ultraleftism
> of the revolutionary intellectuals. . . . I know you are against us. I'm
> not surprised. But we will make the revolution without mention-
> ing socialism but distributing land and fighting imperialism.
>
> Your loyal friend,
>
> Haya

The two men did not speak again. Haya continued his campaign from
abroad, and APRA continued to denounce Mariátegui for Eurocentrism. The alternative, the "revolutionary Americanism" of APRA,
remained a constant of Peruvian politics throughout the succeeding
decades (Haya died in 1978). But its radical credentials did not survive
its first period in power (1985–90), under Alan García, who oversaw the
worst economic crisis in the country's history and whose second administration became synonymous with corruption on a grand scale.

The difference between the two strategies was clearly marked by the
formation of the PSP and the publication of *Labor* in conjunction with
Amauta. In its ten issues, before it was banned, *Labor* included articles
that had appeared in *Amauta,* but it was above all a newspaper for the
working class, carrying news and correspondence from workers' organizations from outside Lima, particularly from the mines. The Morococha mine disaster in December 1928, for example, was reported directly
by Gamaniel Blanco.[22] The *Boletín de Defensa Indígena* continued to
inform and agitate around indigenous struggles too. And a new section,
"Panorama Móvil" provided a roundup of international news.

The trajectory of *Amauta* through its first three phases reflects a
process of clarification and definition of the nature of the proletarian
front, against the populism of APRA on the one hand, and the sectarianism of the Comintern on the other. The magazine's breadth and the
range of issues and the questions it addressed embodied Mariátegui's
intellectual independence and freedom. The future was projected in
Amauta. As Mariátegui argued in his essay "Two conceptions of life":
"The past makes enemies of us all. The future will bring us unity."

José María Arguedas, the Peruvian writer whose work most imaginatively embodied Mariátegui's vision of the indigenous world, said this:

> I declare with great joy that without *Amauta*, the magazine edited by Mariátegui, I would be nothing; that without the socialist ideas that began to be disseminated after the First World War, I would have been nothing. *Amauta* offered the theoretical possibility that one day, through the activities of human beings, social injustice could disappear from the world, and that is what has made it possible for us to write and what gave us the indispensable theoretical instrument to judge these experiences and transform them into material for literature.[23]

After Mariátegui's death, *Amauta* published three more issues under the editorship of Ricardo Martínez de la Torre. Its tone was markedly different; it became, almost instantly, the voice of the new Communist Party, formed at the Comintern's insistence. Although Mariátegui had formed a group around him who argued his case at the meeting in Buenos Aires in 1929, without his personal authority the Comintern proved too powerful to resist, and, for the moment at least, the *Amauta* project died with him.

Chapter Seven

Interpreting Peru: Seven Essays

Seven Interpretative Essays on Peruvian Reality is the best-known work by Mariátegui. He only published one other volume in his lifetime, *The contemporary scene*, a collection of articles, in 1925. His *Complete Works*, and later his *Correspondence*, were published over several decades after his death by his family publishing company, *Editorial* Amauta. Published in 1928, *Seven Essays* was an immediate publishing success and has continued to enjoy an enormous reputation. Yet it had not led, until recently, to the dissemination of the rest of Mariátegui's writings.

A brilliant historical materialist analysis of Peruvian history, Mariátegui announces in the preface that it will be immediately followed by a volume on politics and ideology, the manuscript of which he had sent to his friend César Falcón. The manuscript was never published, and Falcón denied all knowledge of it. It is a highly significant loss. The volume called *Ideology and politics* (Ideología y política), now published together with the *Seven Essays,*[1] is a compilation of earlier writings. The essays had already been published in separate issues of *Amauta*, and together they represent not simply an interpretation, but also a method—a Marxist method.

Mariátegui intuitively understood the necessity for a reading of Marx that embraced the whole "structural" range of his analysis; his attempts to redirect the specific features of a socio-economic formation towards a general model of historical development, which gave Marxism its authentically scientific value, beyond any reading that might deform it in the direction of an idealist historicism. It is that scientific rigor, the necessary dialectical complement to the concrete articulations of historical fact that distinguishes Mariátegui from the crude empiricism of Haya, who was always open to any compromise in practice.[2]

It is that range, as much as its originality, that marks Mariátegui's analysis of Peru; his understanding of the concept of a mode of production interweaves every aspect of human society into a dynamic totality, generating categories and concepts that are specific to that reality and that as a result enrich the "general model." For Mariátegui, culture, politics, and the economy are not separate realms, each with their own prevailing dynamics, history, and theoretical framework; they interact in ways specific in place and time. As Aníbal Quijano puts it, "[T]he quality [of Seven Essays] is as a marker and a point of departure from which to investigate, understand, explain, interpret, and change a concrete historical reality from within."[3]

The centrality of the economy in Marxist analysis, and of the relations of production, had been transformed in the late nineteenth century into a mechanical materialism, economistic and determinist, of which Mariátegui was extremely critical. It was that methodology that Gramsci criticized in his famous essay of 1918, "The Revolution against Capital." Although Mariátegui did not know The German Ideology, he would certainly have agreed with its contention that

> [t]he production of ideas, of conceptions, of consciousness, is at first directly interwoven with the material activity and material intercourse of men, the language of real life. Conceiving, thinking, the material intercourse of men appears at this stage as the direct efflux of the material behaviour.[4]

The essays on religion, education and literature included here are explorations of the formation of consciousness in the framework of a materialist analysis. The conclusions for a Marxist method and a Marxist politics are explored elsewhere, as in *Ideology and politics*, although the latter was not in fact published until significantly later. *Seven Essays* seems to me to be both a model and a vindication of the Marxist method, and an illustration of the new direction announced in "An anniversary and a balance sheet." It is also an answer to the persistent and malicious accusation of Eurocentrism coming from Haya and the Apristas, an accusation based on Haya's drift away from a brief enthusiasm for Soviet Russia and toward the populism that Mariátegui rightly identified at the heart of APRA's new electoral strategy, and that led directly to the split between them. Some of their ideas were held in common while Mariátegui was preparing the essays—indeed, he occasionally quotes Haya on issues where they had agreed. At the same time, the volume is explicitly counterposed to APRA's cross-class populism.

Mariátegui was writing in the late 1920s, with the information available to him at that time, and the analytical tools and conceptual frame to which he had access. *Seven Essays* is not a book of prophecy, nor is it without elements that, nearly a century later, we would want to contest. Yet its approach to the economic history of Peru, and the political conclusions he draws from the analysis, form a political method that remains as vibrant as it was when it was published, and its outcome is a sophisticated analysis that is applicable not just to Peru but to the rest of the continent as a general theory. In that respect, I would echo Jeffery Webber's contention that in many ways it resonates well beyond much of the work of subsequent writers; take the discussions of dependency, for example.[5]

A Colonial Economy

The Peruvian economy was born of an act of destruction; the Spanish conquest destroyed the Inca Empire, whose population in 1532 was estimated at around ten million. In less than two generations, that population was reduced to around one million—a demographic disaster. The Incanato (or Tahuantinsuyu), as Mariátegui describes it, was "a system of stable agrarian communes ... and historical testimony agrees that the Inca people—hard working, disciplined, pantheist and simple—enjoyed material well-being." The basic unit of the society was the ayllu—an extended family or clan unit—grouped in federations called *marcas*.

Although Mariátegui was almost certainly not familiar with Marx and Engels's discussions of the Asiatic mode of production, the pattern he described corresponded very closely to their descriptions of it.[6] For them the "Asiatic" societies rested on a foundation of communal property in which no individual holds property, which evolves toward a unified and organized society embodied in a despot or a "one." As the state power crystallizes, it appears at first as the expression of a social function, a common purpose. Tributes delivered to the despot in this sense may appear as a contribution to the common good. But at some point—and it is a matter of considerable debate at what point—that despotism will be transformed into a ruling, bureaucratic class prior to a transition to private appropriation of the surplus. In the specific case of Inca Peru, Marx and Engels argued, communal property was a function of conquest. The detail of the debate is too extensive to develop here, but Inca Peru clearly did correspond to that designation. It is impossible to know how it would have developed without the conquest. But it is clearly the case that the communal forms of property did survive the elimination of the Inca state. The relationship between the new masters and the old rulers, however, changed dramatically. There was in the colony no sense of a redistribution of the surplus for the common good, of course. Spain ravaged the agrarian system it found. It has been argued that Mariátegui idealized an Inca state that was a slave-holding system. Marx and Engels make the distinction that the slave laborers in fact formed part of the commune:

> Modern communism is a very different thing from Inca communism. . . . Each is the product of a very different historical epoch. They are the elaboration of very dissimilar civilizations. The Incas were an agrarian civilization, Marx and Sorel's an industrial one. . . . In our time autocracy and communism are incompatible, but that was not the case in primitive societies. Today's new order cannot renounce any part of the moral progress that modern society has made. Other societies have produced different types of socialism under different names; contemporary socialism is the antithesis of liberalism, but it is was born in its belly and nourished by the experience. None of its intellectual

achievements should be disdained. Only its limitations should be scorned and denounced."[7]

This key paragraph summarizes Mariátegui's response to a complex set of problems. But in the first instance he distances himself from the various expressions of restorationism or nostalgia for the past that had emerged within the Indigenista movement; and this not simply in regard to the Incas, but in general in his response to history. The advances of the past, technical or political, achieved in the course of capitalism's development, are as much part of the material progress of humankind as are its errors and regressions. The past informs the future, as he says elsewhere, "as cause or origin, but not as a program"; his view is dialectical in the sense that it rejects the positivist view of an inexorable progress, at the end of which lies socialism and whose course is progress itself. That course is replete with contradictions, deviations, and misguided optimisms—they too will illuminate the future, but the engagement with the past is critical and active.

In the controversies surrounding Mariátegui's concept of Inca socialism or communism, some critics have alleged that he ignored or suppressed the fact that the communes, the ayllus, existed within an autocratic state and therefore charged that his vision of Inca socialism was utopian. The allegation became common during his disagreements with the Comintern just before his death,[8] and it was endlessly repeated thereafter by official Communist Party spokespeople, who denounced him as a "romantic" who had idealized the Inca empire.[9] He could not have been criticized for not addressing the "Asiatic mode of production" question, since Marx's writing on the topic had not yet circulated when Mariátegui was writing.

What has moved so many writers to describe Mariátegui as a wholly original Marxist is illustrated particularly in the first two of the seven essays. The European view of economic development and its transitions was treated by both liberals and Marxists, in a post-Enlightenment model, as a universal law—but not, it should be said, by Marx himself. Marx described the evolution of the European economy and analyzed its contradictions and internal conflicts, above all the clash between the evolving forces of production and the relations of production and the class formations, which it produced. That was Marx's method. Mariátegui's originality—and in the end the source of his conflicts with the Communist International—lay in his application of the Marxist method, in its fullness, to a Latin America whose history and political economy did not reproduce the European experience, and in the political consequences he drew from his analysis. As he himself says, it was the first time that Latin America had been subject to a historical materialist analysis.

The basic unit of organization in the Inca Empire was the ayllu; it was both social and physical, both the community and the land it occupied. The collective included the elderly and those unable to work. Mariátegui lays much emphasis on the collective labor of the ayllu members and their sense of solidarity. A large share of their production (there is some disagreement about the exact proportion), however, went to the Inca and the priestly caste, and a smaller share was set aside for the ancestors.[10] In this sense the Inca system was unequivocally autocratic, though Mariátegui insists on the general well-being of its population. It was certainly well ordered and efficient, as the highways, canals and terraces, many of which remain in use today, testify.

The conquest destroyed this successful agrarian economy and eliminated its ruling class (though the new Spanish administration reoccupied some of its spaces), but the communal form remained, albeit now disengaged from central control. The conquistadors destroyed a "formidable productive machine." But theirs was a military and religious enterprise, rather than an economic and social one. The colonizers were not pioneering, in the North American sense, but in the main an unproductive and parasitical class of "viceroys, courtesans, adventurers, clerics, doctors and soldiers."[11] The conquistadors had no substitute project for the indigenous economy they had crushed. The colonial system "seemed less interested in the labor of the Indians than in their extermination." Instead, the indigenous populations were set to work in the gold and silver mines. American gold (and silver) prolonged a feudal order on the Iberian Peninsula and indirectly financed the manufacturing industries of northern Europe whose products, from arms to lace, were consumed by the feudal class.[12] The appalling conditions to which the local populations were subject in part explain the demographic catastrophe that reduced the population of what was the Inca Empire from ten to one million in a generation. The labor shortage on the coastal estates that resulted was later resolved with the importation of Black slaves and Chinese laborers. Slaves were imported in the sixteenth century to supplement the declining Indian labor force. Between 1542 and 1650, Peru held the largest concentration of slaves in Latin America, though the number of slaves reaching Peru declined dramatically after British abolition. In the late 1840s, the flow of Chinese laborers began and accelerated after the abolition of the slave trade in 1854. One hundred thousand Chinese laborers were sent to Peru on four-to-eight-year contracts between 1849 and 1874. Almost half of them died in the course of those years on the coastal plantations or in the construction of the railway.

To illustrate his point, Mariátegui compares the pioneer colonists of North America with the Spanish colonialists. They had come with an intention to produce and a work ethic; they had in the first instance found ways to work with the native populations, whom they described as "nations," though they would later be transformed into "tribes." In Peru, the growth of a coastal agriculture employed (Black) slave labor; in the Andes, the Indian was enslaved by the gamonales, the Andean latifundists. This, however, was an individual slavery in which the surplus value generated by slave labor was not returned in any form.

The imperial structures of the Incas were destroyed, but the communal organizations persisted. Paradoxically, the Spanish Laws of the Indies recognized and protected communal property, though the laws were rarely if ever put into practice. The colonial class within Latin America became the feudal landowners who benefited from Indian labor and land under the *encomienda* system, which theoretically charged the new landowner with a duty of care for the indigenous peoples, whose status as human had been "generously" acknowledged by the church, but only as childlike primitives. What emerged under the viceroyalty, therefore, was a feudal landowning class. The Laws of the Indies, in reality, served to marginalize the indigenous population completely, since although their labor and land could be exploited freely, they were denied access to all the material and cultural benefits of the colony, from the Spanish language to the horse and the mill, though Mariátegui argues (in the essay on religion and elsewhere) that through syncretism the Catholic church in Peru contributed to the conservation of popular religion.

By the end of the eighteenth century, the Spanish monopoly of trade became the major obstacle to the development of Latin America. The creole (white Latin American) elite began to press for independence; though its central concerns were neither humanitarian nor liberal (in a philosophical sense) but commercial—the expansion of trade demanded the ending of the Spanish monopoly. Yet the interests of the Latin American colonies and the interests of Western capitalism, and especially British capital, were in accord. The liberal principles of the independence struggles of the early nineteenth century remained paper promises; the colonial latifundists held on to their feudal holdings, and the ruling class of the new republic entered into an alliance with them, which ensured that the enslavement of the Indian would continue. The evidence of continuation of feudalism in Peru is to be found not in laws or constitutions, but in the reality of the agrarian economy, in the Andes and on the emerging agricultural estates of the coast, where the concentration of land ownership and the absence of a wage system were proof of the continuing colonial heritage.[13]

Mariátegui refers to these relations as "semi-feudal," to differentiate them from the European understanding of "feudalism" as a historically specific formation. Furthermore, the nature of the emerging Peruvian capitalism did not correspond to a new "stage," but rather to an economic system that integrated the semi-feudal with sectors of the local capitalist economy and imperialism. The Indian populations, therefore, remained marginalized and ignored. More importantly, however, their enslavement was the main support of an economic system from which landowners, as well as a new generation of capitalists and their imperialist partners, benefited directly. "The colonial link with Spain had been broken, but colonialism persisted; it had simply become internal"[14].

This is a key insight in his materialist analysis of Latin America. The patterns of capitalist development were not followed in Latin America, and its protagonists played a different role than their trajectory in Europe. Most important for the postcolonial or neocolonial era was the role of the bourgeoisie. The independent republic maintained the colonial structures, including the slave economy, not only in the highlands but also in the more developed coastal economy where pressed Indian labor worked alongside Black and Chinese workers.

There was no bourgeois revolution in Peru. As Aníbal Quijano points out, the only revolution with a real potential for ending the colonial regime, the rebellion of Túpac Amaru II (born José Gabriel Condorcanqui) of 1780–82, had been crushed and the potential leadership of an indigenous uprising had been eliminated.[15] Thus, the indigenous peasantry played no part in the emancipation of Peru from colonial domination, while the bourgeoisie, with no independent political or economic project, conserved the feudal order. Forced labor was formally abolished, but the feudal class continued to impose it. The continuing destruction of communities did not result in a new peasantry, but only in an expanded labor force. The weakness of the bourgeoisie and its fusion with the big landowners made it easy prey for the marauding European (particularly British) capitalist interests when the economic boom based on guano from the islands and nitrates from the deserts of Chile and Peru, both destined for a European market, began. Thus, the Peruvian bourgeoisie threw in its lot with foreign capitalists who then invested in the coastal agricultural economy.

The subsequent emergence of an export agriculture on the coast was also largely financed by foreign capital. The new capitalist bourgeoisie served foreign interests but had no project of its own. It had no proposals for the elimination of precapitalist forms of labor or landholding, no perspective for the freeing of labor, no political manifesto to offer for an independent nation-state. In the 1870s, a sector of the bourgeois class that had begun to open a commercial space around the margins of foreign trade formed the Partido Civilista,[16] which had a modernizing impulse. But the sector was notoriously inept, and the Pacific War with Chile, driven by the hidden hand of British capital, destroyed any possibility of change. The war's disastrous consequences, including the loss of the port of Tacna and of the nitrate fields of Arica, weakened them further, and in 1890, the holders of government bonds forced the Grace Contract on the government, conceding the railways to British interests. Civilismo as an independent project was defeated; instead it now represented the submission of the local capitalist class to foreign capital, a relationship that would deepen and that reinforced its supine dependence on the export industries wholly controlled by foreign interests. The landowning families of the colonial era, the familiar aristocratic

Spanish names, together with the new bourgeoisie and the Andean landowners, became the local associates of foreign capital and invested their profits in British banks and enterprises.

The growth of mining, textiles, wool in the Andes, oil, and (briefly) rubber intensified the exploitation of Indian labor and the expansion of the latifundios into communal lands. Both "freed" indigenous labor for the coastal and mining enclaves, where the virtual slave conditions were reproduced well into the twenties.

The "problem of the Indian," therefore, was not a moral or a juridical one. The dynamic of the system, its motor force, was exploitation of the most extreme kind. But its sustaining mechanism was the ownership of land, since for the indigenous communities the system of land tenure, "the problem of the land," shaped and defined society. The problem of the Indian was socioeconomic, and its solution demanded the transformation of both the economy and society.

The War of Independence from Spanish rule, and the establishment of the new republic in 1821, did not produce a bourgeois state. Though the legal status of the Indian was altered, briefly, the weakness of the bourgeoisie, economically and politically, ensured that the republic would in fact entrench and expand the interests of the feudal landowning class, the gamonales. The achievement of independence could have brought an end to a feudal system and replaced it with a modern capitalism. Instead, as Mariátegui indicates, the Peruvian bourgeoisie was a dependent and servile class, obsessed with dreams of the past in the absence of a vision for the future, while it rode on the coattails of imperialism.

It was to the problem of the land that Mariátegui turned in the third of the seven essays. What was significant for the development of a Marxist politics at the time when he was writing was to analyze the place of the Indian within the relations of production, on the one hand, and on the other, to understand Inca religiosity, as he called it, enshrined in their myths. His discussion of Inca socialism arises out of those two aspects of the Peruvian reality, and their specific history. But he is emphatic in distancing himself from any suggestion of a "backward glance" that might imply the restoration of that past, an accusation that has also frequently been made against him. The founding program of the Peruvian Socialist Party in 1928, for example, which he wrote, asserted:

Just because we encourage the free resurgence of the indigenous people, and the creative manifestations of their native spirit and strength, does not in any way mean a romantic and anti-historical tendency to reconstruct or resurrect Inca socialism, which existed in historical conditions that have now been complete surpassed, and of which all that remains as a factor that can be used within a perfectly scientific framework of production, are the habits of cooperation and socialism of the indigenous peasantry.[17]

The conclusion that Mariátegui draws from his analysis is this: there are two expressions of the survival of feudal relations in Peru—the existence of the latifundio, the large landholding, and the persistence of slavery. On the other side, the basis of Inca communism is the survival of forms of communal organization and a collectivist ideology. The ayllu, after all, which had survived the destruction of the Inca Empire for four hundred years, was an agrarian community.

Any discussion of the Indian problem that doesn't see it as a socio-economic problem are just so many sterile words. . . . And even if they are uttered in good faith, that does not save them. Its roots are in our economic system and our property regime. Any attempt to resolve it by administrative or policing means, or with education or public works are just superficial as long as the feudal regime of the gamonales continues to exist.[18]

And there is here an extremely sophisticated understanding of the interpenetration of race and class. It is in this sense Webber rightly suggests that "a politics of antiracism, and especially of indigenous liberation, proliferates throughout his discussions of emancipatory strategy."[19] The problem of the Indian is not simply symbolic; its resolution is the core of an authentically anti-capitalist strategy in an imperialist age.

The ruling class's racist sentiment acts in a manner totally favorable to imperialist penetration. The [Peruvian] lord or bourgeois has nothing in common with their peons of colour. To class solidarity is added racial solidarity or prejudice to make the national bourgeoisie docile instruments of Yankee or British imperialism. And that feeling extends to much of the middle class, who imitate the aristocracy and the bourgeoisie in their disdain for the plebeian of color, even when it is obvious that they come from a mixed background.[20]

Inca Socialism

In *Seven Essays*, Mariátegui offers a brilliant and comprehensive materialist analysis of Peruvian history; but it is also a characterization of the whole course of Latin American history. The great debates about the autonomy of the national bourgeoisie during the mid-twentieth century are anticipated and answered in this volume. The bourgeoisie—and the Mexican case was another particularly clear and significant one—have always deferred in the last instance to imperialism when called upon to carry through the radical economic and social transformation that would make it possible to found an independent, sovereign state that represented the majority of society. This was the central question in the polemic with APRA. The recent experience of the "pink tide" and the Bolivarian Revolution have once again confirmed that the petty bourgeoisie cannot represent or lead an "integrated nation" by compromising with imperialism.[21] A capitalist state, whatever its background, functions on the basis of exploitation and accumulation. For that reason, Mariátegui insisted, the tasks of a democratic technological and economic development will fall to the united front of the working classes.

In the case of Peru, the argument for Inca socialism or communism is a central concept. Is this a romantic utopian notion, a backward and idealized glance? What he is describing does not belong to the past. The reality is that the ayllu exists, functions, and represents a collective tradition that has survived the destruction of the Inca Empire and the centuries that followed. We have addressed above the accusation that he evaded the reality of Inca autocracy; in fact, he responded clearly that he was not looking to the past in a historical debate. Today, we can assert with particular confidence the existence of sustained collective traditions of indigenous resistance as a motor of struggle and self-organization of indigenous peoples. It has been made dramatically evident across Latin America since the beginning of the twenty-first century. And in the second place, it answers the dogmatic assertion of the mechanical Marxism of the early twentieth century that the peasantry is by definition conservative and opposed to revolution. Its collective traditions resist individual ownership in some cases. For the landless agricultural workers, the *yanacones*, whose union was established with Mariátegui's help and support in the mid-twenties, the demand for land was combined with the issue of the right to organize set out in the PSP program.

The communal tradition, on the other hand, is integral to the socialist vision of society. The ayllu reflects a practice and a principle of solidarity, of social responsibility, and of equality that must lie at the basis of any genuinely democratic form of social organization. That tradition, for Mariátegui, is enshrined in "myth," where collective memory and the shared metaphors of liberation meet. In an "integrated Peruvian nation," these traditions will be as meaningful to the proletariat as to the indigenous community. And they will represent the capacity for self-emancipation that is the heart of socialism. One aspect of the Asiatic mode of production, as Marx and Engels described it, was the passivity of the communal population, a resignation based on the permanence of their social structures and relations. Mariátegui refers to it too. But the history of indigenous resistance, especially since the Huaylas rebellion of 1885 led by Pedro Pablo Atusparia, offers a very different picture. The specific demands that sparked that rebellion were the theft of Indian lands by the gamonales and the burden of taxes on the Indian communities. After presenting their demands to the local prefect in Huaraz, Atsuparia was arrested and tortured. After his release he led a rising, before he was detained again and killed. The rising led by Rumi Maqui in 1916 was also a defense of indigenous land rights, among other issues, in a continuum of rebellion and repression.

> In our Spanish America, semi-feudal still, the bourgeoisie did not know how to carry through the liquidation of feudalism, nor was it interested in doing so. Close relatives of the Spanish colonizers, it was impossible for them to take on the demands of the peasant masses. That will be socialism's task. Socialist doctrine alone can give a modern, constructive sense to the indigenous cause which, located in an actual social and economic terrain, and raised to the level of realistic and creative politics, can rely for the realisation

of that project on a class that today has emerged in our historic process: the proletariat.[22]

This was Mariátegui's most radical proposal. Other writers and theorists had found models of communal living and a culture of peaceful coexistence with nature in other societies, like William Morris and the Arts and Crafts movement in medieval England. But these examples were within the framework of European development. The vehemence of the criticism leveled at Mariátegui might suggest that the reaction had deeper roots. In the first place, the *Seven Essays* had presented a materialist analysis from outside the framework of a Eurocentric Marxism that implicitly called into question the dominant understanding of Marxist political economy. And at the same time, to pose as a model for a successful developed economy the experience of an indigenous people might also have offended the economism of many Marxists. Yet Marx, in his brief correspondence with Vera Zasulich, sees no *necessary* contradiction between individual and communal agricultural production, especially as modern technology becomes available:

> Communal land ownership offers it the natural basis for collective appropriation, and its historical context—the contemporaneity of capitalist production—provides it with the ready-made material conditions for large-scale cooperative labor. It may therefore incorporate the positive achievements developed by the capitalist system, without having to pass under its harsh tribute. It may gradually replace small-plot agriculture with a combined, machine-assisted agriculture which the physical configuration of the Russian land invites. After normal conditions have been created for the commune in its present form, it may become the direct starting point of the economic system towards which modern society is tending; it may open a new chapter that does not begin with its own suicide.[23]

And in the following year, in the preface to the Russian edition of the *Communist Manifesto*, Marx reinforces the point:

> But in Russia we find, face to face with the rapidly flowering capitalist swindle and bourgeois property, just beginning to develop, more than half the land owned in common by the peasants. Now the question is, can the Russian obshchina, though

greatly undermined, yet a form of primeval common ownership of land, pass directly to the higher form of Communist common ownership? Or, on the contrary, must it first pass through the same process of dissolution such as constitutes the historical evolution of the West?

The only answer to that possible today is this: if the Russian revolution becomes the signal for a proletarian revolution in the West, so that both complement each other, the present Russian common ownership of land may serve as the starting point for communist development.

Marx's correspondence with Zasulich was his reply to the Narodnik claim that the *obshchina* was a peculiar expression of the Russian soul. Here he offers a general insight; the discussion about a future communist society centers on a variety of unknowns, among them the creative and unpredictable responses of a proletariat that is no longer in contention with a bourgeoisie bent on defending private property.

In 1929, Mariátegui presented three documents to the meeting of the Latin American Communist Parties. "The problem of race in Latin America"[24] opens with the argument he has presented in *Seven Essays*— that the problem of the Indian is essentially a question of ending the semi-feudal system in Latin America. The ruling classes of the region have presented it as a problem of the inferiority and backwardness of the indigenous peoples, a racist diversion from the fundamental socioeconomic question. Most Indians are not proletarians, but servants, outside the wages system. What elements of civilization exist in their communities have survived from precolonial days. As long as the feudal landowning class has them in thrall, there can be no national integration, no nation to speak of, since the "feudal and bourgeois classes in our countries feel the same contempt for the Indians as well as others as the white imperialists," and the feeling extends to some of the middle classes. It is the indigenous peoples themselves who will eliminate racism through their own actions and their acceptance of socialist ideas. But that must operate together with a sustained working-class campaign against a socioeconomic order that deploys racism as a weapon in its maintenance, a racism, furthermore, that upholds the alliance of landowners, bourgeoisie, and imperialists:

The "communities" that have demonstrated under the harshest repression an astonishing and persistent capacity for resistance represent a natural factor in favour of the socialisation of the land. The Indian has deeply embedded habits of cooperation. . . . The "community" can be transformed into a cooperative with minimal effort. The transfer of of feudal lands to the "communities" is, in the Andean region, the solution that the agrarian problem demands.

Mariátegui understood that these arguments must be rooted in the vernacular traditions, the social and cultural survivals from precapitalist communities, and in the practices of solidarity, collective ownership, and social responsibility in them.[25]

As Flores Galindo points out,[26] these arguments, framed as they were, were anathema to the Stalinist Comintern, who accused Mariátegui of romanticism, as well as APRA, who denounced them as "Eurocentric." In fact, as Löwy shows, this was Mariátegui's attempt to overcome the dualism that separated the specific and the universal, arguing instead that the relationship between the two must be fluid, dialectical, and above all concrete and rooted in the material realities in which these cultures and ideas have evolved. Had he known the Russian introduction to the *Communist Manifesto*, he would surely have found there an echo of his own views.

Mariátegui goes on to say:

> It is true that socialism is not an Indoamerican doctrine. But no contemporary doctrine or system is or could be that. And socialism, though it was born in Europe, like capitalism, cannot be specifically or particularly European either. It is a world movement, from which no country that moves within the orbit of western civilization can be alien. This civilization leads with a strength and means at its disposal that no civilization has ever had, towards universality.[27]

And yet he does see socialism within the Latin American tradition. He asserts that the most advanced primitive communist organization in history was the Inca. This trenchant opinion is debatable, since there are now many examples to refer to. But the general point he makes holds well. There are communal traditions that have held firm through time and laid down a "social myth" that refers both to the past and the future. These myths survive from very different worlds. Luis Vitale, in a very interesting discussion, argues that Mariátegui exposed in the clearest terms that in Peru it was not possible to envisage a national project led by the bourgeoisie.[28] The "national formation" to which he refers is surely a new and different structure, multiple and creative. The struggle for land would make the Indian community a key actor in the transformation and in its unfolding.

To envisage that new "nation-people" is an act of imagination now. The pluricultural constitutions of the twenty-first century, in Bolivia, Venezuela, and Ecuador, certainly enacted important cultural changes. But the nation-state remains, albeit fractured and subject to the powerful pressures of the global market. What lies beyond may be currently in construction, emerging from the new struggles of the indigenous communities.

One example is the organization of popular justice, an element that has become extremely controversial recently in the course of the indigenous resistance of the early twenty-first century.

> In an individualistic regime, the administration of justice is bureaucratic. It is in the hands of a magistrate. Liberalism atomizes it, makes it the individual responsibility of a judge. That creates a caste, a bureaucracy, a hierarchy of judges. By contrast, in a regime of the communist type the administration of justice is a function of the whole society—and as in the case of Indoamerican communism, it is the role of the elders, the yayas.[29]

Nelson Manrique takes a critical view of Mariátegui's position:

> Mariátegui cannot resist that vision which considers the disappearance of the Indian (in this case the cultural disappearance) a condition for integration into the nation. This is less an expression of Mariátegui's personal limitations than the limitations of the world view that he shared with his contemporaries—a mentality established with European modernity and which marked social thought in Latin America until the recent crisis of Marxism."[30]

This seems to me to be a misreading of Mariátegui, who was careful to separate taking advantage of technological and cultural developments in the West from an acceptance of the Western model of development. As to the survival of the indigenous community as a partner on equal terms with other sections of society, that was surely the core of his political project.

In some ways the recent period of intensifying indigenous struggle has moved in an opposite direction. As it has proved, cultural assimilation and legal recognition have still not addressed the central problem—that the condition of the Indian is not an issue of recognition, or education, or morality, but of exploitation. In Bolivia and Ecuador, for example, the struggle itself has demonstrated not simply the resilience of indigenous communities, but the alternative forms of organization that they have evolved.

And there is a deeper and more fundamental point to be made, as Quijano affirms in his compelling introduction to the *Seven Essays*.[31] Whatever developments and discoveries might have called into question some of his detailed conclusions, the subversive thrust of the *Seven Essays* remains untouched. Despite the accusations of Eurocentrism and Indigenismo leveled at him from opposite sides, the concept of Indoamerican socialism remains the cornerstone of a Latin American Marxism because the materialist analysis tests Marxism against a different reality, a different history, and finds it the most effective analysis of that reality. That is what *Seven Essays* demonstrates in practice, and what might explain the vehemence of the denunciations delivered not just by European Marxists, but by all those within the Stalinist tradition.[32]

The *Seven Essays* also include further work on public education, the "religious factor," regionalism and centralism, and literature.[33]

Like so many of his writings, the essay on public education seems oddly contemporary. In 1920, with the end of civilismo and the beginning of the Leguía regime, and against the background of the university reform movement, it seemed that the education system would change and modernize. "You cannot democratize the education system of a country without democratising its economy and its political structures"; and the ambitious new plan for education never moved beyond theory. But the movement continued to be driven by what he calls the "proletarianization" of the middle class and its increasing identification with the working-class movement—in the Popular Universities for example—a point that Quijano reinforces. Two external groups of assessors, from the United States and France, were called in to respond to the aspirations of

the bourgeoisie on the one hand, and the old ruling class on the other—
the one practical and vocational, the other aristocratic and academic.

But the debate did not address the high levels of illiteracy among the
indigenous population, or the low number of students applying to be primary school teachers. They would have been held back by the prospect of
facing the landowner and his acolytes as soon as they entered any rural
school. But in any event, the problem of Indian education is far greater
than a problem of pedagogy. It becomes clearer every day that "teaching
literacy is not educating." The primary school is not there to redeem the
Indian morally or socially. The first step in his redemption must be to
bring an end to servitude.[34] As González Prada had put it, in his "Nuestros indios," "If someone says schooling, answer 'schooling and bread.' The
problem of the Indian, more than pedagogical, is social and economic."[35]

The nature of the education to support that process is political,
and its material must be the experience of the exploited class itself—the
core of what Paulo Freire called "the pedagogy of the oppressed."[36] But
the most radical education will not change the situation of the Indian
until the "problem of the land is addressed." Mariátegui reserves special
scorn for the widely disseminated idea of *mestizaje* as a solution—since
this is a veiled racist strategy for the effective elimination of the Indian
community. The idea, says Mariátegui, must have come from some sheep
farmer. The assimilation of what is beneficial and progressive in Western
culture will occur to the extent that the process is one of mutual enrichment, rather than a mask for imperialism or genocide.

Chapter Eight

Literature and Politics

The German critic Adalberto Dessau has calculated that 40 percent of Mariátegui's writings were concerned with literary and aesthetic issues. Certainly, it was a central concern of his early years, his "stone age" as he called it, though a little unfairly to himself. The reality is that he continued to interweave issues of art and politics throughout his life. The final essay of his *Seven Essays*, which is also the longest, addresses what he calls "the process of literature" in Peru. So, his interest in literature cannot be consigned to an early pre-Marxist period; there is no "epistemological break" in his work, though a number of writers have ignored his early writings, citing that reason.

The failure of the Peruvian bourgeoisie to produce an ideological and economic project of their own is a core theme in Mariátegui's analysis of the Peruvian reality. The alienation and marginality of the avant-garde artists were symptoms of the absence of an independent vision of the nation, or of a strategy for change. It was, of course, what Leguía had promised in 1919 in the aftermath of the collapse of civilismo. But it had failed, and by the latter part of his regime, he had subordinated Peru to the economic aspirations of imperialist capital and turned his repressive machine against all those who resisted.

Before 1919 the Bohemian circles, the avant-garde, which Mariátegui joined, were defined by their hostility to a conservative and superficial bourgeois culture shaped largely by its "backward glance."[1] It looked back, but in a very different way from Mariátegui's understanding of a past to be interrogated for its intimations of the future. This art of conformity questioned nothing, merely addressing the present as eternal and the past in continuity with it. The avant-garde writers, by contrast, expressed their discontent as boredom, as "ennui" (the very origin of the term in French signaled its rejection of a colonial, Hispanic culture), "spleen"—that consciousness described as "fin de siècle," a weariness and indifference to the facile optimism, materialism, and frivolity of a bourgeois age. It was ironic, irreverent to the point of heresy,[2] indifferent to bourgeois values in the reflected and diluted form in which they appeared in Peru. Mariátegui expressed it in his own poem "Spleen":

> *A disdain for life, a vague unease*
> *In the knowledge I am bound to die*
> *An indolent tedium . . . stops me from struggling*
> *and buries me in the sterile lassitude of dreams*

Futurism was the first of the new European avant-garde movements to reach Peru through Abraham Valdelomar, editor of *Colónida*, who had a spent a year as a diplomat in Italy—though he did not have a particularly high opinion of Marinetti, the founder of the movement. Mariátegui himself returns to Futurism a number of times, as an example of how artistic experimentation and radicalization could nevertheless turn in reactionary directions. If the common root of Modernism was its shared disillusionment with bourgeois rationalism, in the case of Futurism, the outcome of its initial assault on all that was antiquated, all that was old, was to throw in its lot with Mussolini's fascism and its militant restorationism. Having watched all that was solid melt into air, it colluded in the rebuilding of what had already collapsed. In the year of his death, Mariátegui wrote a scathing epitaph on an artistic vanguard that had failed to look to the future, despite its name:

> Marinetti and his followers claimed to represent, artistically as well as in politics and feeling, a new Italy. But looking at it from a distance, futurism makes one smile. . . . it is some time now since

it entered the academy and the political order; fascism has swallowed it whole, effortlessly, which is no credit to the digestive system of the Blackshirts but proof of how fundamentally innocuous the futurists are.[3]

In contrast, Russian Futurism, above all in the shape of its outstanding writer Vladimir Mayakovsky, interpreted futurism in exactly the opposite way. In dismantling the thought of the past, literature contributes to the shaping of the future:

This is for you—
Who put on little fig leaves of mysticism
Whose brows are harrowed with wrinkles—
You, little Futurists,
Imaginists,
Acmeists, entangled in the cobweb of rhymes.

This is for you—
Who have exchanged rumpled hair
For a slick hairdo,
Best shoes for lacquered pumps,
You, men of the Proletcult,
Who keep patching
Pushkin's faded tailcoat

. . .

There are no fools today to crowd, open-mouthed, round a maestro *and await his pronouncement.* Comrades,
Give us a new form of art;
An art
That will pull the republic out of the mud.[4]

Futurism had its representatives in Peru—Alberto Hidalgo and Carlos Oquendo de Amat, as well as Xavier Abril before his conversion to Surrealism. All three had their work published in *Amauta*, together with the most apolitical and "purist" poet of the generation, José María Eguren.

Writing about the Argentine poet Oliverio Girondo, Mariátegui described the avant-garde as the "ambiguous flora of a world in decay." He said: "In the ultramodern schools the old art decomposes, becomes chaotic and dissolves in exasperated searchings and tragic-comic acrobatics. The vocation of the avant-garde is negative, is dissolution. Their role is to dissociate and destroy all the ideas and all the feelings of bourgeois art."[5]

So, the new art was anti-bourgeois, but that did not necessarily mean that it was revolutionary. If language is always dialogue, just as the human is always social, it is a contradiction to pursue a "pure" language, disengaged from history. Language and literature do not exist outside time. If Modernism and its expressions represent an assault, a dismembering of bourgeois reason, the vocation of literature is not fulfilled by that act of destruction alone, though it can be a prelude to a new art. As the divergence between Italian and Russian Futurisms had shown, however, it can look backwards rather than forward, though that was, in Mariátegui's view, a betrayal of literature itself.

Like myth, literature interrogates and challenges social being and suggests alternative possibilities. In the words of the Russian linguist Roman Jakobson, it "makes language strange." Mariátegui's interest in literature was more than a secondary diversion. It was integral to his Marxism, and to the emergence of the alternative, anticipatory thinking, the "myth," that would point to a socialist future. Imagination was an indispensable element in its creation.

It is in this sense that he is critical of socialist realism and questions the theory of reflection which the later Lukács articulated. His withering critique of Zola and of Naturalism is that it "annuls the critical potential of all artistic praxis."[6] "A work of art cannot inaugurate any heroic period, but it can signal latent possibilities that can only be realised at the political level through the concrete transformation of reality."[7]

Naturalism simply reflects the present and renders it as reality. But that reality, as the seven essays powerfully illustrate, is dynamic. Language, art, and literature are not simply mirrors of the world but active components of that reality in a dialectical process. That material world, after all, neither precedes humanity nor exists outside it. History, to recall Marx's famous phrase, is made by human beings, albeit in circumstances not of their own choosing. It is transformed through their actions, in the course of which human beings are themselves transformed. And those actions can be *both* reactions to the real *and* the potential attempts to change it, anticipated in myth and literature. For Mariátegui, that was the key to any art worthy of the name; literature is always the expression of the potentialities and aspirations of the spirit—or as he sometimes puts it, of a faith, a passion. But unlike the romantic theory that separates the artist and his creative practice from other human activities, Mariátegui insisted on the interrelationship between them. And its significance grows in tumultuous periods like the decade in which he was writing. In writing much later about Aleksander Solzhenitsyn, Lukács located his work in a moment between the "no longer" (*nichtmehr*) and the "not yet" (*nochnicht*). In this moment of ideological crisis, there is no bourgeois "absolute," no overriding social narrative; in its absence there is decadence and disorientation:

> If society is a structured whole, its destruction must necessarily imply the simultaneous collapse of all its sustaining pillars; not just its economic oligarchy, but the myths, artistic forms and cultural expressions that permit that oligarchy to maintain its hegemony over the dominated classes. To destroy a society everything that makes people believe in it, its absolute, must be destroyed.[8]

"Not all new art is revolutionary, nor truly new. Today there exist two souls—the revolutionary and the decadent. Only the presence of the first can give a poem or a painting the value of new art."[9] The critical element of the avant-garde was emerging in Peru before Mariátegui's departure for Europe. Once there he met with writers and artists,[10] many of whom would later contribute to *Amauta*. And it was in the emerging surrealist movement that he found a revolutionary impulse:

> The surrealist insurrection arose in a phase that demonstrates that it is no mere literary phenomenon, but a complex spiritual one, not an artistic fashion but a protest from the spirit. The surrealists move on from the artistic field into the political. They denounce not only the compromises of art with the decadent bourgeois thought. They denounce and condemn capitalist civilization as a whole.[11]
>
> The surrealists exercise their "scandalous subjectivity,"[12] in their art. But they do not confine themselves, as their predecessors did, to that activity. They believe in the autonomy of art, but they do not cut art off from other activities.

The Argentine novelist Julio Cortázar put it this way: "You can't denounce anything if you're doing it from within what you are denouncing. Writing against capitalism with the mental baggage and the language that derive from capitalism is a waste of time."[13]

Surrealism proposes to travel the road of fantasy and imagination, with the aim of creating a new reality, a new possibility. To renounce "fantasy," Mariátegui insists, would mean that bourgeois realism was the only option. It is not possible to discover the real without a refined sense of the imaginary and the mythic. It is that link that places Mariátegui's discussion of literature and art at the heart of his Marxism, rather than peripherally to it.

Mariátegui had learned a great deal from the American writer Waldo Frank, who confirmed for him the importance of fantasy and dream, and of Freud, whose individualist perspective did not stop Mariátegui from interpreting his insights as the perceptions of the collective imagination that Alfred Adler would go on to discuss. The key was that this journey into the subconscious, whether personal or collective, did not indicate a withdrawal into the irrational but a more complex understanding of thought that could include both knowledge and desire, intelligence, and feeling.[14]

The iconoclasm and bohemianism of the avant-garde arise with the crisis in bourgeois culture and contribute to it. But by definition, the crisis is transitional. In Italy, as Mariátegui describes, the bourgeoisie were happy to echo the belligerent fantasies of Mussolini, but they attempted to withdraw from their temporary alliance when they lost control of the fascist movement. But by then it was too late.[15] The interregnum cannot last—it is a "catastrophic equilibrium." Mariátegui's relationship with the avant-garde artistic movements has to be understood against that background. They could be won to the revolution, and integrated into the united front of intellectuals, for a time. But with no independent project of their own, they would grow weary all too soon, and succumb to flattery or bribery or threat, unless they became organic to the movement for change. The surrealists, for him, by contrast, were genuine revolutionaries of the spirit.

But this does not mean, as Proletcult argued in Russia in the early 1920s, that everything must begin again and the past be renounced.

Lenin argued fiercely against them that the art and the advances of the past, despite the fact that they had occurred under capitalism, belonged to humanity as a whole. They had only been temporarily appropriated, privatized we might say, by the capitalist class. Bach, Mozart, Beethoven, the steam engine, internal combustion, belonged to the future that would build on and with them. In his fine essay on the fifteenth-century Spanish poet Jorge Manrique,[16] Mariátegui returns to the theme of tradition to distinguish it from traditionalism. Tradition is vital and dynamic, constantly rediscovered and renewed by subsequent generations. The latter is preserved as fixed and dead, a collection of dead relics and extinct symbols. "The tradition of these times is being forged by the iconoclasts who at times seem to be denying it. . . . Without them, society would have been abandoned, abdicating the will to live in constant renewal and overcoming."[17]

As Eric Hobsbawm[18] and others have argued, each age recreates the tradition that illuminates its present and points toward its future. Walter Benjamin, to whom Mariátegui has been compared as a cultural critic and a creative Marxist thinker, addressed the same issues in his *Theses on the Philosophy of History.* "The movements of the future can contribute to repairing the sufferings of the past," he writes, "by recovering the history of the oppressed"—and, we might argue, by recovering its own narratives and stories. A realism of the future, for Mariátegui, must embrace not simply what is visible to the observing eye, but also what is buried and sensitive to the "pulse of the times."

The United Front of Culture

The founding statement of *Amauta*, as we have seen, offered an open forum, a debate around the central issues that confronted "a Peruvian nation still in formation." Although his earlier writings on art and culture offered sharp opinions and judgments, Mariátegui's journal had a different purpose. The united front of the working class would grow in the practice of class struggle, though it would be a long, slow process, shaped by external material forces. Its transformation into a revolutionary front, however, would hang on the building of a leadership of organic intellectuals. The absence of a bourgeois culture in Peru, which is explored in detail in the seventh of the seven essays, left those who were critical of the deeply conservative vision of the country that it rested on, the iconoclasts, only with negation and withdrawal. It was, in a limited sense, a critique of capitalism and its values; the limitation was an absence of any alternative. In *Seven Essays* he takes as an example the influence of Manuel González Prada.

Prada was a member of the aristocratic elite, imbued with all the elements of classical and Hispanic culture, and a positivist committed to the ideas of liberal progress propagated by Auguste Comte, which were highly influential in the Latin America of the late nineteenth century. It was a period spent in Europe that changed his ideas, and he returned a convinced advocate of the anarchist ideas of Peter Kropotkin.

Mariátegui, like all the members of his generation, expressed enormous admiration for González Prada as a rebel who turned against his own class. He represented, as he puts it, "the first lucid moment in Peruvian consciousness,"[19] where "Peruvian" refers to "the new nation still in formation." He was a precursor, a herald of a change to come—but he was too aristocratic, and his language too married to rhetoric, his attitude too individualistic, for them to become expressions of collective aspirations. He embodied the restless spirit of rebellion, of rejection of the deeply conservative Peru of the "civilistas." His lectures and writings were an inspiration to Mariátegui's generation in that sense. But, despite the formation in 1901 of the Unión Radical, he left behind him on his death, in 1918, neither a program nor an organization for the succeeding generation. There was, in González Prada, a profound contradiction: on the one hand, a determinism derived from his positivist conviction in the inevitable scientific and material progress of mankind; and on the other, an almost Nietzschean belief in the power of the individual will. The new generation had moved on from his ideas, but it celebrated his spirit.

That spirit of rebellion and renewal informed the new Peruvian generation, but it had not yet found its political and cultural expression—its future. *Amauta*'s mission was to forge the intellectual expression of that future. It is worth recalling that the original name for the publication was to be "Vanguard." At this stage, Mariátegui did not see the intellectuals in Leninist terms, but as a layer functioning within the proletarian movement in a united front where debate, discussion, and criticism were the material out of which the revolutionary organization would emerge over time. His reluctance to set up that organization too early is well known, and his ambivalence proved to be justified. But the contribution of *Amauta* to the creation of a Marxist understanding of culture and literature in Latin America cannot be overestimated. It was not just a matter of the aesthetics of the magazine—the design, the illustrations by the Indigenista artist José Sabogal, the inclusion in its pages of revolutionary intellectuals from across the world. It was read widely, and it maintained an influence after its brief duration. And it shifted the terrain of political and philosophical argument in Latin America definitively.

By including a spectrum of political and artistic positions, Mariátegui widened the debate to embrace both literature and politics. While other Modernist and avant-garde journals did proliferate in the decade, *Amauta*'s commitment to integrating revolutionary artists with the political vanguard was unique.

Marinetti, for example, figured in the journal, despite the trenchant critique of his politics that Mariátegui had given in earlier writings. The Peruvian Futurist poets Alberto Hidalgo and José Parra de Riego were also published in the journal. Martín Adán, author of *La casa de cartón* (The cardboard house), arrived at Mariátegui's home as a twenty-year-old, carrying his manuscript; Mariátegui's immediate advice to him was that the young man should change his aristocratic name to the pseudonym he eventually used. *La casa de cartón* is certainly a work of the avant-garde, an evocation, without dialogues or names, of the Barranco district of Lima where Adán grew up. In his afterword to the published work, Mariátegui says of him: "Martin Adán is not properly speaking an avant gardist, neither is he a revolutionary nor an indigenista. . . . he humorously describes himself as a reactionary, but his skepticism gives the lie to that. . . . Skepticism today is bourgeois, as it once was aristocratic . . . I believe Martin Adán's work is a heresy, and that is why I have not hesitated to call it a sign."[20]

It is a sign in the sense that "Martin Adan is not concerned with the political factors that determine, though he doesn't know it, his writing." It is not a matter of its form or its technique, but of its content. In an earlier time, he would not have treated his own social milieu with such bitter irony. Here Mariátegui found "corroboration of my ideas as an intellectual agitator." Like Manuel González Prada, Adán expressed the "spirit of the age"—its anti-Romanticism, skepticism, and (especially in his poetry) a withdrawal into poetry as a pure space, in the manner of José María Eguren. And yet, like the German Expressionists, or Pablo Neruda and Jorge Luis Borges, all found space in *Amauta*, because it was the reflection of the complex and multifaceted spirit of the age.

James Higgins describes Mariátegu's socialism as "based on collaboration and tolerance."[21] He was clear on the ideological differences between himself and the avant-garde artists, but he saw them as a symptom of the crisis of the bourgeois order, their marginality at once a rejection of the existing conservative culture and of the absence of a project for the future, in which they could nevertheless play an important role. In Surrealism he found the synthesis between artistic and political revolution, and in particular in the work of the extraordinary poet César Vallejo. Mariátegui discusses Vallejo's first two books of poetry—*Los heraldos negros* (1919) and *Trilce* (1922); two more volumes of poetry were published in the thirties. "His poetry contains the pessimism of the Indian; his hesitation, his restlessness, resolved in a sceptical 'What is it for?' But his writing always rests on a foundation of human compassion." Vallejo is a difficult poet, and hard to translate. He was not indigenous and did not belong to the Indigenista school that Mariátegui discusses later in his essay. What Vallejo captured, in Mariátegui's view, was the spiritual experience of a nation, an experience marked by abandonment, orphanhood, and emptiness—that which has been taken and has left only a shadow. In one of Vallejo's most famous poems, "To my brother Miguel" the game of hide and seek ends with his brother's unexplained disappearance and a line of dots that suggest that there will be no solution. A Catholic with the religious sensibility that Mariátegui describes as spiritual rather than theological, "this-sided" rather than otherworldly, Vallejo's God is no more able to control events then he is— in "the eternal game of dice" God is as susceptible to the unpredictable as any ordinary human being. Here and throughout, there is, as Mariátegui says, an overwhelming nostalgia for a past both unnamed and irretrievable. That is the content of the poetry, which Jean Franco identifies in the frequent metaphors of emptiness—the zero, the unfinished sentence, the language that in *Trilce* breaks down into incoherence.[22] This is not a neoromantic contrivance, however, nor the turning back toward an idealized past that Mariátegui so often criticizes, even in the poets of his own generation, like José Santos Chocano. Vallejo's melancholy is tender, concerned, a sadness that is the sadness of all human beings. If language is social, the material that makes us human, the collapse of language is a profound and definitive loss. His search is for a freedom from suffering, for a life and a poetry stripped of artifice.

Vallejo later visited Soviet Russia and became a communist, though a critical one. His *Spain take this cup from me* (1937) is a work of extraordinary intensity written while he was a participant in the Spanish Civil War. His final, posthumous, work, *Poemas humanos* (1938) is the most explicitly political. But his doubts, his fears, are expressed in the title poem of *Spain*. "Children of Spain—if Spain falls—it is just a thought—but if Spain falls..." "Masa" comes from his final work; in it a dying combatant is surrounded by people who ask him not to die—but "the corpse, just went on dying" until everyone on earth begged him not to die, "and the corpse rose up and began to walk." This was an avant-garde poetry on which the past weighed heavily, as pain, yet for which the future, a collective future of solidarity, of a common language, could be imagined.

The literature of Peru, or rather its spirit, was in a process of transformation. After González Prada came the experiments with other European schools in what Mariátegui calls the *Colónida* insurrection against academicism. In Lima it produced

> the imitation in many cases of corrosive Western decadence and the adoption of some anarchic fin de siècle fashions. But in this precarious flux a new sentiment, a new revelation is making itself felt. Along the universal, ecumenical road, for which we are so criticized, we are coming ever closer to ourselves.[23]

The "we" of the essay is the new Peruvian culture, a product of a fusion or encounter of elements. Both national and international, both male and female, both white and indigenous. In the present, Indigenismo turned its attention to the unacknowledged, hidden Peru, without which there can be no national culture.

With the publication in September 1927 of "Aniversario y balance" (An anniversary and a balance sheet), *Amauta* explicitly changed direction, declaring its socialist politics—and effectively ending its "ecumenical" phase. As we discussed in an earlier chapter, the new line reflected the sharp and definitive break with APRA. *Amauta*, in many ways, was an expression of the alliance between Mariátegui and APRA, since Haya's organization represented the emergent petty bourgeois intelligentsia. The relationship had remained open and relatively friendly until the formation of the Partido Nacional de Liberación (PNL) in 1928 consolidated the ill-defined anti-imperialist alliance into a party with a distinct perspective. The tensions were already evident in the field of working-class organization. In the cultural arena, the new series of the magazine marked a change of direction, above all with the publication of the articles that would become *A defense of Marxism*. There was still a range of poetry and a number of articles and illustrations of Peruvian and Mexican art. Eguren, the least political of Peru's poets, appears, but it is Xavier Abril, the Futurist turned Surrealist, who figures centrally. Anatoly Lunacharsky and Larissa Reissner represent a greater emphasis on Soviet politics and society. Yet Mariátegui holds to his position on literature, despite the drive toward socialist realism led in the Soviet Union by Stalin's son-in-law Zhdanov:

> Literary populism is essentially demagogic, supplying the people with a literature that adapts to its tastes and explores its feelings. But on the desk of a revolutionary critic, independently of any question of hierarchy, a book by Joyce will always be a more valuable document than anything written by any neo-Zola.[24]

In contrast, together with the Surrealists, he argues that "we can only find reality through fantasy." But fantasy, or the imagination, does not operate in a separate realm: "By proposing that literature take the road of imagination and dreams, the surrealists are doing no more than inviting it (literature) to discover and re-create the real." As Manuel Muñoz Navarrete underlines,[25] this new literature that discovers reality through fantasy, dream, and imagination, points ahead to the Magical Realism through which Latin America reencountered the European dream with the instruments of a different reality. The first novel of the genre is possibly the Cuban novelist Alejo Carpentier's *The Lost Steps* (1953), but the proposal for a "marvelous realism," as he calls it, comes in the preface to

The Kingdom of This World, a novel of the Haitian rebellion published in 1943. After him, Gabriel García Márquez's iconic *One Hundred Years of Solitude* (1967) brings face to face the realist and the mythic, the world turned upside down, the "History" of the conqueror retold in the imaginative recreations of a collective voice. Mariátegui would certainly have felt vindicated in his predictions of thirty years before.

The writing of José María Arguedas is not usually located within the framework of Magical Realism, yet his whole body of work is an invitation to discover aspects of the Peruvian reality as unfamiliar to most Peruvians then, and even today, as any dreamscape. In his essay on the "the process of literature," Mariátegui devotes relatively few pages to the literary school of Indigenismo, though the first issue of *Amauta* included an extract from Luis Valcárcel's *Storm over the Andes*, and he was a regular contributor to the magazine throughout its existence. Mariátegui says of Valcarcel's book:

> His work is neither theory nor criticism. It is evengelical and apocalyptic. It is the work of a believer. The principles of the revolution that will restore to the indigenous race their place in history are not present; but its myths are . . . and this is an aspect of the struggle that, within the most perfect realism, we cannot afford to neglect.[26]

In a footnote, he recalls an earlier piece in which he pointed out, in a gentle critique, that Valcárcel's lyrical vision of an Inca world to which it should be possible to return is "excessively romantic"—because the wheel of history cannot be turned back. But Valcárcel's passionate advocacy of the Indian cause, and his detailed knowledge, as an anthropologist, of the inner life of the community, ensured him his place among the most significant writers of his time. His work is more poetic and evocative than in any sense realist. "The character of this literary current is neither naturalist nor 'costumbrista' (a narrative of customs and practices) but rather lyrical," Mariátegui says of the Indigenista writers. Yet as a school it was still developing and had not yet produced "its flowers or its fruit." The writers that he discusses are Valcárcel and López Albújar, whose representation of the dry, harsh world of the mountain communities is highly naturalistic. Valcárcel, by contrast, writes lyrically. But the problem is that it remains a mestizo literature, written *about* the Indian, albeit from a perspective of sympathy and solidarity. Indigenous literature will arise only when the indigenous people are in a position to write for themselves.

In 1935, José María Arguedas published his first book, a collection of short stories called *Agua*. His whole body of work thereafter concerns the world of the Andean sierra and the life of the indigenous communities. A mestizo himself, he spoke Quechua from an early age and in fact only learned his Spanish when he was sent to school in Abancay. Critics have argued that his background disabled him from being considered something other than an Indigenista writer, yet his literary project was to find a means of writing the community from within. The problem of language was central. The imaginary, philosophy, the shared memory of the community, is embedded in language; to translate it into Spanish would certainly betray the nuances of language (and Arguedas has not been well served by his translators). His literary experiment was to reproduce, as far as was possible, the rhythms, visions, and nuances of Quechua in Spanish. In my view he succeeds to an extraordinary degree, though others disagree. And in the end, his most complex novel, *El zorro de arriba y el zorro de abajo* (The highland fox and the lowland fox), in which indigenous and white worlds are in dialogue, failed him in his aspirations. Later additions were prefaced with a suicide note he left in despair at what he regarded as that failure.[27]

A Question of Theory

Amauta included a number of contributions from and about the new Soviet culture, and Mariátegui had written admiringly of Anatoly Lunacharsky and of Trotsky's contributions to the discussion of art in the revolution. Lunacharsky, he noted, "knew that the creation of new social forms was a political rather than a literary task."[28] Elsewhere he cites Oscar Wilde's less earnest comment: "Art nourishes life and life nourishes art. It is absurd to try to separate them and isolate one from the other."

At the same time, Mariátegui was highly critical of the theory of reflection, as it was now beginning to be used by Marxist writers applying a mechanical interpretation of the base-superstructure relationship. For him literature and art were in a dialectical relationship with the real, since ideas were elements of the real in themselves. Human beings did not merely reflect the material world; they were part of that world and equally shaped it. What view of the human did Zola's Naturalism present, for example? Society was presented there as a single biological organism whose features are products of an objective, external process. The famous cycle of the *Rougon-Macquart*, for example, represents the working out of biological necessity through generations of two families, motivated unknowingly by those forces. Among Modernist works, Mariátegui highlights John Dos Passos's brilliant novel *Manhattan Transfer*, in which the protagonist is a multitudinous city in which the individual inhabitants are subordinated to the anonymous totality, isolated in an urban landscape much like that reflected in the art of Edward Hopper. The two idioms were very different, but the relationship between the human and the environment were much the same.

A Raymond Williams puts it:

> At the very heart of Marxism is an extraordinary emphasis on human creativity and self-creation. Extraordinary because most of the systems with which it contends stress the derivation of most human activity from an external cause—from God, from an abstracted nature or human nature, from permanent instinctual systems, or from an animal inheritance. The notion of self-creation. . . . was radically extended by Marxism to the basic work processes and thence to a deeply (creatively) altered physical world and a self-created humanity.[29]

This corrresponds closely to the concept of the philosophy of praxis, derived from Labriola and Gramsci, to which we shall return in the final chapter. Literature did not simply hold up a mirror to the world; it intervened in the social reality to mold or judge it, or to introduce into its representation alternative potentialities. Modernism, as we have seen, in many cases signaled those alternative potentials as absences, empty spaces, language as far as possible shorn of its social referent. That was to deny literature, or the imagination of which it was a product, its function in consciousness—or perhaps to deny consciousness itself.

Bertolt Brecht responded to Georg Lukács in the same terms; if bourgeois theater represented the world as given and unchangeable, Brecht retorted that "the role of theatre was not to 'reflect' a fixed reality but to show how character and action were produced in history." In Adolfo Sánchez Vázquez's view: "By means of art, man as a particular, historical being universalizes himself, but not on the level of an abstract, impersonal or dehumanized universality. Instead he enriches his human universe, conserves and reclaims his concrete being and resists all dehumanization."[30]

A wonderful illustration of the general point, and of the sensitivity of Mariátegui's critical writing, is his essay on Chaplin's *The Gold Rush*.

> The gold rush was the romantic, Bohemian phase of the capitalist epic. It begins at the moment when Europe stops looking for theoretical gold and begins to search for the real thing. Capitalism's was certainly a technological revolution. . . . but it has never been able to break free from gold, despite the tendency of the forces of production to reduce it to a symbol. . . . Chaplin has sensed something that still lives in the world's subconscious.
>
> In film Chaplin is the embodiment of the Bohemian; he needs the poverty and the hunger of his creation. . . . Chaplin is the anti-bourgeois par excellence, always ready for adventure, for change, for the journey. It is impossible to imagine him with a savings account. . . .
>
> It was logical that Chaplin should turn to capitalism's Bohemian Project, the gold rush. . . . He would never find it, like a good capitalist, in trade, industry or finance. This was the only way we could imagine him getting rich. . . . No force, no accident could stop him; neither avalanche nor storm can defeat him. And who else should share his journey, other than Jim McKay, the gold prospector who, crazy with hunger on the mountain, tries one day to kill his companion to eat him. The first duty of the prospector is to survive. His reasoning is Darwinian and implacably individualist.
>
> Chaplin, the perfect English clown, is measured, mathematical; blessed with perfect English dignity. . . . he goes to Hollywood. The health and the energy of North America entrance him; but its bourgeois childishness, its prosaic arrivisme, disgust the romantic

Bohemian. And North America rejects Chaplin too. The Hollywood chiefs see him as subversive, hostile. There is something in him that escapes them. For the neo-Quakers of Yankee finance and industry, Chaplin will always be tainted by Bolshevism

> Chaplin's smile and appearance relieve the sadness of the world. And he understands the wretched happiness of men better than all the statesmen, philosophers, industrialists and artists.[31]

Like myth, the act of imagination is anticipatory, reclaiming the creativity of the human from a capitalism that has rendered it a commodity, and divided praxis against itself, between the mechanical and the creative. Revolution is the moment when the division is overcome, when practice and imagination are reconciled.

Chapter Nine

The Question
of the Party

In October 1928 a small group of seven people met on the beach at Chorrillos, outside Lima. These were the founders of the Peruvian Socialist Party. José Carlos Mariátegui, the person responsible for bringing them together, was not present; he was too ill to attend. The specific moment of the PSP's formation had to do with the recent angry split between Mariátegui and Haya de la Torre. The two men had been friends since before the foundation of APRA in 1924, though they had grown more distant since Haya's enthusiasm for the Russian Revolution began to fade. The clash that produced the bitter correspondence between them[1] was Mariátegui's response to the news that APRA had created a new party (the PNL, or National Liberation Party) to support Haya's presidential ambitions for elections two years later. In Mariátegui's view, Haya had revealed himself as just one more ambitious bourgeois politician, and not the anti-imperialist with whom he could sustain a debate around principled disagreements.

The creation of a socialist party had long been Mariátegui's project. The newspaper that César Falcón and José Carlos had founded in 1919, *La Razón*, had declared itself the organ of an Organizing Committee for a Socialist Party. The paper was closed after just two issues, in response to

161

its support for workers on strike, and the two men were exiled to Europe shortly afterward. In the combative year of 1919, when a general strike had paralyzed the city of Lima and protests over the high cost of living had filled the streets, the founding of a socialist party might have been a real possibility, though both Mariátegui and Falcón had opposed the proposal to form the party that came from one of their supporters, Luis Ulloa. There was no further discussion on the question of the party until 1922, while they were in Italy, when Falcón and Mariátegui, with two others, formed what they called the first Peruvian Communist Party cell, though this was almost certainly a gesture of solidarity with the new PCI, and a symbolic act rather than a serious organizing initiative. There was no more activity around the proposal, though Falcón later argued, in an angry correspondence, that the initiative should have gone further. Mariátegui's answer, it might be said, was his concept of the united front.

When Mariátegui arrived back in Lima in early 1923, the political situation was very different from what it had been in 1919. The level of working-class militancy had declined, and the Leguía regime was increasingly repressive. The Universidad Popular, which Haya had organized two years earlier (with Leguía's support), had drawn in some of the leaders of the workers' movement of 1919, as well as young students and intellectuals from the generation of university reform. But at the same time, some of the leading anarchists had moved toward collaboration with the regime. Mariátegui's lectures on the world crisis at the university were well attended but controversial; his old anarchist comrades were unhappy to hear him describe himself as a Marxist. But his seminal public statement of the following year, "The First of May and the United Front," emphasized the united front as the main organizational principle for a movement where the working class was small and still in its infancy. "We are too few to be divided," he wrote.

The Italian Communist Party, formed after breaking away from the Socialist Party, the PSI, in 1921, had accepted the Twenty-One Conditions imposed by the Comintern for their admission to the Communist International. The debate around the Russian Revolution had divided both the reformist parties and the anarchist movement across the world. The role of the Bolsheviks in the overthrow of tsarism, but more importantly in the seizure of state power, gave the Soviet Communist Party an incontestable political authority and represented a successful model of revolutionary organization—the Leninist vanguard party. The creation of the Comintern in 1919, an international communist organization led by Russia, was a political initiative, creating parties committed to supporting the October Revolution. At the same time, it represented a mechanism of defense of the new soviet state, in that the national communist parties could exercise pressure on their own ruling clases, all of whom were actively engaged in supporting the counter-revolution besieging the Soviets at the time.

His lectures at the Universidad Popular made very clear, ending as they did with a final session on Lenin, that Mariátegui was a fervent supporter of the Russian Revolution. He had planned to travel to Moscow, but in the end he was prevented from going by a family illness. Yet he was less convinced of the wisdom or applicability of the Twenty-One Conditions to Latin America and specifically to Peru. His reports on events in Europe had appeared in the Lima newspaper *El Tiempo*, and were later published as *Letters from Italy* (Cartas de Italia);[2] the political and theoretical conclusions he drew from the experience, and specifically from Italy, were contained in his lectures at the Universidad Popular (*History of the world crisis*), and in the articles collected in his first published volume, *The contemporary scene*, in 1925.

The opening lecture on the world crisis provides, indirectly, an indication of his response to the demand for the immediate creation of a communist party—despite his involvement in the organization of a communist cell in Italy the previous year. What he had seen in Europe was a working-class movement seriously divided against itself in its attitudes toward the Russian Revolution. He had seen the confusion and disorientation of Marxists of the Second International in the wake of the First World War. And many in the anarcho-syndicalist movement were ambivalent about the revolution, despite the enthusiastic support for Lenin and the Bolsheviks of Mariátegui's mentor, Georges Sorel, who was a major influence among anarchists and socialists (including Gramsci) at the time. In the aftermath of the factory council's experience in Turin, the anarchists who took control of the internal union organizations were deeply contemptuous of the communists, for example. And the division at Livorno had weakened the revolutionaries. As he put it in his opening lecture:

> Part of the proletariat does not believe the moment is revolution-
> ary, that the bourgeoisie has not yet exhausted its social function
> and is still strong enough, in fact, to hold on to political power,
> that the hour of the social revolution has not yet arrived. Another
> part believes that the historic moment of revolution has arrived,
> that the bourgeoisie is incapable of reconstructing the social
> wealth destroyed during the war and is thus unable to resolve the
> problems of the peace, that the war has produced a crisis whose
> only solution is a proletarian one, a socialist one, and that the Rus-
> sian revolution has marked the beginning of the social revolution.[3]

The problem, as he saw it, was that the young Peruvian working-class
movement was unprepared organizationally or politically to address
these huge issues. Its knowledge of the socialist movement, and thus of
the implications of the Russian Revolution, was limited, as he put it, to
prewar literature. There had been no debate in Peru around the issues of
reform or revolution, as there had been in Europe. At that moment, and
until the working class had begun to build its own class organizations
and a leadership with knowledge and understanding of the issues they
faced, the creation of a communist party would be premature, formalis-
tic, and authentically sectarian rather than advancing the revolutionary
cause. There was little understanding, until Mariátegui began his work,
of the class nature of Peruvian society, of its historical evolution, or of
the relations of production that prevailed there. Without that it would
be imposible to develop a socialist strategy. In that sense, his *Seven Essays*
was a key *political* contribution to the movement.

His closest political companion, César Falcón, disagreed violently
and wrote to José Carlos to tell him so. He argued that there was no
need to adapt the idea to the reality, that theory was strong enough in
itself. Communism was a universal, he argued, whose time had come; it
was time to prepare for the conquest of power, and Mariátegui's hesita-
tions were simply "nationalist illusions." He was even more disparaging
about his friend's insistence on the need to build a clear theoretical position and an intellectual vanguard. Ideas, he declared, disseminate themselves. He insisted that they were correct to form their cell the previous
year in Italy in line with the Third International, and that they should
have affiliated to it.

Falcón's criticisms were echoed at the end of the decade by the Stalinist leadership of the Comintern at the 1929 Communist Conference in Buenos Aires, where Mariátegui was viciously denounced for very similar reasons.[4] Falcón was clearly articulating the views of that section of the Bolshevik leadership that would launch the "theory of the offensive" within the Comintern, arguing (as Falcón does) that an imminent capitalist offensive would confirm the fundamental instability of capitalism and produce a revolutionary response from the working class. Falcón's reaction was sectarian and ultraleft. Mariátegui's answer came directly in the form of his article on the united front, and indirectly in his tireless activity in building both the intellectual leadership and the class organizations that were the cornerstones of a meaningful revolutionary movement. Worsening conditions would certainly produce rebellion, resistance, and struggle "spontaneously." A revolution, by contrast, is an act of conscious transformation, in which the exploited classes become the subjects of their own history.

In the debate at the Third Congress of the Comintern in 1922, Leon Trotsky spoke "On the Question of the United Front." I am not suggesting here that Mariátegui was aware of it, nor that he was a supporter of Trotsky, though he expressed admiration for his role in the revolution. But at this stage, in February 1922, Trotsky was speaking on behalf of the Comintern leadership, and his views reflected the general line that prevailed at the congress. Addressed at the time to the French and Italian parties, it was particularly appropriate for Peru. And it shows that Falcón's position was by no means the official one at the time.

> What task confronts these parties? To conquer the overwhelming majority of the proletariat. And to what end? To lead the proletariat to the conquest of power, to the revolution. When will this moment be reached? We do not know. Perhaps in six months, perhaps in six years. Maybe the interval will differ for the various countries between these two figures. But speaking theoretically, it is not excluded that this preparatory period will last even longer. In that case, I ask: What will we do during this period? Continue to fight for the conquest of the majority, for the confidence of the entire proletariat. . . . The workers who belong to our party and those who do not join it, like the members of the social-democratic

party and others, all of them—depending on the stage and the character of the working class in question—are disposed and able to fight for their immediate interests; and the struggle for their immediate interests is always, in our epoch of great imperialist crisis, the beginning of a revolutionary struggle.[5]

In fact, there were several more letters exchanged between the two friends, and the correspondence grew increasingly acrimonious. Falcón dismissed José Carlos's position on the indigenous question, for example, and he was very critical of *Amauta*. Mariátegui was equally uncomplimentary in his commentary on Falcón's article on the conflicts in the British mining industry in 1926.[6]

But it seems that Falcón's criticisms were correct in one respect. Mariátegui was opposed to the creation of a Leninist party *at that time*. His later critics would suggest that his reluctance is evidence that he was never a Leninist but rather a populist. Yet this seems hard to reconcile with a comment made shortly before his death in the continuing debate with APRA:

> We have nothing to add to what we said earlier; the vanguard of the proletariat and the conscious workers, faithful to their actions in the class struggle, repudiate any tendency that represents a fusion with political forces or organizations of other classes. We condemn as opportunism any policy that proposes the temporary surrender by the proletariat of its independent program or action.[7]

Given its rather formulaic language, it could be argued that Mariátegui was simply yielding to Comintern pressure. But as the article's title suggests, he was reproducing a position he had repeatedly taken in the argument with APRA from 1928 onward.

Trotsky's speech on the united front set the tone of political debates at the first two congresses of the Comintern, where debate was extremely lively, untrammeled by diplomacy, and wide-ranging. And the position of the Comintern at that point was confirmed by discussions around the question of the struggles taking place in the colonial world, especially in Asia and Africa. If Latin America was of less apparent concern, it was because the primary issue in the debate was the role of struggles in the colonies in weakening the imperialist powers, Britain and France, and diverting them from their attacks on Soviet Russia and their support for the counter-revolution there. In that context, Lenin argued that communists should participate in national liberation struggles led by elements of the local bourgeoisie, where they were clearly anti-imperialist, though without, as he put it, "giving them communist coloration."[8] This was clearly the application of the united front thesis on the colonial and national question. Mariátegui's position at this time was therefore entirely consistent with the Comintern's line on the issue, and it would also explain the collaboration with Haya de la Torre, and APRA, while it was still claiming to be a national anti-imperialist front. But in another respect, he disagreed with the general thesis in the case of Peru; the Peruvian bourgeoisie would never lead a movement for national liberation, though he clearly had a different view of the role of the petty bourgeoisie around Haya. As soon as it proved to be a bourgeois-nationalist organization whose aim was the establishment of a state capitalism collaborating with imperialism, however, Mariátegui broke with it in a dramatic and definitive way:[9]

> It would be utopian to think that proletarian parties, insofar as it is at all possible for them to arise in these countries, will be able to carry out Communist tactics and Communist policies in the backward countries without having a definite relationship with the peasant movement, without supporting it in deeds. . . . The point about this is that as communists we will only support the bourgeois freedom movements in the colonial countries if these movements are really revolutionary and if their representatives are not opposed to us training and organising the peasantry in a revolutionary way.[10]

The 1924 document for the first of May set out the immediate strategy, as Mariátegui saw it. It had two critical elements; the first was to build effective trade unions among the working class, independently of the conservative mutualist tradition and the corporate unions Leguía had created in his 1920 Constitution. Some of the anarchist leaders of the 1919 strikes, chief among them Arturo Sabroso, had accepted positions in the state unions; and he would later join APRA. The second element concerned the Indian question. Mariátegui had begun to seriously investigate the condition of the Indian and to analyze its historical origins as soon as he returned from Europe, and systematically from 1924 onward. His proposal for a united front was a project that would embrace and connect the urban and rural working class, the peasantry, and the indigenous community, as well as a layer of radical intellectuals associated with the Universidad Popular and therefore influenced by Haya de la Torre. Until the actual formation of APRA, this group was not organized beyond the student federation that Haya led. As we have seen, *Amauta*, in its first phase, was directed at these layers, though the magazine's content reflected the broader alliance Mariátegui was concerned to build.

The issue of indigenous liberation, signaled in the journal's title and increasingly in its content, was not a liberal humanitarian question, but the key to the growth of the united front. As he elaborated in his *Seven Essays*, central to that liberation was land, because the origin of the oppression and exploitation of the indigenous communities was a system of land tenure that maintained a semi-feudal landowning class, the gamonales. The issue of land—in that sense—and the demand for its redistribution to the indigenous communities collectively or, in places, individually to small peasants or agricultural workers—was anti-imperialist in the sense that it struck directly at the bizarre mode of production in Peru whose historic structure Mariátegui was the first to analyze. A revolutionary anti-imperialism, therefore, could not arise without addressing the land tenure system and its economic and social effects. It is in that sense that Mariátegui insists that the Indian problem is socioeconomic, and neither moral nor juridical. We have seen in more recent times that the resolution of administrative and educational problems can leave indigenous populations as alienated and exploited as they were before.

A revolutionary organization not founded on the combination of these struggles and these demands, of class-based working-class organization and indigenous and peasant mobilization, could not hope to succeed—and the united front was the expression of that project. But there was also the matter of timing. Mariátegui's constant emphasis on preparation was an indication of how far the movement was from uniting its different sectors, and how ideologically unprepared it was. The petty bourgeois intellectuals were in the throes of disengaging from Leguía, and APRA had not yet enticed them to support its still very vague positions—though that vagueness may well have been one of its most seductive features. The working class was young, small, and still attached to a very recent artisan experience. The mine workers were in the early stages of trade union organization in the most difficult and isolated of conditions, and both they and the oil workers were facing a ruthless foreign management. There was still very little physical contact between them and the urban workers, partly for very basic geographical reasons. The workers in the coastal latifundios were still in many cases marginal to the wage system. The organizational problems facing the class were daunting, and the simple declaration of a party with no established roots anywhere in the class—which is what Falcón and the Comintern were calling for—would have been an abstract gesture. It was evidence that a clear understanding of the specific conditions socialists faced was fundamental. And Mariátegui's instincts in this respect were right.

When Mariátegui took over as editor of the newspaper *Claridad*, the organ of the Universidad Popular, he announced the imminent publication of another paper, to be called *Vanguardia*. Its publication was long delayed, and when it did emerge it had been renamed *Amauta*. The change of title was significant, since it reflected the centrality of the indigenous communities and the peasantry for the project. It was still intended as part of the strategy for building an intellectual vanguard and a working-class political leadership. The vanguard would be the most combative section of the class, but it would be part of the class, formed in the course of its practice and representing its emerging class consciousness. He still did not speak in terms of a vanguard party, though the role that the vanguard should play had clear Leninist echoes. And when the Socialist Party was formed in 1928, the communists were to be a semi-clandestine cell within the organization—it is not clear that it was ever formally organized, but there was certainly a leading group around Mariátegui, some of whom would represent him at the key 1929 conferences.

Although it was not directly articulated in this way, the strategy seemed closer to to Lenin's famous formulation in "What Is to Be Done?":

> The Social-Democrat's ideal should not be the trade union secretary but the tribune of the people, who is able to react to every manifestation of tyranny and oppression, no matter where

it appears, no matter what stratum or class of the people it affects. . . . who is able to take advantage of every event, however small, in order to set forth before all his socialist convictions and his democratic demands in order to clarify to all and everyone the world-historic significance of the struggle for the emancipation of the proletariat.[11]

The Peruvian working class was in its infancy, its knowledge of the wider realities of Peru sparse; it was struggling still with the transition from a craft economy, and the majority of the population were only beginning to enter the wage system. The model Falcón was arguing for, the Bolshevik model, was utopian in the Peruvian context. Yet it was the clearly the long-term objective of Mariátegui's organizing work to build revolutionary organization attuned to the Peruvian reality. It was clear, however, that while it would learn from the history of the Bolsheviks, it would take a different, as yet undetermined form.

In 1924 Mariátegui wrote:

The united front does not eliminate the personality or the affiliation of any of its components. It does not signify the confusion or amalgamation of every doctrine into a single one. It is a contingent, concrete, practical action, concerned only with the immediate reality, leaving all abstractions and utopias aside. . . . Within the united front each will maintain his own affiliation and ideas, each will work for his own credo. But all should feel united by class solidarity, by the same revolutionary will, and by an urgent necessity.

The emphasis he puts on the word "concrete" is significant, as Higa suggests. As opposed to the abstract, the concrete reality is "the synthesis of a vast series of factors which present themselves to the analyst as a unitary whole."[12] Mariátegui notes that divisions and contradictions will inevitably arise later as the organization absorbs different groups and experiences; this is not a problem, but on the contrary "a sign of the advance of the revolutionary process." But it will and must arise out of the specific conditions of Peru. Against Falcón and the dogmatic Marxists who would turn against him, Mariátegui was elaborating and building on the debates that were taking place in Europe, but resisting a precipitate imitation (a "calco y copia") that would learn nothing from its own reality and obstruct the building of a revolutionary working-class movement. As Trotsky said in 1921, the timing could not be predicted, and the circumstances would certainly change, but the revolution would be socialist or it would be nothing.

Mariátegui's illness and operation that year does not seem to have reduced his work rate very much. While he was recovering in the more comfortable climate of Miraflores, a coastal suburb of Lima, he was receiving a constant stream of visitors. Clearly he felt the urgency of the task.

The subject of history that would be forged in and by the united front was the "multitude." Higa explains that Mariátegui's definition bears no resemblance to the multitude of Hardt and Negri, nor to the multitude as the formless and undifferentiated mass of fascism, deferring always to its leader. Mariátegui specifically rejects a politics based on leaders—for instance, the caudillo figure had dominated Peruvian politics in the first half of the nineteenth century—and he would later be savagely critical of Haya's twentieth-century version of the phenomenon:

> The multitude is the social location of political action, its point of departure and arrival. . . . It is the privileged space of the praxis of solidarity; it is in the joint praxis of the multitude that there develops with the greatest intensity what Alfred Adler defines as the "sense of community," in part won through the disciplined labor in the factories imposed by capital, in part brought in from the long peasant tradition of communal life, later integrated into the proletariat.[13]

But this praxis would have to be developed, built on and articulated if it was to fulfill its historic mission. In this sense the role of the vanguard was not to lead from without—because that vanguard must be the most conscious and combative element of the multitude itself—but to make it conscious of its own potentiality. Internationalism was central to that consciousness, but he was emphatic that it would come through the particular, and therefore that the first task of the movement was to discover its own identity, its own singularity. The reality of the multitude, its diversity and internal differences, would necessarily be reflected in the vanguard. But the organic connection between the vanguard and the class, and its accountability, was fundamental. He wrote, "The first task, therefore, is to overcome the anarchoid, individualistic, egotistical spirit that, aside from being deeply anti-social, is nothing other than the exasperation and degeneration of the old bourgeois liberalism."[14]

By 1925 Mariátegui was already preparing his study of the Peruvian economy and his work on the Indian that would emerge in the *Seven Essays*. But the central task of these times was the building of the organizations of the working class. 1925, however, was a year of intensified repression, with new arrests of workers' leaders. At this stage, according to Rouillon, Mariátegui was considering forming a left group within APRA,[15] which was having some small success in recruiting leading working-class militants as well as developing contacts among the workers in the coastal export agricultural sector. The publication of a letter to the Kuomintang from Haya, however, gave Mariátegui pause, and the decision was never made. In any event it would have constituted a critical left current within APRA, at a time of emerging distrust of both Haya's personal ambitions, and his growing distance from the Soviets soon after declaring an interest in Marxism.

Mariátegui would later be criticized for persisting in his attempts to work in alliance with APRA until the final and definitive break in 1928. It was clear, even before its formation as a party, that it was an organization wholly subject to the caprices of Haya. Its political leadership was almost entirely outside Peru, and Haya himself mainly resident in Mexico. The Mexican experience had a major influence on Haya in his formulation of the kind of broad cross-class alliance that APRA represented.[16] The Latin American dimension proclaimed in its title was symbolic rather than real; though Haya claimed influence over a number of national sections, for example Sandino in Nicaragua, it was not an organized or coordinated network. When he was criticized on this count, he replied, "[I]f twenty Russians can make a revolution there, then nineteen Peruvians can make one here." Haya's contact with Russia was pragmatic and his Marxism skin-deep. He was more interested in raising APRA's profile on the international Left than in drawing political lessons from the Russian experience, but the Russian connection at that point gave him access to the Anti-Imperialist Congresses.

Mariátegui, by contrast, had made his political sympathies clear in his lectures to the Universidad Popular, and especially the last of them devoted to Lenin.[17] The decision to develop the united front was consistent with positions taken in the early congresses of the Communist International, and indeed with Lenin's arguments around the national liberation struggles in the colonies. Although there was barely any reference to Latin America at those conferences, Mariátegui extrapolated the tactical debate to Latin America. And he then argued that the nascency of the working class, the situation of the Indian and the peasantry, meant that the proletarian front, with the characteristics he was proposing, was more appropriate to the building of a revolutionary consciousness and revolutionary organization in Peru. *Amauta* was part of the same project—and was developed side by side with trade unions, for example among state employees and the yanacones, the agricultural laborers. And the line of growth from the Workers' Congress to the formation of Peru's first national trade union congress, the CGTP, was pursued with equal consistency until its foundation in 1928.

If Mariátegui hesitated over the break with APRA, it was for political reasons and not sentimental ones. There had been a drift of some workers' leaders toward APRA under the more repressive conditions after 1925, and a growth of its influence in the state sector and in export agriculture. It was important to continue to work with these groups. When Julio Portocarrero went to Moscow in 1927 to attend the Profintern conference, carrying a letter for the International asking for their view of the situation of the Peruvian working class, however, the curt and unhelpful reply was that "the Peruvian comrades must form their own party with a class orientation and cease to cooperate with the APRA alliance."[18] The letter added, "The conditions of the working class and the masses of peasants in Peru are identical to those faced by the working and perasant masses in the majority of Latin American countries."[19]

The dismissive reply makes very clear both the lack of meaningful contact between the International and Mariátegui, and, more significantly, its ignorance of Latin America and its indifference to it.[20] The first Latin American meeting of the International on Latin America was the conference in Buenos Aires in 1929, and the attitudes of the Comintern representatives there, led by Codovilla, were as dismissive as its 1927 response. The Soviet Union's foreign policy was centrally concerned with Asia and Africa, and with European imperialism. Flores

Galindo is emphatic that there was no relationship between Mariátegui and the International prior to Portocarrero's visit to Moscow in 1927.[21] When the Peruvian Socialist Party was formed in 1928, the first clause of the new party's program was its affiliation to the Communist International. The timing of the announcement suggested that the priority had been the construction of a united front with a broad base among peasants, indigenous peoples, agricultural and industrial workers, as well as some sectors of the petty bourgeoisie, including artisans and intellectuals. The new party would be a further stage in that process, rather than a deviation from it. The existence of a "secret" Marxist cell at its core may well have been linked politically to the revolutionary socialist perspective of Mariátegui and his circle, and affiliation to the International was a unilateral determination. The reaction of the Comintern executive was certainly less than encouraging. It may be that the new party was precipitated by APRA's decision and the consequent split between Mariátegui and Haya. It was critical that the distinction between the two versions of the political front be clarified.

Mariátegui's commitment to internationalism was consistent and unwavering. That was clear in his Universidad Popular lectures and through all of his writings. There was no contradiction between that internationalism and his concern to locate his socialist perspective in the concrete reality of Peru. Trotsky and Lenin's interventions in the early congresses of the international acknowledged the necessity of addressing the particular conditions under which socialist organization would be built, and the strategic flexibility and intelligence that this required. Mariátegui's Italian experience certainly shaped his conviction that there was no national solution to the construction of socialism and his clear understanding that it would be built in specific socio-cultural and historical conditions. To ignore the latter could lead to a premature division of the working and peasant classes as had happened in Italy, or the separation of the vanguard from the wider class forces. The consequence in Italy had been the rise of fascism, as Mariátegui so graphically and thoroughly described. That possibility remained in the forefront of his thinking.

When *Amauta* was shut down by the Leguía regime in June 1927, and Mariátegui was accused of participating in a communist plot, he responded by saying that he was a Marxist but that he had no connection with the Communist international.[22] Since Mariátegui never concealed his convictions or his commitments, there is no reason to suppose that this was simply a tactical denial. It had been clear in the Twenty-One Conditions, for example, that membership of the International was dependent on declaring a communist party. The correspondence with Falcón and the insistence on the centrality of the united front—but a united front in which distinct currents could coexist and organize—emphasized Mariátegui's sustained resistance to the premature declaration of a communist party.

The Comintern of 1927 was in its sectarian "third period" phase. The events of these last two fraught years of Mariátegui's life and the actions of the Comintern were analyzed in a work that is fundamental to any understanding of Mariátegui's life and death—Alberto Flores Galindo's outstanding book *La agonía de Mariátegui*, first published in 1992 and expanded thereafter.

The first Latin American communist parties were formed in Mexico (1919), Argentina (1920), Uruguay (1921) and Chile (1922). There was no attempt to set one up in Peru—almost certainly in part because of Mariátegui's influence, but also because the emphasis on building the party among the industrial proletariat in societies with a tiny and unorganized working class, like Peru, made very little sense. For that reason, the Comintern showed little interest in Latin America through most of the 1920s. Peru was placed in a category of "semi-colonies," whose feudal character placed them in a precapitalist phase. In accord with this thesis, these countries must pass through a period of capitalist development, and a bourgeois-democratic revolution, before socialism could be on the agenda.

Mariátegui, by contrast, emphasized the "semi-feudal" character of social relations in the Andes. The term was descriptive rather than scientific; it pointed to the *capitalist* character of the Peruvian economy in which, nonetheless, an advanced capitalist sector coexisted with a rural economy engaged with foreign capital and interlocked with the oil, mining, and manufacturing sectors, while the social conditions and labor relations continued to be characterized by semi-slavery. The twenty-first century has again reminded us that even the most advanced sectors of the global economy consume products produced under conditions of slave labor in poor countries. But the Comintern would have none of that. Thus, at the Comintern's Latin American Conference in June 1929, Victorio Codovilla, presiding, dismissed Mariátegui's analysis and the three documents he had sent to the conference with Julio Portocarrero and Hugo Pesce. In fact, he attacked them as "populism."

There are multiple paradoxes here. Mariátegui is insisting on a socialist strategy because, in however distorted a form, what exists in Peru under Leguía is capitalism, with specific characteristics. The bourgeois revolution has happened, albeit in an unequal alliance with foreign capital. Yet the Communist International attacks him and ignores the careful analysis that has led Mariátegui to that conclusion. Codovilla's counterproposal—the "proletarianization" of the cadres—would destroy the united front of workers and peasants that Mariátegui has patiently built over the previous six years, isolate the most advanced sectors of the class, and abandon the peasant and indigenous communities to their fate. The subsequent line—the creation of independent indigenous republics—consummated that isolation, ensuring the deeper separation from their class allies, and delivered the rest of the class into the arms of APRA, a cross-class populist alliance dominated by the petty bourgeoisie. It would be futile to explore the might-have-beens, had Mariátegui lived. But the ultimate irony, of course, is that within four years Stalinism had abandoned the ultraleftism of the third period and turned toward a popular front strategy that subordinated the working classes to yesterday's enemies.

The new Socialist Party was invited to attend the Profintern Congress in March 1929, and Portocarrero and Armando Bazán represented the party there. The Peruvians, it seems, were not intimidated by the leadership of the world revolution. They refused to sign a document condemning Andreu Nin, the Spanish revolutionary, and they also refused to denounce APRA, insisting that that was a decision that could only be reached in Peru. This assertion of independence by the Peruvian delegates provoked a new and equally scornful response from Jules Humbert-Droz on behalf of the Executive Committee.

The issue was not whether the organization was revolutionary socialist in its orientation, but whether it would continue to be in a

position to win workers to Marxist politics. In other words, its political leadership, in Mariátegui's view, had to grow with and out of its
praxis. In the interim, a group—Resurgimiento—had formed in Cuzco
around the magazine *Pututo*. They rejected the Indigenista thesis and
the political line argued by Mariátegui; though they had had very little contact with him, he was associated with Luis Valcárcel, whom they
had suspended from the group. The pressure from the Comintern had
swayed some other younger members of the group, among them the
future leader of the Communist Party, Jorge del Prado, and the group
around *Vanguardia* at the University of San Marcos. Del Prado claims
that Mariátegui had a death bed conversion to the Communist Party;
others say that Mariátegui, who was confined in Lima and extremely
ill, agreed to the long-term objective of creating the party. It is difficult
to imagine what else a sick man watching his life's project undermined
could say. In any event, he wrote to Glusberg to ask him to prepare for
his move to Buenos Aires. The journey was projected for March 1930,
but Mariátegui was too ill to go, and he died some days later in Lima.[23]

But this was 1928, and the Communist International, which had
not met for four years, was now moving into what was called its "third
period" and to a politics of "class against class." Speaking from the point
of view of the APRA leadership, Eugenio Chang-Rodríguez explains the
split as a sign of Mariátegui's subordination to the Comintern, and more
generally to Eurocentrism, carefully avoiding the fundamental point of
principle at stake.[24] Indeed, that was the position taken by all the Aprista
writers contributing to *Amauta*. The treatment that Mariátegui and his
representatives would receive at the hands of the Comintern after the
formation of the PSP was eloquent testimony to Mariátegui's independence of mind, and to his courage in facing a sustained assault at a time
when the deterioration in his health made it impossible for him to travel
to defend his ideas personally. Nonetheless his two spokespersons at the
Latin American Trade Union Conference (CLAS) in Montevideo in
May 1929 mounted a vigorous defense on his behalf.

Julio Portocarrero, a textile workers' leader and a key figure in
Mariátegui's group of close collaborators, went to Montevideo to present his theses on the Indian question, "The problem of race" (El problema de las razas), but he was ignored. "They just treated the community

in general terms, as something primitive that existed in lots of countries" and said that capitalism would eliminate them.[25] In May, Portocarrero and Hugo Pesce moved on to Buenos Aires to represent Mariátegui and the PSP at the Comintern's first Latin American Conference. The meeting was presided over by Victorio Codovilla, who would become the International's chief hatchet man in Spain and later in Argentina. It was quite clear that it was a prime purpose of the meeting to discipline and crush Mariátegui. In his opening address, Codovilla criticized the PSP for failing to take a position on the question of the loss of Tacna and Arica. The other delegates seconded the criticism; it would have been unthinkable for them to oppose Stalin's personal representative. Portocarrero went on to read Mariátegui's "Anti-imperialist perspective" to the delegates, explaining that the PSP was a Marxist and revolutionary party:

> Taking into consideration our economic situation and our political level we believed it was correct to found a socialist party that could draw in the broad mass of artisans, poor peasants, agricultural workers, workers, and some honest intellectuals. We believed that the party should be rooted primarily in the proletariat. . . . We have formed the socialist party as a tactic, as a means of uniting with the masses. . . . We have been called reformists without looking at the issue in the depth it merits. . . . If our (communist) group can control the party and direct its actions, is it not a good means of linking up with the masses?[26]

Portocarrero and Pesce argued that the correct perspective was the gradual incorporation of the indigenous masses into the socialist movement, fusing modern socialism with comumunal traditions. The arguments were rejected outright. In fact, the meeting showed little interest in the Andean region, focusing instead on Argentina and Uruguay, and on Brazil and Mexico. Humbert-Droz described Mariátegui's ideas as "dangerous," and another delegate argued that the creation of an "ideologically monolithic" communist party was the precondition for serious revolutionary work among the masses.

Mariátegui's response is set out in his document "The anti-imperialist perspective."[27] It is specifically directed at APRA and the fallacy of its revolutionary perspective. In South America, he argues, APRA's slogan of "a second independence" has a special irony in the light of Mariátegui's analysis in *Seven Essays*. The first independence movement, he argues, was led by a bourgeoisie that continued the pattern of colonial exploitation and then delivered the country into the hands of imperialism in the guano and nitrate booms. The Peruvian bourgeoisie has collaborated with both imperialism and the landowning classes and continues to do so under Leguía; it has no independent project and has no connection, cultural or otherwise, with the mass of the people. APRA's appeal is directly to a middle class and petty bourgeoisie; its program for a state capitalism working together with imperialism can neither represent nor defend the interests of workers and peasants. Thus, their project to launch a new phase of capitalism in collaboration with imperialism will not end class struggle but intensify it. Imperialist capital would have no difficulty in ending its alliance with the old landowning class and creating alliances with a new petit bourgeois leadership. The Mexican example showed clearly where such an alliance will lead: "We are anti-imperialists because we are Marxists, because we are revolutionary, because we oppose capitalism with socialism which is destined to replace it, because in the struggle against foreign imperialisms we fulfil our oblgations to the revolutionary masses of Europe."[28]

The document is a sophisticated presentation of a Latin American Marxism. Ironically the class-against-class line of the Comintern at this time was at least in part a response to the catastrophic outcome of a collaboration with the Kuomintang, who then turned on the Communists in Canton in late 1927 and murdered them in their hundreds. There was no acknowledgment of the failure of the policy, and the reaction to APRA should be seen against that background. But, in fact, Mariátegui's document was a withering denunciation of the cross-class alliance and of the opportunism of APRA and Haya de la Torre—but also of the Comintern's opportunist position. His conclusion, however, was not what the Comintern representatives wanted to hear. The argument for a revolutionary strategy based on the reality of the Andean republics of Latin America, on the integration of the indigenous communities into a socialist alliance led by the working class, was of no interest. The formula of "separate republics and self-determination" was the response;

a politics of national liberation was offered to replace the creation of a class-based alliance. In fact, the focus on land tenure engaged the indigenous peoples both as Indians and as peasants in a key platform of a socialist program—the socialization of land—that would have immediate and dramatic effects for agricultural and industrial workers. But it did not fit the dogma.

When Portocarrero and Pesce presented Mariátegui's other two documents—on "The problem of race in Latin America" and "Antecedents and development of class action"—he was again simply dismissed. Codovilla devoted some time to attacking the *Seven Essays*, arguing that there was no specific "Peruvian reality," simply a global semi-colonial situation. On the Indian question, his argument, later applied with disastrous results, was for the formation of independent Aymara and Quechua republics, while at the same time repeating Stalin's arguments that in the semicolonial countries there must be a bourgeois democratic stage prior to socialism.[29] The argument for separate indigenous republics isolated the indigenous communities from the class struggle at a key moment. Separation (and isolation), after all, had been the experience of indigenous communities ever since the conquest. How could this fail to appear as a new form of segregation, of discrimination? Mariátegui understood clearly the relationship between oppression and exploitation—the Comintern, it seemed, did not.

Mariátegui's stubborn refusal to bend to the Comintern's insistence that he immediately form a communist party in Peru had an enormous personal and political cost. But it was entirely consistent with the politics he had pursued from the moment he returned from Europe. He has often been described, and correctly so, as anti-Jacobin. Time and again he emphasized that the vanguard must arise from the class and its praxis, and change with it. A Leninist in many ways, he did not adhere to the Stalinist version of a Leninist party, rigid, centralist, and married to orthodoxy. He always emphasized the issue of discipline, in the sense of the suppression of the subjective in favor of the collective. But the party he was concerned to build would be a spur to joint struggle between each sector of the exploited class, and a forum of debate, respectful of a diversity that reflected the working-class movement itself, and capable of drawing together the experiences, visions (or passions as he was inclined to call them), and demands of the peasantry and the indigenous communities, as well as those of workers. The imposition of an organization formed out of general principles, or a model conceived under very different circumstances, could not prosper; the process of building was dialectical—the national in engagement with the international, as his famous final paragraph of "The Anti-imperialist perspective," quoted above, suggests.

There has been a great deal of speculation about why he refused to abandon the Socialist Party for a Communist Party. One suggestion is that he was convinced that calling it "Communist" would bring down the full weight of Leguía's repressive machinery upon it. After all, just two years previously, Leguía had used an alleged communist plot to persecute Mariátegui and the leaders of the working-class movement and close down *Amauta*. That might have been one tactical consideration. But it seems to me that much more significant was the response of the International in its first communications in 1927. Mariátegui did not acknowledge obedience to any international organization; the idea of a party shaped by and around its leader was anathema to him. Portocarrero says of Mariátegui: "I saw him as someone who was prepared to share his ideas, his desire to create something. . . . I never saw him place himself above anyone."[30]

Mariátegui's loyalty was to a Marxist politics he saw represented by Lenin, in his flexibility of thought and tactical creativity. His Marxism was a political method, one that could never be a rigid orthodoxy in a world in constant movement.

Other commentators have seen him as a Trotskyist, largely based on his concept that the tasks of the bourgeois revolution in Peru would be realized by the working class in revolution, which was close to Trosky's theory of permanent revolution.

After Mariátegui's death in April 1930, the International moved quickly to impose its theory, and it instructed the Lima leadership of the PSP to change the party name to "Communist" immediately. The vote to do so was overwhelming, with only Ricardo Martínez de la Torre dissenting. He would go on to edit the last three issues of *Amauta*, and his *Apuntes para una interpretación marxista de la historia social del Perú* is an indispensable documentary history of the movement. One of Mariátegui's closest collaborators, he moved toward the Comintern line quite soon after his mentor's death. The new secretary of the party was Eudocio Ravines, originally a member of APRA who then joined the PSP. Mariátegui had placed enormous faith in Ravines, who had very recently turned to Mariátegui, having failed in a bid for leadership of APRA at a meeting from which he was finally physically ejected. He would very soon renounce his communism and publish his memoir of an ex-communist, *La gran estafa* (The great confidence trick) in 1952 in Mexico.

The Comintern then embarked on what it called the "de-Mariáteguization" of the Communist Party. Its line would later be presented by Moreshewski in an article entitled "Populism in Peru."[31] The virulence of Stalinism's attacks begs the question: Why did they launch such a sustained attack on a revolutionary socialist thinker who had contributed so much to the Peruvian trade union and socialist movements? His independence as a thinker, his insistence that a Marxist method demanded a clear understanding of the historical and cultural circumstances of Latin America and their political effect, were a challenge to the new "Marxist-Leninist" orthodoxy. And Mariátegui's unorthodox views on religion, on myth, and on the subjective elements of revolution, were a heresy. How wrong they were, and how much damage they did, are evidenced in Mariátegui's stubborn refusal to be buried by history.

Chapter Ten

Mariátegui's Marxism

There have been as many characterizations of Mariátegui's Marxism as there are writers. There is one area of agreement, however, among almost all the more supportive commentators; that it is a multiple, complex, and historically specific development of Marx's method, framed by a concept of totality. Mariátegui was fond of asserting that he was not an academic, that he had "acquired" his ideas through experience, reading, discussion, and the test of practice. When he described himself as an "anti-academic," he was not sneering at the radical students and intellectuals to whom part of his work was directed, but referring to the academic institutions, and above all their method of separating aspects of human history into named compartments—or disciplines—each of which were deemed to possess autonomous laws of motion, rules of conduct, and discourses. The enormous body of writing and the range of activities that he left behind are organic. And Mariátegui's restless, dynamic personal and political journey carried him so quickly through phases of its own development that it can leave the reader breathless. He drew on contemporary sources and moved beyond them as he progressed. But he was not eclectic; there was a direction in his thinking and his activism that was constant—and shaped by Marxism. The power of the Marxist method, for him, was its capacity to identify relationships between phenomena—both material and spiritual—within the totality of history and society.

In the second decade of the twenty-first century, we have easy access to Benjamin, Gramsci, Korsch, and Lukács, not to mention the entire oeuvre of Marx, Engels, and Lenin. But that should not allow us to underestimate the insight and sensitivity required of a young man working under limited personal and material conditions and at an enormous distance from the regions where Marxism originated. Many of these seminal writings of Marxism were not available at the time, nor had Latin America yet developed an interpretation of Marxism from its specific conditions; that would be Mariátegui's greatest contribution. A century later there is an enormous body of Marxist writing to consult, but there is also a history of its uses and misuses that hangs like a pall of smoke between the contemporary reader and Mariátegui. The smoke will need to clear before it is possible to assess the contribution he has made to the understandings that nourish revolutionary socialism in these times.

We discussed earlier how Mariátegui came to revolutionary socialist ideas. His first encounter was with anarcho-syndicalism, a philosophy of action whose subject was the working class but which did not address the question of state power. He came to question those ideas and to move toward socialism, which could offer a vision of a different social order. He encountered Marxism in Europe. He was already an enthusiastic supporter of the Russian Revolution with a sense of the profound effect of the First World War on bourgeois ideas, which had laid bare the contradictions of a social democracy that still claimed the legacy of Marx. Although the conflict had a direct and developmental impact on the Peruvian economy, the devastation and human costs were distant thunder in Lima. In an odd way, its first echoes in the life of the adolescent Mariátegui were in the decadent artistic styles adopted, in imitation of Europe, by some members of Lima's bohemian circles. In Europe, Mariátegui would come to fully understand that this Modernism also marked an ending—the final and definitive collapse of a bourgeois rationality that lay buried in the mud of Flanders. For this was where the promise of an expanding capitalism that would finally flower in a socialist order—the dominant interpretation of Marxism in the Second International—had foundered.

A Definition of Marxism

In Mariátegui's own words,

> Marxism, which many people talk about but few know or, more importantly, understand, is a fundamentally dialectical method, that is, a method that rests integrally on reality, on the facts. It is not, as some people wrongly suppose, a body of rigid principles and their consequences, identical for every historical age and and all social latitudes. Marx pulled his method from the very guts of history. Marxism in every country, in every people, operates and acts in the ambience, in the environment, neglecting none of its modalities.[1]

This short paragraph in some senses contains many of the principles that made Mariátegui's Marxism creative and original, heterodox and challenging. He developed the key points in his final work, *Defense of Marxism* (Defensa del marxismo),[2] a reply to and critique of "Beyond Marxism," by the Belgian revisionist Henri de Man. It is a ferocious response. "The true revision of Marxism, in the sense of a renewal and a continuation of Marx's work, has been realised, in practice, by a different category of revolutionary intellectuals."[3]

Against de Man's "negative and defeatist" book, "which "ignores and evades the emotion and *pathos* (in the sense of strength) of revolution," he sets Sorel's "return to the dynamic and revolutionary concepts of Marx." He describes Sorel as "the most energetic and productive restorer of Marxism." As we discussed earlier, Mariátegui's unstinted and consistent praise for Sorel is and has been highly controversial, giving rise to some of the most critical assessments of his thought.[4] It should be said that references to Sorel are almost invariably placed side by side with his admiration for Lenin's revolutionary practice. It was through Sorel that Mariátegui first encountered Marx, and he found that the Frenchman, for all his divergent and sometimes contradictory ideas, was held in high esteem by the revolutionaries he met in Europe, and particularly in Italy, Gramsci among them. That respect was not shared by Lenin, to whom Mariátegui ascribes, quite wrongly, a recognition of Sorel. In fact, Lenin had described Sorel as a "confusionist." But the new Communist movement that grew out of the wider response to the

Bolshevik Revolution included in its ranks a range of people who had encountered revolutionary socialism in different environments, including the revolutionary syndicalist circles who took Sorel most seriously, as well as members of socialist and other left parties. So Mariátegui's route to Marxism was not especially unusual for its time, though his unflinching loyalty to his intellectual mentor (who died in 1918) probably was.

Mariátegui's defense of Marxism was, in the first place, a reiteration of his early denunciation of reformism, of Second International Marxism, which had become bourgeois and bureaucratic, and worst of all, positivist. The process of history that it had come to represent was wholly external to the human—the transformations of the material reality would, in this version of Marxism, automatically produce social change. And the socialism that was its end point was defined simply as a material goal. These "rigid principles and their consequences," to which humanity was subordinated, eliminated from Marxism the element of consciousness as a dynamic, motivating force in history. It was that awareness that Mariátegui found in Sorel. And if he repeatedly returned to the Frenchman, it may have been because Leninism and Marxism, as he understood them, with their active principles, were in the course of the decade of the 1920s increasingly distorted by bureaucratic regulations and revolutionary consciousness located outside the working class, who was the true subject of Marx's version of history. What other meaning could the concept that "socialism is the self-emancipation of the working class" possibly have?

Marx, Mariátegui says, "pulled his method from the very guts of history." But that was not a single process following identical paths in multiple environments. Marxism derived its concepts from a complex European experience—from French socialist traditions, English political economy, and German philosophy. Marx drew from their combination patterns of economic development and technological changes in social circumstances, shaped by the contradictory relations between the different social forces engaged in and affected by those changes. Or as he put it, by the encounter of forces of production and the relations of production. Those encounters in the class struggle were shaped by exploitation and accumulation, but also by the values and explanations that were offered for them, and by the ideological and philosophical universes inhabited by all the protagonists of history. What made Marxism more than just another analytical instrument was contained in that deceptively simple eleventh thesis on Feuerbach: "The philosophers have only interpreted the world in various ways—the point however is to change it."

Within the general process of human affairs, there are particular histories, in specific settings and circumstances. The European experience yielded critical insights into the process of social life, which could be applied to other realities—but not mechanically. History, after all, was lived, experienced, by living human beings, all of whom inhabited a universe of thought, belief, emotion, aspirations, and purposes. Most importantly history was *made* (not merely observed) by human beings collectively—though not in circumstances of their own choosing. There is no history outside that human experience of it, beyond the description of external data.

Thus, the process of analyzing social change is "a fundamentally dialectical method," as Mariátegui puts it. George Lukács had argued, in his groundbreaking 1922 essay "What Is Orthodox Marxism?,"[5] that revolutionary action must be grounded in "a dialectical knowledge of reality . . . not in isolated facts but in the totality."[6]

"The dialectical principle on which the whole Marxist conception is based excluded the reduction of the economic process to a pure mechanics. . . ."[7] This may provide the key to the question that Quijano[8] and many others have asked over time: Why, despite the inconsistencies in his thought, and whatever gaps there may have been in his political education, does Mariátegui remain alive and relevant for those who came after him? There were, after all, other Marxist thinkers in Latin America, including Luis Emilio Recabarren, Julio Antonio Mella, and Aníbal Ponce, for example. But what differentiates Mariátegui is the creativity of his application of Marxism to the Peruvian reality. There had been no historical materialist approaches to Peruvian history, no application of Marxist analysis to it, until his work began. There was, as we have suggested, no socialist tradition in Peru out of which that discussion might have arisen. But Mariátegui did not simply take the general principles embodied in Marx and apply them—he elaborated and tested them against his reality. And paradoxically, he was punished for precisely that lack of orthodoxy and that independence of mind by Stalinism on the eve of his death. Others followed the Comintern's scornful dismissal of Mariátegui, laying emphasis on his enthusiasm for Sorel, the controversial concept of myth, his religiosity, and other elements to discredit that thought.[9] But these were secondary issues, of interest at different levels, but leaving unaffected that rich revolutionary analysis that articulated a Latin American reality from within, rather than reiterating tired formulas that came from without. His "within" was not simply about being and living in Peru, but in seeing the country and its history from the perspective of popular tradition and history, from the largely silent spaces unacknowledged in the history written by the powerful. And that, in Walter Benjamin's view, was precisely the responsibility of Marxism—to rediscover the history of the oppressed, and "to brush against the grain of history."[10]

We know now, since the publication of the writings of the period by Lukács, Korsch, and Benjamin, and the gradual publication of Marx's early work, that Marxism was far more than the economic determinism characteristic of its prewar epigones, like Karl Kautsky and Georgi Plekhanov. Before the "cult of technological progress" took hold, under Stalin's rubric of Marxism-Leninism the debate around Marxism in the early years of the revolution was rich and creative.

The crisis that followed the ending of World War I was, as Mariátegui discussed in his lectures at the Universidad Popular and the articles of *The contemporary scene*, that the bourgeois rationality to which it was promised Europe would return had collapsed in the face of the realities of that war. Second International Marxism, whose complicity in the war had meant its demise, still occasionally attempted to reemerge, as de Man's volume showed. But there was no way back for evolutionary Marxism after the Russian Revolution of October 1917. Mariátegui encountered Italian Marxism at a point where it still retained a relationship with other ideologies, and when Gramsci could still reject mechanical determinism in his famous essay "The Revolution against 'Capital'" (1918). The impact of October was extraordinary, but its political consequences for the rest of Europe were complex. The Communist International reflected Lenin's compelling conviction, in principle and in the circumstances, that the isolation of the revolution by the reactionary forces supported by capitalist Europe could still strangle it in its infancy. But beyond the specific moment, Lenin was in every sense an internationalist by conviction. The international character of capitalism had also generated an international working class whose theory and practice was Marxism. Russia demonstrated the actuality of revolution, and each capital's assault on the revolution could be undermined by being forced to confront its own working class at the expense of the siege of the Soviets.

The universal assertion of working-class solidarity, however, could not hide the vastly different forms that capitalist exploitation adopted across the globe. The Russian Revolution as a formula for revolution, applicable to every country, confronted those differences in the International. The debates around the revolution in the colonial world, at the Congress of the Peoples of East at Baku in 1921[11] and in the congresses of the International in 1921 and 1922 exposed the contradictions. In the debate between the Indian Marxist M. N. Roy and Lenin, for example, Roy's radical proposals were amended by Lenin, but the final versions acknowledged his concerns.

Roy's original proposal was that "the European working class will not succeed in overthrowing European capitalism until its . . . colonial profits have been definitively stemmed." The amended motion read, "As long as European capitalism has not been deprived of that source of surplus, *it will not be easy* for the European working class to overturn the capitalist order."[12]

In his report on the commission on nationalities to the Congress of the International in 1920, Lenin argued, "The Communist Interntional should advance the proposition, with the appropriate theoretical grounding, that with the aid of the proletariat of the advanced countries, backward countries can go over to communism, without having to pass through the capitalist stage."[13]

Yet Mariátegui's affirmation of the same principle moved some to condemn him as a Trotskyist. And Lenin went on to argue that "it would be utopian to believe that proletarian parties in these backward countries, if indeed they could emerge there, can pursue Communist tactics and a Communist policy without establishing definite relations with the peasant movement and without giving it effective support."[14]

After Lenin's death, and after the catastrophe of Shanghai in 1927, the line of the International changed to the "class against class" position advocated by Stalin, effectively reversing Lenin's arguments and proposals. It is not clear how closely Mariátegui had followed the discussions at the 1921 and 1922 congresses, but it is very clear that in his subsequent polemic with Haya de la Torre and APRA, the crisp summary of his position in "The anti-imperialist perspective" repeats many of Lenin's arguments. Taking his evidence from the specific history of the Peruvian bourgeoisie elaborated in the *Seven Essays*, probably his single most important contribution to Marxism, Mariátegui emphatically rejects the alliance with the national bourgeoisie that APRA represented. While APRA argued that imperialism could drive forward the consolidation of Peruvian capitalism and the creation of a state capitalism, in effective alliance with the bourgeoisie, Mariátegui demonstrated the incapacity of that class to produce a capitalist transition. Their die was already cast. Historically and under Leguía's modernization drive, the Peruvian capitalist class had already entered into an alliance with imperialism. Its effect, far from accelerating national development, was to deepen the relation that we would now describe as "dependent," integrating the Peruvian economy, as a source of raw materials for the industries of the developed world and a market for its products, without producing equivalent development internally. He also gave short shrift to APRA's argument that imperialism could not relinquish its alliance with the landowning classes, who guaranteed cheap and disciplined labor for the extractive industries and the coastal export agriculture that was the most dynamic sector of the economy. Mariátegui again offered evidence that imperialism would have no difficulty at all with a capitalist agriculture or a new class of landowning peasants:

> Do the interests of imperialist capitalism in our countries necessarily and inescapably coincide with the feudal and semi-feudal interests of the landowning class? . . . . It certainly exploits the power of the feudal class, insofar as it sees it as the dominant class. But its economic interests are not identical. . . . Finance capital will feel more secure if power is in the hands of a larger social class which, by satisfying certain urgent demands and placing obstacles in the way of class orientation of the masses, will be in a better position than the hated old feudal class to defend the interests of capitalism.[15]

"The Anti-imperialist perspective" dates from 1928—yet its argument could be used virtually without amendment in the latter part of the second decade of the twenty-first century, as imperialist capital—American, Chinese, and Russian—reimposes the reliance on extractive industries and subverts the attempts at endogenous development and national sovereignty encapsulated most recently under the ambiguous heading of "the pink tide." It reads: "[T]he danger of an economic prosperity based on the possession of a natural resource exposed to the greed and assaults of a foreign imperialism or to the decline of its applications due to the continuous changes in the scientific advances produced in the industrial field."[16]

The argument with APRA, which was a central impulse in the clarification of Mariátegui's Marxism, was reinforced by the Mexican experience. The objective of the Mexican Revolution of 1910–17 was, in the view of most historians, an agrarian revolution, symbolized by the movement in Morelos Province led by Emiliano Zapata under the slogan "Tierra y Libertad" (Land and liberty). The working class, which was more numerous and advanced than in Peru, played a reactionary role in Mexico, where workers' battalions were sent to attack the Morelos Commune under instructions from General, later President, Obregón.[17] The Mexican Constitution of 1917 recognized communal land rights (in the form of the ejido) and workers' rights, yet by the mid-1920s, the nationalism of the post-1917 governments functioned only as ideology as a new ruling class renegotiated its relationship with imperialism under president Plutarco Elías Calles.[18]

> The political movement that overthrew Porfirio Diaz in Mexico was driven in its advance towards a victory over feudalism and its oligarchy, by the feelings of the masses, rested on their forces and was driven by an undeniable revolutionary spirit. In all these senses it was an extraordinary and instructive experience. But the character and objectives of this revolution, of the men who led it, by the economic pressures to which it was subject and by the nature of its process, are those of a bourgeois-democratic revolution. Socialism can only be activated by a class party; it can only be the consequence of a socialist theory and a socialist practice.[19]

When Mariátegui presented his paper on anti-imperialism to the 1929 Buenos Aires conference, it was dismissed by a Communist International that had on the one hand discarded the politics of the united front and on the other combined the politics of "class against class" with a renewed stagist theory, which argued that Latin America must first pass through a bourgeois-democratic stage. The most tragically damaging expression of the line was the insistence on advocating separate Quechua and Aymara national republics, directly sabotaging Mariátegui's patient construction of a common front of workers, peasants, and indigenous peoples, and effectively condemning the indigenous communities to struggle in isolation for more than a generation thereafter.

In the program of the Socialist Party, Mariátegui restated his analysis of the relationship between imperialism and the local bourgeoisie. That relationship confirms the conclusions he had drawn from the Mexican experience:

> Capitalism is in its imperialist stage. It is the capitalism of the monopolies, of finance capital, of imperialist wars over the control of markets and of the sources of raw materials. . . . The precapitalist economy of Republican Peru, in the absence of a vigorous bourgeoisie and because of the national and international circumstances that have determined the country's slow advance towards capitalism, cannot be liberated under a bourgeois regime, tied in to imperialist interests, that colludes with the feudal gamonales and clergy and remains in thrall to colonial feudalism. . . . Only the actions of the proletariat can first stimulate and later fulfil the tasks of the bourgeois-democratic revolution, which the bourgeois regime is incapable of developing and completing.[20]

It is not clear whether Mariátegui knew Trotsky's writings on permanent revolution, though Trotsky's *The New Course* of 1923 was part of his library and annotated. Lenin had argued that "the democratic revolution will not extend beyond the scope of bourgeois democratic social-economic relationships," but the disagreement between the two Bolshevik leaders was around the possibility that the peasantry might form an independent, reactionary party. Trotsky disagreed, arguing that the internal differences within the peasantry would drive the majority of poor peasants to ally with the working class because of its strength. Mariátegui reached his conclusion independently, as a result of his analysis of the specific role played by the Peruvian bourgeoisie, and its absolute lack of contact with the popular movement. The task of development would fall to the proletariat in alliance with the peasants, the indigenous peoples and advanced sections of the petty bourgeois intelligentsia.[21] It is interesting that Mariátegui also echoes Trotsky's dismissal of the arguments about the technical unpreparedness of the working class.

In fact, Mariátegui referred to Trotsky several times in his writing. Acknowledging him as a key leader of the revolution, he clearly saw him as an intellectual slightly apart from the mass working-class movement, as a brilliant military strategist and as a rounded intellectual "pensante y operante"—in thought and action—whose breadth of ideas allowed him to write on literature and revolution, just as Lenin had found time and space to discuss philosophy and specifically to critique the ideas of Kant in *Materialism and Empirio-criticism.* In addressing the rise of Stalin, Mariátegui, whose direct contact with events in Russia up to that point seems to have been minimal, offers an apology for Stalin's *behavior,* arguing that Trotsky's horizons were too broad, too cosmopolitan for the Russian leadership, whose concerns were more local and narrow. It is an odd criticism for Mariátegui to make, if indeed it is a criticism rather than a veiled expression of concern. Later, he returned to Trotsky in far more sympathetic terms. He was certainly in contact, through *Amauta,* with Pierre Naville and the Trotskyist Verité group in France. But he can neither be denounced nor claimed for a Trotskyism he never professed. He wrote four articles on Trotsky.[22] The first, in 1925, described him as part of "a defeated fraction within Bolshevism," echoing the official Moscow line. In January 1927, *Amauta* published Trotsky's portrait of Lenin, with an approving caption. A year later, in a markedly different tone, his piece on "Trotsky and the opposition" described the important role Trotsky had played in the revolution.

"The exile of Trotsky," however, published in February 1929, began on a note that proved premonitory. "Revolutionary optimism could never accept the possibility that this revolution might conclude, like the French, by condemning its heroes." The Trotskyist opposition, he said, fulfills an important function. It reflects the feeling of the urban working class;

and internationally, Trotsky's brilliant analysis of the world system has achieved recognition of the Russian Revolution as the precursor of a new civilization. But Trotsky, much admired abroad, does not enjoy the full confidence of the party within Russia. He attributes that to the Trotsky's early history as a Menshevik, though he recognizes that Lenin and he worked well together. But with Trotsky as its leader, the Left Opposition had, in his view, adopted a more combative "insurrectionary" tone. The revolution is in its phase of national organization, and Stalin is more in tune with the nature and problems of Russia, he argues. Yet neither Stalin nor Bukharin, he says, are far from Trotsky's positions. In the end, a decade after his death, the revolution did condemn its heroes, and Mariátegui's confidence in Stalin proved to be misplaced. He would discover, within weeks of writing this article, that Stalin also had him in his crosshairs.

Mariátegui, of course, was not a Trotskyist, but his conception of revolutionary organization embraced difference, debate, and open disagreement, as did that of both Lenin and Trotsky. This was not a liberal principle based on freedom of expression; liberal precepts could not be deployed where ideas formed part of a philosophy of praxis. Mariátegui had identified earlier in the Russian Revolution, and beyond, a propensity for bureaucratism, for principles to become regulations and instruments of a party discipline over and above the discipline of the struggle itself. But Marxism saw history as a dialectical process in constant movement; the ideas that were to be introduced into the political debate between revolutionaries were not distinct from the reality from which they emerged. Ideas do not have a separate history from the historical forces that generate them. This was the essential meaning of the philosophy of praxis. To restrict the ideas and arguments that may be presented in political debate is to deny that part of reality that they reflect.

But the process may also operate in reverse. Ideas, visions, expectations generated in a process of imagination, of thought, will in turn act upon the world to transform it. The source of those ideas is not metaphysics, however, but philosophy, ideas applied to the understanding of man in the world. This is what Marx referred to as the "this-sidedness" of thought in the "Theses on Feuerbach," and it is what Mariátegui refers to as "materialist idealism." Quijano among others refers to Mariátegui's readiness to introduce into his understanding of Marxism non-Marxist elements and thinkers, from Sorel and William James to Kant and Schopenhauer. Does that make his Marxism eclectic? Mariátegui anticipates the criticism by reminding his readers that Marx himself acknowledged three different sources of Marxism—German philosophy (and especially Hegel), French socialism (including Lasalle) and English political economy (from Mill to Bentham). From the amalgam of these originating schools, Marx produced (dialectically) a wholly new product, Marxism itself. But the addition that Marxism brings to the mix is history, the restless movement and transformation of the world by the action of living forces. In a sense the key answer to the accusation of idealism is his analysis of the Russian Revolution as theory and praxis. But beyond that is his designation of Marxist method as a "process," rather than a body of fixed conclusions.

This is a reflection of a theoretical constant in Mariátegui—his "anti-Jacobinism," which I understand to mean his suspicion of a vanguard leadership not subject to the control of the grass roots. It emerges very clearly in his polemic with APRA, but it is present throughout his work. It may reflect his early anarchism or indeed the influence of Sorel. It does not arise out of a principled opposition to leadership; in his political practice and in his discussions of the role of intellectuals, he does not avoid the issue of leadership, but he does insist on the emergence of leaders from the movement itself, and on their accountability. The vanguard must earn its right to lead. Although he refers to the notion of the vanguard party in the PSP program, it is not the Stalinist variant. Indeed, according to Flores Galindo, he consciously avoided the label "Marxist-Leninist," describing it instead as "militant Leninist."[23]

In *The contemporary scene*, Mariátegui argues: "I don't believe it is possible to to contain in a single theory the broad panorama of the contemporary world. We have to explore it and know it episode by episode, facet by facet. Our judgment and our imagination will always lag behind the totality of the phenomenon."[24]

It is worth comparing these words with Lukács's assertion that "revolutionary action is correct which is grounded upon a dialectical knowledge of reality, which discovers the tendencies pointing towards the ultimate objective not in isolated facts but in the dynamic totality."[25]

In writings prior to his iconic volume, *History and Class Consciousness*, Lukács counterposed "opportunism," a vulgar empiricism that saw only "facts," and "utopianism," referring to a goal conceived abstractly, a "beyond" or a moral "ought." In the revolutionary dialectic to which he now refers, that class consciousness "is an objective possibility, the rational expression of the proletariat's historical interests."[26]

It is in this sense that it becomes possible to speak of a "materialist idealism," as Mariátegui does.[27] Mariátegui employs a different terminology, of course, and it is his sometimes-eccentric use of language that occasionally causes confusion. He consistently refers to "religion" or "religiosity," for example, yet he insists that this is not metaphysical. It is not, in other words, a conception of a "beyond" but the accretion of historical experience, shared memory, and collective goals enshrined in the most controversial of his concepts, the "myth." The fact that he derives it from Sorel adds to the confusion, especially since Sorel himself was less than clear on the objective of revolutionary violence beyond the destruction of bourgeois liberalism. Mariátegui, in contrast, was interested in the overthrow of that order, insofar as it would be the prelude to the construction of a new socialist society. And he regularly addressed future problems in relation, for example, to a socialist regime of land tenure, or to the use and development of technology in the new society.

According to Robert Paris, and a number of far less sympathetic, Stalinist critics, Mariátegui "spiritualized" Marxism. Mariátegui refers to a letter from someone who commends de Man for doing just that and responds with angry, biting wit, satirizing the new bourgeois fashions for exotic "Eastern" mysticism. The biographies of Marx, Lenin, Sorel, and a thousand other socialists stand second to none in their moral beauty and affirmation of the power of the spirit, he says. Marxist idealism incorporates all the possibilities for moral, spiritual, and philosophical improvement. The charge was based on the centrality of the Sorelian "myth" in his thinking, but effectively it was the familiar accusation of idealism—that his Marxism was a utopian concept. In a very different sense, Michael Löwy describes him approvingly as a "Romantic revolutionary," recalling his essay on "Man and myth" in *El alma matinal*:

> The strength of revolutionaries is not in their science, but in their faith, their passion, their will. It is a religious, mystical, spiritual

power. It is the power of Myth. The revolutionary emotion is a religious emotion. But the objectives of religion have moved from heaven to earth. They are not divine but human, social.

The Romantic movement of the nineteenth century was anti-capitalist and anti-bourgeois in its impulses. It was a protest against the quantification of the world, the transformation of human beings into mere extensions of the machine. And it expressed that rejection in a backward glance, an evocation of precapitalist worlds and communities. But what Mariátegui called "neoromanticism," while equally critical of capitalism, looked forward from the basis of a collective vision. Solidarity and community are key precepts. For Mariátegui, the ethical and spiritual dimension of the struggle for socialism is the expression of its resistance to economism, to mechanical Marxism, to positivism: "Marxism, where it has been revolutionary—that is where it has been Marxist—has never given way to a passive or rigid determinism."[28]

Revolutionary transformations are events in consciousness, the realization of imagined alternative futures, as well as the initiation of changes in material conditions. Without the element of imagination, of creativity, there would be resistance and struggle in reaction to capitalism's depredations. But without a myth, an inspiration, revolution would be a mere fiction, a dream. It is significant that Mariátegui expressed an increasing interest in Freud and psychoanalysis, finding there some resonance of the collective will.

In that sense his definition of Marxism as a philosophy of praxis has been described as simply another version of the utopian deviation, both by the official Soviet writers in the 1940s and by Posadas, writing in Havana in 1968. The term most often used in relation to Mariátegui is "heterodox," itself an ambiguous epithet; it suggests that his ideas derive from a number of different sources, but it can equally refer to the conscious distance between his ideas and orthodox Soviet Marxism after Lenin, a distinction he would certainly have made.

Perhaps the best starting point is the essay "Two conceptions of life":

> What distinguishes the people of this epoch is not just doctrine, but above all feeling. . . . Two conceptions of life, the one prewar the other postwar, affect the intelligence of people who appar-

ently serve the same historical interests. That is the central feature of the contemporary crisis.

He quotes the opinion of Adriano Tilgher, the Italian historian, to the effect that "the generation that grew up before the war lived in a world that seemed consolidated forever and assured that it would not change. And they adapted effortlessly to this world." But the First World War destroyed that bourgeois complacency, and in its aftermath, "'I struggle therefore I exist' replaces the Cartesian reassurance, 'I think therefore I am.' No-one knows when the good life will return. And skepticism and nihilism give birth to the harsh, brutal urgent necessity for a faith and a myth that can move men to live dangerously."[29]

The positivist vision that held ideological hegemony over both classes before 1914 was exposed by the war and was replaced by the class struggle inspired by the Russian Revolution. But what moves working people to pursue the transformation of their world? Resistance and rebellion are a response to the exploitation and oppression that they suffer under bourgeois rule. But revolution is not mere resistance. It is above all an action born of consciousness, but consciousness itself is not a mere reflection of the material world.

> To Hegel, the life process of the human brain, i.e., the process of thinking, which, under the name of "the Idea," he even transforms into an independent subject, is the demiurge of the real world, and the real world is only the external, phenomenal form of "the Idea." For me, on the contrary, the ideal is nothing other than the material world reflected by the human mind, and translated into forms of thought.[30]

It is the material world reflected but also transformed in the dialectics of history, for ideas are also material forces insofar as they exist in the minds of the active human subjects who bear them. It is true that the cruder interpretation of the theory of reflection reduced all acts of the imagination to mere mirror images on the wall of Plato's cave. Of course Marx also went on to say that it is not consciousness that determines social being, but social being that determines consciousness. Everything rests on the nature of the determination. But it is not proposed as a mechanical response, but as a response in consciousness. In his vigorous and lifelong refutation of positivism and its dehumanizing impact, Mariátegui espoused the philosophy of "praxis."

The author of the term was Antonio Labriola, the Italian philosopher, whom Mariátegui had read at the same time as he had encountered Sorel. It is of itself a controversial term, since Gramsci's use of it was described by his colleague Togliatti as a "camouflage" in order not to use the term "Marxism" in his letters from prison. It seems even less convincing given the content of the *Prison Notebooks*, and Gramsci's acknowledgment of Labriola's influence. Adolfo Sánchez Vázquez rejects the suggestion trenchantly:

> Gramsci used the denomination in order to clarify his understanding of what Marxism meant. It enabled him to distinguish Marxism from both mechanistic materialism on the one hand and from speculative philosophy which was divorced from actual history and from practical human activity (and particularly politics) on the other. Further it was a means of stressing the role in actual history of the subjective factor, of the revolutionary consciousness and activity of the proletariat under the leadership of their party; in this he was reacting against a prevalent "lazy" Marxism which used objective factors and the development of productive forces to justify a rejection or postponement of revolutionary activity which was then translated into the crudest kind of opportunist reformism.[31]

Sánchez Vázquez goes on to make an important distinction between theoretical activity—even that which describes itself as a theoretical instrument of praxis, but which "cannot transform the world"—and praxis, "a material, transforming activity," "one of whose conditions is the production of the ends that characterise theoretical activity."

Among many Marxists of the immediate post-October period, Marxism was discussed well beyond economic matters. For Lukács's generation, for example, art and religion were central topics, just as ideology and hegemony preoccupied Gramsci's generation. Mariátegui seems in many ways to have been in tune with that debate, though that was less a product of his knowledge of that intellectual current than the result of his close and intimate reading of his own culture.

200 IN THE RED CORNER

His Marxist method, which it seems to me very hard to question, lies precisely in his exploration of the knowledges and aspirations that workers, peasants and indigenous people, and the intellectuals of an incipient anti-capitalism brought to the revolutionary discussion. Those knowledges were informed by specific actual or historical experiences conserved in the collective memory and ritualized or universalized through time—that is, in social myths. It is true they are often located within an alternative, mythic time, though to return to an earlier point, that time is not a *beyond*, a metaphysical space. It is rather an alternative narrative, which will lay hold of whatever speculative language is available in that time and place. That space may be an imaginative universe, a new language (or as Roman Jakobson, the Russian linguist, put it, in discussing poetry, a language made strange), a metaphor, or perhaps a religious discourse—useful in its very abstraction. The use in many radical movements in Latin America today of the term *mística*, for example, is by no means limited to radical religious movements like the Brazilian base communities or the theology of liberation. What all these examples have in common is what Higa calls their *anticipatory* power.[32]

"Myth," however, is not merely an idea; it impels action, intervention in the world. In *Defense of Marxism*, Mariátegui makes the important distinction between a moral position and praxis. It is clear that the central features of his thought are an opposition to bourgeois rationalism, on the one hand, and on the other a relentless critique of economism. But this "anti-rationalism" as Higa describes it,[33] is not to be confused with de Man's "moral" socialism. For him, "'moral' socialism and its antimaterialism lead only to falling back into the most sterile and lachrymose humanitarian romanticism, the most decadent defence of the 'pariah,' in the most sentimental and inept plagiarism of the evangelical language of the poor of the earth."[34]

The pariah becomes the object of the actions of others, humanitarians, saviors, and the power of the masses to liberate themselves, and become the subject of history, is abandoned—and with it the very meaning of revolutionary socialism. For Mariátegui, the subject of revolution is the proletariat. De Man's position, he says, smacks of the sense of that aristocracy that, having entertained itself by dressing up as shepherds and joining the liberal ranks, dreamed of leading a revolution of the ragged armies of the poor.

Mariátegui spoke of revolution as "heroic creation," that was neither imitation nor copy of other experiences. It was heroic in the sense that it was an advance into unknown territory, what Bloch had called the "not-yet," and Lukács the "ought." That future was not the automatic outcome of material development; that was the false promise of economistic Marxism that was also the consequence of the transformation of Leninism into a Stalinism that claimed to be its continuity. The proletariat again became subject to forces outside itself—be it the laws of capitalist accumulation or the control of the bureaucracy. His understanding of revolution was a process of creation and self-creation, as the proletariat transformed itself from object into subject. There was a moral force at work here, but it was what Mariátegui called "the morality of the producers:" "The ethical function of socialism is to be found, not in the grandiloquent decalogues or the philosophical speculations that in no way represented the necessity of theorising Marxism, but in the creation of a morality of the producer in the process of anti-capitalist struggle itself."[35]

It is not the mechanical product of economic interests, but the outcome of the class struggle and "the heroic spirit and passionate will" of the producers. Lenin's famous phrase "without revolutionary theory there is no revolutionary action" is interpreted by Mariátegui as a reference to the relationship between the present struggle and the future purpose. And that future purpose is the product of creativity in thought and action. His models of a revolutionary are Lenin, Trotsky, and in a passionate essay, Rosa Luxemburg. These were "pensante y operante," thinkers and actors, the "new persons" that would lead and represent a socialist world. It was not simply anecdotal that each was creative, imaginative, and fascinated by every aspect of human experience. Like Mariátegui himself, their intense relationship with reality produced imaginative responses at the level of ideas. But this was not utopianism, because the idea existed as realization in the act of transformation—in that sense it was a philosophy of praxis. To see Marxism in that way is an important corrective to its distortions under Stalinism and the later evacuation of practice to leave a curious, so-called postmodern version of de Man's empty moralism.

Mariátegui drew on a wide range of sources for his ideas, from philosophers and historians through writers and artists, from Latin

America to the rest of the world. Some writers have argued that this is a
weakness, a simple accumulation of ideas. It seems to me that this is an
unfounded criticism. What he certainly did was draw on every source
of knowledge, in theory and in practice, in order to make sense of his
own world. In doing so he enriched Marxism in a global sense and wrote
what was undeniably the first Marxist interpretation of the reality and
the political economy of Latin America. Jaime Massardo, a Chilean
critic, attributes five particular elements to a Latin American Marxism,
all of which can be traced back to Mariátegui's analysis of Peru.[36] The
characterization of a national bourgeoisie that cannot achieve national
liberation—that task must fall to other classes. The issue, of course, has
been the subject of intense and bitter argument in Latin America. Many
Marxists insisted that the vocation of that class was to carry through a
national liberation movement and the creation of a strong nation-state.
In every case, from Mexico to Argentina, that has proved to be illusory.
The recent experience of the "pink tide" and the Bolivarian Revolution
could be seen to reinforce that assertion, even though in these cases the
project was led by the petty bourgeoisie. Thus, the task will fall to other
classes, in a particular dialectical relationship of class and race that sees
a central role for an indigenous community within a united front with
the working class.

The development of Marxism is a process of change, just as the
historical reality in which it functions is subject to change. After two
generations in which Marxism was an orthodoxy applied in essentially
mechanical ways, Mariátegui's references to faith and religiosity could
be easily misunderstood, and have been by critics who have suggested
that these terms pointed to a residual Catholicism he had never relin-
quished. But there is another way of making sense of that spirit or that
faith. Opponents of Marxism have always derided it as a kind of religion,
meaning a blind and unthinking devotion to an unchanging scripture.
What Mariátegui means by it, however, is exactly the opposite—a will to
change informed by visions of a future born out of the accumulated experience of a community. It is anticipatory, mythic, but not metaphysical:

> Socialism and syndicalism, despite their materialist conception of
> history, are less materialist than they might appear. They rest on

the interests of the majority, but they tend to ennoble and dignify life. Western people are mystical and religious in their own way. Is revolutionary emotion not a religious emotion? It so happens that religion in the west has moved from heaven to earth. Its motives are human, social, not divine. They belong to life on earth and not to life in heaven.[37]

Acknowledgments

I am grateful to the Leverhulme's Emeritus Research Program, which allowed me to carry out research for this book in Amsterdam and Lima. The staff at the Casa Museo José Carlos Mariátegui were extremely helpful and welcoming, for which I give many thanks. Ricardo Portocarrero was a guide and a source of great knowledge in Lima, and I was glad to have his company. In Lima, I met three young scholars from Brazil—Ricardo Streich, Bernardo Soares, and Demi Alfaro Rubio—from whom I learned much.

Nella, my partner, has accompanied me through the peaks and troughs of these times, and the journey was not always easy, but it was richer for her company.

Yet I alone am responsible for this text.

Abbreviations

APRA—American Popular Revolutionary Alliance

BBC—British Broadcasting Corporation

Comintern—Communist International

CONAIE—Confederation of Indigenous Nationalities of Ecuador

CGTP—Confederación General de Trabajadores del Perú (General Confederation of Peruvian Workers)

CGIL—Confederazione Generale Italiana del Lavoro (Italian General Confederation of Labor)

FIOM—Federazione Impiegati Operai Metallurgici (Metallurgical Workers Employees Federation)

IMF—International Monetary Fund

NAFTA— North American Free Trade Agreement

PCI—The Communist Party of Italy (Partito Comunista d'Italia)

PCP—the Communist Party of Peru, aka Maoist Shining Path organization

PNL—Partido Nacional de Liberación

PSP—Peruvian Socialist Party

WTO—World Trade Organization

Selected Bibliography

Writings of Mariátegui

Mariátegui, José Carlos, *Complete Works/Obras Completas,* available at
www.marxists.org
——. (1925), *La escena contemporánea* (The contemporary scene) (*Amauta*, Lima)
——. (1928), *Siete Ensayos de interpretación de la realidad peruana (Seven
interpretative Essays on Peruvian Reality)* (*Amauta*, Lima)
——. (1950), *El alma matinal* (The dawning of the soul)(*Amauta*,Lima)
——. (1959), *Historia de la Crisis Mundial* (History of the world crisis)
(*Amauta*, Lima)
——. (1967), *Defensa del marxismo* (A defence of Marxism) (*Amauta*, Lima)
——. (1969), *Cartas de Italia* (Letters from Italy) (*Amauta*, Lima)
——. (1970), *Figuras y aspectos de la vida mundial* (Figures and aspects of
international life) (*Amauta*, Lima)
——. (1970a), *Peruanicemos el Peru* (*Amauta*, Lima)
——. (1971), *Ideología y política* (Ideology and politics) (*Amauta*, Lima)
- (1984), *Correspondencia* (Bibl *Amauta*, Lima)
⸺ ·tos juveniles (*Amauta*, Lima)
¹ vol 1: Siete Ensayos and Ideología y Política

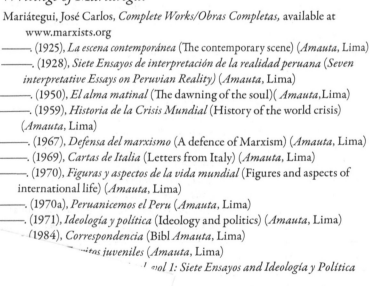

ne—MG)

in socialismo indo-americano: Ensayos esco

dos de Mariátegui (Minerva, Lima)

Mariátegui, J. C. (1988), *Seven Interpretive Essays on Peruvian Reality (trans Marjory Urquidi)*

Vanden, H. and Marc Becker (eds) (2011), *José Carlos Mariátegui: An anthology* (Monthy Review, New York)

Writing on Mariátegui

Adrianzen, Catalina (1974), *Marxism, Mariátegui and the women's movement* (Lima)

Arico, J. (1978), *Mariátegui y los orígenes del marxismo latinoamericano* (Pasado y presente, Mexico)

Baines, John M. (1972), *Revolution in Peru: Mariátegui and the myth* (U of Alabama Press)

Bazan, Armando (1939), *Biografía de José Carlos Mariátegui* (ZigZag, Santiago)

Becker, Marc (1993), *Mariátegui and Latin American Marxist Theory* (Ohio UP)

Beigel, Fernanda (2005), https://seer.fclar.unesp.br/estudos/article/view/113

Berger, V. (ed) (1980) *Ensayos sobre Mariátegui: Simposio de Nueva York* (*Amauta*, Lima)

Carnero, Checa G. (1980), *La acción escrita: José Carlos Mariátegui periodista* (*Amauta*, Lima)

Chang-Rodríguez, E. (1957), *La literatura política de González Prada, Mariátegui y Haya de la Torre* (Mexico)

Cornejo Polar, A. (1980), *Mariátegui y la Literatura* (*Amauta*, Lima)

Del Prado, Jorge (1946), *José Carlos Mariátegui y su obra* (Eds Nuevo Horizonte, Lima)

Del Prado, J. et al. (1972), *Vigencia de José Carlos Mariátegui* (Campodónico, Lima)

Falcón, Jorge (1978), *Anatomía de los Siete Ensayos* (Lima)

———. (1980), *Mariátegui, arquitecto syndical* (Lima)

Flores Galindo, A. (1992), *La agonía de Mariátegui* (Ed Revolución, Lima)

Forgues, Roland (ed) (1993), *José Carlos Mariátegui y Europa* (*Amauta*, Lima)

———. (1995), *Mariátegui: la utopia realizable* (*Amauta*, Lima)

García Salvatecci, H. (1979), *Georges Sorel y J. C. Mariátegui* (Ed Universo, Lima)

Garrels, Elizabeth, *Mariátegui y la Argentina: Un caso de lentes ajenos* (Eds Hispamérica, Gaithersburg)

Higa, J. Oshiro (2013), *Razón y mito en Mariátegui* (Congreso del Peru, Lir

Kossok, Manfred (1967), *José Carlos Mariátegui y el desarrollo del pensa⁊ marxista en el Peru* (Lima)

Larco, Luis Felipe et al. (1995), *El marxismo de José Carlos Mariáte* (*Amauta*, Lima)

⁊a Vegas, R. (1975), *Introducción a Mariátegui* (Ed Causac⁊

Massardo, Jaime (2010), "En torno a la concepción de la historia de José Carlos Mariátegui," available at http://www.rebelion.org/noticia.php?id=114989

Melgar Bao, R. (1997), *Mariátegui y los indígenas*

Melis, Antonio (ed) (1984), *José Carlos Mariátegui, Correspondencia 1915–1930*

———. (1999) *Leyendo Mariátegui* (Amauta, Lima)

Meseguer Illan, Diego (1974), *José Carlos Mariátegui y su pensamiento revolucionario* (IEP, Lima)

Miró, César (1995), *Elogio y elegía del Amauta* (*Amauta*, Lima)

———. (1989), *Mariátegui, El tiempo y los hombres* (*Amauta*, Lima)

Monereo, Manuel (1995), *Mariátegui 1884–1994* (Talasa, Madrid)

Moore, Melissa (2014), *José Carlos Mariátegui's Unfinished Revolution: Politics, Poetics and Change in 1920s Peru*

Muñoz Navarrete, M. (2012), *La creación heróica: Marxismo y crítica literaria en José Carlos Mariátegui (Ed TrincheraCaracas)*

Nuñez, E. (1994), *La experiencia europea de Mariátegui* (*Amauta*, Lima)

Paris, Robert (1972), *El marxismo latinoamericano de Mariátegui* (Eds Crisis, Buenos Aires)

———. (1981), *La formación ideológica de Mariátegui* (Siglo XXI, Mexico)

Posadas, Francisco (1968), *Los orígenes del pensamiento marxista en América Latina* (Casa de las Americas, Havana)

Quijano, Aníbal (1982), *Introducción a Mariátegui* (ERA, Mexico)

Romero, Emilio et al. (1979), *7 Ensayos: 50 años en la historia* (*Amauta*, Lima)

Rouillon, Guillermo (1975), *La creación heróica de José Carlos Mariátegui*, vol. 1 (Ed Arica, Lima)

———. (1963) *Bio-bibliografía de José Carlos Mariátegui* (Lima)

Stein, William E. (1997), *Dance in the cemetery: José Carlos Mariátegui and the Lima scandal of 1917* (UPA)

Tauro, Alberto (1960), *Amauta y su* influencia (*Amauta*, Lima)

Unruh, Vicky (1989), "Mariátegui's aesthetic thought." in *Latin American Research Review* 24/3

Vanden, Harry E. (1975), *Mariátegui: influencias en su formación ideológica* (*Amauta*, Lima)

Villafañe (2009), *Mariátegui, la revolución bolivarana y el socialismo nuestroamericano* (El Perro y la Rana, Caracas)

Semionov, D. and A. Shulgovski (1959), "El papel de Mariátegui en la formación del Partido Comunista del Peru," in *Documentos Politicos*, no. 14, Bogota.

On Peru and Peruvian History

Basadre, Jorge (1931), *Peru, problema y posibilidad* (Lima)

———. (1971), *Introducción a las bases documentales para la historia del Perú* (Lima)

Bernabe (2006), Palais Concert

Bourricaud, Francois (1970), *Power and Society in Contemporary Peru* (Faber, London)

Caballero, José Maria (1980), *Agricultura, reforma agrarian y pobreza campesina* (IEP, Lima)

Del Prado, J. (1976–7), *Interview by Denis Sulmont* (Universidad Católica, Lima)

Flores Bordans, Lourdes Eddy (2015), "Mariátegui, los comunistas y el movimiento sindical minero en el Peru (1928–31)," available at https://dspace .unila.edu.br/bitstream/handle/

Flores Galindo, Alberto (1973), *Los mineros de la Cerro del Pasco 1900–1930* PhD thesis, Universidad Católica, Lima

———. (2010) *In Search of an Inca: Identity and Utopia in the Andes*

Haya de la Torre, V. R. (1936), *El APRA y el antiimperialismo* (Ercilla, Santiago)

———. (1933), *Politica aprista* (*Amauta*, Lima)

Hirsh, S. (2011), "Anarcho-syndicalism in Peru, 1905–1930," available at https://libcom.org/library/

Kapsoli, Wilfredo (1976), *Las luchas obreras en el Peru 1900–1919* (Ed Delva, Lima)

———. *Los movimientos campesinos de Cerro del Pasco 1880–1963* (Lima)

Mella, J. A. (1928), *Qué es el ARPA?* (Mexico)

Martínez de la Torre, Ricardo (1928), "El movimiento obrero en 1919," *Amauta* nos. 16–18.

———. (1949), *Apuntes para una interpretación marxista de la realidad peruana* (Empresa Editora, Lima) (first edition 1935)

Pareja, Piedad (1978), *"La Protesta": contribución al estudio del anarquismo en el Peru (1911–1926)*

Parra, Pedro (1969), *Bautismo de fuego del proletariado peruano* (Eds Horizonte, Lima)

Parssinen, Martti (1992), *Tawantinsuyu: The Inca State and Its Political Organization* (Tiedekirja, Helsinki)

Peru: Paths to Poverty (1984), (Latin America Bureau, London)

Podesta, Bruno (1975), *Pensamiento político de González Prada* (INC, Lima)

Poole, D. and Gerardo Reñique (1992), *Peru: Time of Fear* (L A Bureau, London)

Portocarrero, Julio (1987), *Sindicalismo peruano* (Gráfica Labor, Lima)

Reyna, Ernesto (1932), *El Amauta Atuspario* (Lima)

Sulmont, Denis (1976–77), *Entrevista a Jorge del Prado: Historia del PCP* (Centro de Documentación, Universidad Católica, Lima)

———. (1975) *Historia del movimiento obrero en el Peru 1890–1956* (Universidad Católica, Lima)

Thorp, Rosemary and G. Bertram (1980), *Peru 1890–1977: Growth and Policy in an Open Economy* (Columbia UP, New York)

Selected Bibliography

Writings of Mariátegui

Mariátegui, José Carlos, *Complete Works/Obras Completas,* available at www.marxists.org

———. (1925), *La escena contemporánea* (The contemporary scene) (*Amauta,* Lima)

———. (1928), *Siete Ensayos de interpretación de la realidad peruana* (*Seven interpretative Essays on Peruvian Reality*) (*Amauta,* Lima)

———. (1950), *El alma matinal* (The dawning of the soul)(*Amauta,*Lima)

———. (1959), *Historia de la Crisis Mundial* (History of the world crisis) (*Amauta,* Lima)

———. (1967), *Defensa del marxismo* (A defence of Marxism) (*Amauta,* Lima)

———. (1969), *Cartas de Italia* (Letters from Italy) (*Amauta,* Lima)

———. (1970), *Figuras y aspectos de la vida mundial* (Figures and aspects of international life) (*Amauta,* Lima)

———. (1970a), *Peruanicemos el Peru* (*Amauta,* Lima)

———. (1971), *Ideología y política* (Ideology and politics) (*Amauta,* Lima)

———. (1984), *Correspondencia* (Bibl *Amauta,* Lima)

———. (1994), *Escritos juveniles* (*Amauta,* Lima)

———. (2012), *Mariátegui Total, vol 1: Siete Ensayos and Ideología y Política* (Minerva, Lima)

Translations

(All translations in the text are mine—MG)

Löwy, Michael (ed) (2006), *Por un socialismo indo-americano: Ensayos escogi-*

dos de Mariátegui (Minerva, Lima)

Mariátegui, J. C. (1988), *Seven Interpretive Essays on Peruvian Reality (trans Marjory Urquidi)*

Vanden, H. and Marc Becker (eds) (2011), *José Carlos Mariátegui: An anthology* (Monthy Review, New York)

Writing on Mariátegui

Adrianzen, Catalina (1974), *Marxism, Mariátegui and the women's movement* (Lima)

Arico, J. (1978), *Mariátegui y los orígenes del marxismo latinoamericano* (Pasado y presente, Mexico)

Baines, John M. (1972), *Revolution in Peru: Mariátegui and the myth* (U of Alabama Press)

Bazan, Armando (1939), *Biografía de José Carlos Mariátegui* (ZigZag, Santiago)

Becker, Marc (1993), *Mariátegui and Latin American Marxist Theory* (Ohio UP)

Beigel, Fernanda (2005), https://seer.fclar.unesp.br/estudos/article/view/113

Berger, V. (ed) (1980) *Ensayos sobre Mariátegui: Simposio de Nueva York* (*Amauta*, Lima)

Carnero, Checa G. (1980), *La acción escrita: José Carlos Mariátegui periodista* (*Amauta*, Lima)

Chang-Rodríguez, E. (1957), *La literatura política de González Prada, Mariátegui y Haya de la Torre* (Mexico)

Cornejo Polar, A. (1980), *Mariátegui y la Literatura* (*Amauta*, Lima)

Del Prado, Jorge (1946), *José Carlos Mariátegui y su obra* (Eds Nuevo Horizonte, Lima)

Del Prado, J. et al. (1972), *Vigencia de José Carlos Mariátegui* (Campodónico, Lima)

Falcón, Jorge (1978), *Anatomía de los Siete Ensayos* (Lima)

——. (1980), *Mariátegui, arquitecto syndical* (Lima)

Flores Galindo, A. (1992), *La agonía de Mariátegui* (Ed Revolución, Lima)

Forgues, Roland (ed) (1993), *José Carlos Mariátegui y Europa* (*Amauta*, Lima)

——. (1995), *Mariátegui: la utopia realizable* (*Amauta*, Lima)

García Salvatecci, H. (1979), *Georges Sorel y J. C. Mariátegui* (Ed Universo, Lima)

Garrels, Elizabeth, *Mariátegui y la Argentina: Un caso de lentes ajenos* (Eds Hispamérica, Gaithersburg)

Higa, J. Oshiro (2013), *Razón y mito en Mariátegui* (Congreso del Peru, Lima)

Kossok, Manfred (1967), *José Carlos Mariátegui y el desarrollo del pensamiento marxista en el Peru* (Lima)

Larco, Luis Felipe et al. (1995), *El marxismo de José Carlos Mariátegui* (*Amauta*, Lima)

Luna Vegas, R. (1975), *Introducción a Mariátegui* (Ed Causachun, Lima)

Massardo, Jaime (2010), "En torno a la concepción de la historia de José Carlos Mariátegui," available at http://www.rebelion.org/noticia.php?id=114989

Melgar Bao, R. (1997), *Mariátegui y los indígenas*

Melis, Antonio (ed) (1984), *José Carlos Mariátegui, Correspondencia 1915–1930*

——. (1999) *Leyendo Mariátegui* (Amauta, Lima)

Meseguer Illan, Diego (1974), *José Carlos Mariátegui y su pensamiento revolucionario* (IEP, Lima)

Miró, César (1995), *Elogio y elegía del Amauta* (*Amauta*, Lima)

——. (1989), *Mariátegui, El tiempo y los hombres* (*Amauta*, Lima)

Monereo, Manuel (1995), *Mariátegui 1884–1994* (Talasa, Madrid)

Moore, Melissa (2014), *José Carlos Mariátegui's Unfinished Revolution: Politics, Poetics and Change in 1920s Peru*

Muñoz Navarrete, M. (2012), *La creación heróica: Marxismo y crítica literaria en José Carlos Mariátegui* (Ed TrincheraCaracas)

Nuñez, E. (1994), *La experiencia europea de Mariátegui* (*Amauta*, Lima)

Paris, Robert (1972), *El marxismo latinoamericano de Mariátegui* (Eds Crisis, Buenos Aires)

——. (1981), *La formación ideológica de Mariátegui* (Siglo XXI, Mexico)

Posadas, Francisco (1968), *Los orígenes del pensamiento marxista en América Latina* (Casa de las Americas, Havana)

Quijano, Aníbal (1982), *Introducción a Mariátegui* (ERA, Mexico)

Romero, Emilio et al. (1979), *7 Ensayos: 50 años en la historia* (*Amauta*, Lima)

Rouillon, Guillermo (1975), *La creación heróica de José Carlos Mariátegui*, vol. 1 (Ed Arica, Lima)

——. (1963) *Bio-bibliografía de José Carlos Mariátegui* (Lima)

Stein, William E. (1997), *Dance in the cemetery: José Carlos Mariátegui and the Lima scandal of 1917* (UPA)

Tauro, Alberto (1960), *Amauta y su* influencia (*Amauta*, Lima)

Unruh, Vicky (1989), "Mariátegui's aesthetic thought." in *Latin American Research Review* 24/3

Vanden, Harry E. (1975), *Mariátegui: influencias en su formación ideológica* (*Amauta*, Lima)

Villafañe (2009), *Mariátegui, la revolución bolivarana y el socialismo nuestroamericano* (El Perro y la Rana, Caracas)

Semionov, D. and A. Shulgovski (1959), "El papel de Mariátegui en la formación del Partido Comunista del Peru," in *Documentos Politicos*, no. 14, Bogota.

On Peru and Peruvian History

Basadre, Jorge (1931), *Peru, problema y posibilidad* (Lima)

——. (1971), *Introducción a las bases documentales para la historia del Perú* (Lima)

Bernabe (2006), Palais Concert

Bourricaud, Francois (1970), *Power and Society in Contemporary Peru* (Faber, London)

Caballero, José Maria (1980), *Agricultura, reforma agrarian y pobreza campesina* (IEP, Lima)

Del Prado, J. (1976–7), *Interview by Denis Sulmont* (Universidad Católica, Lima)

Flores Bordans, Lourdes Eddy (2015), "Mariátegui, los comunistas y el movimiento sindical minero en el Peru (1928–31)," available at https://dspace.unila.edu.br/bitstream/handle/

Flores Galindo, Alberto (1973), *Los mineros de la Cerro del Pasco 1900–1930* PhD thesis, Universidad Católica, Lima

———. (2010) *In Search of an Inca: Identity and Utopia in the Andes*

Haya de la Torre, V. R. (1936), *El APRA y el antiimperialismo* (Ercilla, Santiago)

———. (1933), *Politica aprista* (*Amauta*, Lima)

Hirsh, S. (2011), "Anarcho-syndicalism in Peru, 1905–1930," available at https://libcom.org/library/

Kapsoli, Wilfredo (1976), *Las luchas obreras en el Peru 1900–1919* (Ed Delva, Lima)

———. *Los movimientos campesinos de Cerro del Pasco 1880–1963* (Lima)

Mella, J. A. (1928), *Qué es el ARPA?* (Mexico)

Martínez de la Torre, Ricardo (1928), "El movimiento obrero en 1919," *Amauta* nos. 16–18.

———. (1949), *Apuntes para una interpretación marxista de la realidad peruana* (Empresa Editora, Lima) (first edition 1935)

Pareja, Piedad (1978), "*La Protesta*": contribución al estudio del anarquismo en el Peru (1911–1926)

Parra, Pedro (1969), *Bautismo de fuego del proletariado peruano* (Eds Horizonte, Lima)

Parssinen, Martti (1992), *Tawantinsuyu: The Inca State and Its Political Organization* (Tiedekirja, Helsinki)

Peru: Paths to Poverty (1984), (Latin America Bureau, London)

Podesta, Bruno (1975), *Pensamiento político de González Prada* (INC, Lima)

Poole, D. and Gerardo Reñique (1992), *Peru: Time of Fear* (L A Bureau, London)

Portocarrero, Julio (1987), *Sindicalismo peruano* (Gráfica Labor, Lima)

Reyna, Ernesto (1932), *El Amauta Atuspario* (Lima)

Sulmont, Denis (1976–77), *Entrevista a Jorge del Prado: Historia del PCP* (Centro de Documentación, Universidad Católica, Lima)

———. (1975) *Historia del movimiento obrero en el Peru 1890–1956* (Universidad Católica, Lima)

Thorp, Rosemary and G. Bertram (1980), *Peru 1890–1977: Growth and Policy in an Open Economy* (Columbia UP, New York)

Valcárcel, Luis (1927), *Tempestad en los Andes* (Minerva, Lima)
———. (1964), *Ruta cultural del Peru* (Eds Nuevo Mundo, Lima)
Vargas, L. and Oscar Jara Holliday (1975), "Desarrollo del capitalismo.
   Mariátegui y la organización de la clase obrera en el Peru," Talleres Cien-
   cias Sociales, Universidad Catolica, Lima, September
Yepes del Castillo, E. (1971), *Peru 1820–1920: Un siglo de desarrollo capitalis-
   ta* (IEP, Lima)
"Zitor" (1976), *Historia de las principales huelgas y paros obreros habidos en el
   Peru 1896–1946* (Lima)

Other Works Consulted

Anderson, Benedict (1991), *Imagined Communities* (Verso, London)
Arico, J. and David Broder (2015), *Marx and Latin America* (Haymarket,
   Chicago)
Barekat, H. and M. Gonzalez (2013), *Arms and the People* (Pluto Press, London)
Benjamin, Walter (1970), *Illuminations* (Verso, London)
Bureau Sudamericano de la Internacional Comunista (1932), *La situación
   revolucionaria del Peru y las areas del PCP* (Buenos Aires)
Claudin, Fernando (1975), *The Communist Movement: From Comintern to
   Cominform* (MR Press, New York)
Fitzpatrick, Sheila (1970), *The Commissariat of the Enlightenment: Soviet
   Organization of Education and the Arts under Luncacharsky, 1917–21*
   (Cambridge UP)
Franco, Jean (1976), *César Vallejo: The Dialectics of Poetry and Silence*
   (Cambridge UP)
Gilly, Adolfo (2006), *The Mexican Revolution* (New Press, New York)
Gramsci, Antonio (2010), *Prison Notebooks* (Columbia UP, New York)
———. (1978), *Selections from Political Writings 1921–26* (Lawrence and
   Wishart, London)
Hamilton, Earl (1934), *American Treasure and the Price Revolution in Spain,
   1501–1650*
Higgins, James (1989), *César Vallejo en su poesía* (Seglusa, Lima)
Hobsbawm, Eric (1983) (ed with T. Ranger), *The Invention of Tradition* (Cam-
   bridge UP)
Knight, Alan (1986–1990), *The Mexican Revolution* (Univ of Nebraska Press,
   Lincoln)
Lih, Lars (2009), *Lenin Rediscovered: What Is to Be Done?* (Haymarket, Chicago)
Lukács, Georg (1967), *History and Class Consciousness* (Merlin, London)
Malek, A. Abdel (1981), *Social Dialectics, vol. 2, Nation and Revolution* (Mac-
   millan, London)

Mosler, Volkard (2013), "An Army in Revolt: Germany 1918–19," in Bourekat
    and Gonzalez (2013) 35–57
Pearce, Brian (ed) (1977), *Baku: Congress of the Peoples of the East* (New Park,
    London)
Portis, Larry (1980), *Georges Sorel* (Pluto, London)
Ravines, Eudocio (1952), *La gran estafa* (Venero, Mexico)
Sánchez Vázquez, Adolfo (1977), *The Philosophy of Praxis* (Merlin, London)
———. (1973), *Art and Society* (Merlin, London)
Spriano, Paolo (1975), *The Occupation of the Factories* (Pluto Press, London)
Trudell, Megan (2013), "Nation against Italy: Italy 1919–21," in Bourekat and
    Gonzalez (2013), 58–78
Vitale, Luis (1997), "Mariátegui and 'the problem of the Indian," available at
    http://www.socialistvoice.ca/?p=1344
Webber, Jeffery (2011), *From Rebellion to Reform in Bolivia: Class Struggle, In-
    digenous Liberation, and the Politics of Evo Morales*, (Haymarket, Chicago)
———. (2017), *The Last Day of Oppression and the First Day of the Same* (Hay-
    market, Chicago)
Williams, Gwyn A, (1975), *Proletarian Order: Antonio Gramsci, Factory
    Councils and the Origins of Communism in Italy, 1911–21* (Pluto Press,
    London)
Williams, Raymond (1977), *Marxism and Literature* (New Left Books, London)

Notes

Introduction: A Revolutionary Rediscovered

1. Frederick Pike, by no means a sympathetic commentator, called him "perhaps the only original Marxist thinker that Latin America has produced."

Chapter One: The Resurrection of José Carlos Mariátegui

1. Naomi Klein, in her 2015 book *This Changes Everything: Capitalism vs the Climate.*
2. Mariátegui 2012a, 424–5.
3. That is the term used by Vanden and Becker in the introduction to their anthology of his writings; Vanden 2011.
4. Benedict Anderson 1991
5. Luis Vitale 1997.
6. See Jeffery Webber 2011.
7. "Marxism and Romanticism in the Work of Jose Carlos Mariategui," by Michael Löwy and Penelope Duggan, in *Latin American Perspectives.*
8. "Dos concepciones de la vida," in Mariátegui 1950.
9. See his "Emile Zola y la nueva generación francesa," published in *Variedades,* February 5, 1930, shortly before Mariátegui's death.
10. Mariátegui 2012a, 41.
11. Mariátegui 2012a, 12.

Chapter Two: Learning His Trade

1. Glusberg, letter, November 1929, in *Correspondencia*.
2. Yepes 2013, 41–42.
3. In his *Seven Essays*.
4. See below.
5. The atmosphere of the times is recreated in José Eustasio Rivera's 1924 novel *La Vorágine* (*The Vortex*). The translation was published in 2003. Greg Grandin's fascinating book *Fordlandia* (2009) gives another insight into the years of the rubber boom.
6. See Thorp 1980 and Yepes del Castillo 2013. See, in general, Sven Beckert's ambitious *Empire of Cotton* (2015).
7. See Pareja 1978, and, more generally, her work on Peruvian anarchism.
8. Steven Hirsh, "Anarcho-syndicalism in Peru 1905-30," available at www.libcom.org.
9. Ibid.
10. Vargas 1975.
11. Kapsoli 1976.
12. Martínez de la Torre 1928.
13. César Miró 1989, 23.
14. E. Chang Rodriguez, "La superación del anarquismo en Mariátegui," in Berger 1980, 47–57.
15. Later reproduced in *Amauta* no. 16 (July 1928), 13–14.
16. Manuel González Prada, "Discurso en el Politeama," available at www.voltairenet.org.
17. Mariátegui 1928, 254.
18. See "The question of religion," in Mariátegui 1928.
19. We will look in detail at this key concept in Mariátegui's work in chapter 3.
20. Bazan 1939, 88 (quoted in Higa, 51).
21. Rouillon ref
22. Mariátegui 1987, 340.
23. Bernabé 2006, 88.
24. "La Mariscala" and "Las Tapadas."
25. See Stein 1997.
26. Mariátegui 2012, 282–3; JCM uses the Gallicism "pompier."
27. Chang-Rodriguez, in Berger 1980; see Steven Hirsh on anarchism.
28. This adds special significance to G. Carnero Checa's *La acción escrita* (Carnero 1980), which examines his early journalistic career. In the 1990s, edited by Alberto Tauro, his early work was published in *Escritos Juveniles* (1994).
29. Quoted in Higa, 38.
30. Chang-Rodriguez certainly thinks he did.

31. *Historia de la crisis mundial*, lecture 1.
32. Martínez de la Rosa, quoted in Carnero Checa 1980, 116.

Chapter Three: *The Discovery of Marxism*

1. They would only reappear in 1994 in the collection *Escritos juveniles*,1994.
2. Rouillon 1975, 32.
3. For an account of this period, see Spriano 1975 and Williams, 1975. See also Trudell 2013.
4. Gwyn Williams, introduction to Paolo Spriano 1975.
5. Williams, ibid.
6. Quoted in Antonio Melis 1999, 156.
7. In Mariátegui 1950.
8. "Mussolini and fascism," in Mariátegui 1925.
9. See his "The forces of socialism in Italy," in Mariátegui 1969.
10. Mariátegui 1925.
11. "Scenes from a civil war," in Mariátegui 1969.
12. "The Italian press," in Mariátegui 1969.
13. Rouillon 1963, 44.
14. See Hirsch 2011.
15. See Fernanda Beigel 2005, available at https://seer.fclar.unesp.br/estudos/article/view/113.
16. Mariátegui 1959, 15.
17. See chapter10.
18. Mariátegui 1969, 109.
19. See V. Mosler on Germany, in Barekat and Gonzalez, *Arms and the people*.
20. See the section "The crisis of democracy," in Mariátegui 1950.
21. In Mariátegui 1925.

Chapter Four: *The World Crisis*

1. The Battle of Caporetto (October 24–November 19, 1917) brought Italian troops face to face with an Austro-Hungarian force, with German support. The result was a rout of the Italian troops, made especially humiliating by the systematic use of poison gas against them. It was described as "the greatest defeat in military history"; 10,000 troops were killed, 30,000 wounded, and 265,000 taken prisoner.
2. Letter to Samuel Glusberg, April 30, 1927 in Mariátegui 1984, 274.
3. "La crisis de la democracia," in Mariátegui 1950, 32
4. "El 1 de mayo y el frente único," in Mariátegui 2012, 421–4..

5. "1 de mayo," Mariátegui 2012a, 422.
6. See chapter 10.
7. Oshiro Higo 2013, 68.
8. As Gramsci argued for in the Lyons Theses, for example.
9. Ibid, 130.
10. Mariátegui 1959, 99.
11. Meseguer 1974.
12. Mariátegui 1959, 135.
13. Higa 2013, 110.
14. Ibid., 119.
15. Ibid., 120.
16. Ibid.
17. Cf. Lauer et al.
18. Flores Galindo 1982a, 18
19 Ibid..
20. He was using the term in the sense that Marx and Engels spoke of "the masses." Its use here is not be confused with the way the term is used by Hardt and Negri.
21. Mariátegui 1925, 27; O. Higa 2013, 170–1
22. Refer back to it.
23. Sánchez Vázquez 1977.
24. Refer to Harman on Gramsci and Voloshinov.
25. Lecture no. 17 in Mariátegui 1959.
26. Boothman, 132.
27. Gramsci 1971, 328
28. If it is, in fact, praise to compare him to Peter the Great, as he did!

Chapter Five: Building the Movement

1. He appears as a character in Walter Salles 1997 film, *The Motorcyle Diaries*.
2. Leon Trotsky "The Question of the United Front" (February, 1922), at www.marxists.org.
3. Flores Galindo.
4. "Pesimismo de la realidad optimism del ideal," in Mariátegui (1950).
5. The Party of the National Revolution—PNR, later the Party of the Mexican Revolution—PRM—under Lazaro Cardenas 1934–40, and finally the PRI—the Institutional Revolutionary Party—which continues to exist.
6. "Al margen del nuevo curso de la política mexicana," in Mariátegui (1970a).
7. Bergel
8. Ibid..
9. On this section, see Fores Galindo 1973 and Flores Bordans 2015.

10. Those conditions were later dramatically described by Ciro Alegría in his iconic novel *Broad and Alien Is the World* (*El mundo es ancho y ajeno*) published in 1941.
11. Julian Laite 1981.
12. Flores Galindo 1974.
13. Blanco was arrested at the 1930 protests, and murdered in jail.
14. del Prado 1976–77, 14.
15. Published in *Amauta* 22.
16. Flores Galindo 1974.
17. The key work on the working class in Peru is Denis Sulmont 1975.
18. Sanchez 1934, 166.
19. Laite 1981.
20. "Manifesto of the 1st May Committee," in Mariátegui 2012a, 432.
21. In Mariátegui 2012a, 419–20.
22. An interesting article in no. 7 (February 21, 1929) argues the case for factory committees and industrial unions, for example.
23. See chapter 9.
24. Sulmont 1975, 151–3.

Chapter Six: Amauta

1. Mariátegui 2012a, 525–6.
2. See A. Tauro 1960 for a comprehensive index of the contents of the magazine.
3. In "Anniversary and balance sheet," in Mariátegui 2012a, 531.
4. Mariátegui 1925, 117–18.
5. The Russian poet Aleksandr Blok is taken as an example of this kind of avant-garde artist. See ibid.
6. On the cultural debate in Russia, see Fitzpatrick 1970.
7. On Barbusse, in Mariátegui 1925, 120.
8. Flores Galindo 1978 quoted these figures in a recorded public lecture, "La crisis del 30 y el movimiento obrero," delivered at the Universidad Católica del Peru, at Library of the Universidad Católica in Lima..
9. David Wise, "Amauta 1926–30: Una fuente para la historia cultural peruana," in Berger 1980, 132.
10. Mariátegui 1959b, 125; quoted in Higa 2013, 186.
11. See chapter 7.
12. In Mariátegui 2012a, 527.
13. In Martin Bergel 2010.
14. The notorious Eudocio Ravines, who will be discussed below, disputed Haya's claims that he was leading a movement of students and workers in Peru. According to him, certainly an unreliable witness, Mariátegui was

220 IN THE RED CORNER

an intellectual, and Haya an activist leading a group of young demagogues who were not the communists they claimed to be.

15. Sánchez 1934, 166.
16. Haya de la Torre *Qué es el Apra?*, 1936.
17. Sánchez 1979, 166.
18. Bergel, 320.
19. Flores Galindo, "La crisis del treinta y el movimiento obrero," a recorded lecture.
20. In 1930 the US embassy had described Haya as a Bolshevik. In 1931, he was defined as an acceptable ally for the US.
21. Mariátegui 1984, 372–3.
22. See www.pueblomartir.wordpress.com/catástrofe de Morococha.
23. Arguedas speaking at the first Congress of Peruvian Writers, Arequipa, 1965. Quoted in Muñoz Navarrete 2012, 13.

Chapter Seven: Interpreting Peru

1. Mariátegui 2012a.
2. "Mariátegui, Latin America's first Marxist," in Antonio Melis 1999, 22.
3. Quijano 2012, 379. My emphasis.
4. *The German Ideology* available in www.marxists.org.
5. Webber 2016.
6. For a full discussion of the issue, see Draper 1977 515–71 and 629–65.
7. Mariátegui 2012a, 102.
8. See chapter 9.
9. See, for example, Francisco Posada 1968. Published by Casa de las Américas in Havana and therefore reflecting a more or less official communist view of Mariátegui, though with a strong Althusserian leaning, it presents a very negative assessment of his Marxism.
10. According to Conrad and Demarest's *Religion and Empire* (Cambridge 1984), the dispute between Atahuallpa and Huascar over the succession, which the Spaniards stumbled upon, centered on an argument around the cult of ancestor worship.
11. *Nueva corónica y buen gobierno* (The new chronicle and good government) by Felipe Guaman Poma de Ayala (1535–1616?), translated as *Letter to a King*, is an extraordinary document, beautifully illustrated with his drawings, and unmasking the realities of life in early colonial Peru.
12. Earl Hamilton 1934 remains the standard work on this.
13. His thesis is brilliantly summarized in his response to a questionnaire from the Seminar of Peruvian Culture that appeared in the newspaper *La Sierra* in June 1929. It is reproduced in Vanden and Becker as "On the character

of Peruvian society," 243–54.

14. Henri Favre, "Etat, capitalisme et ethnicité: La cas peruvien," ERSIPAL, Document de travail 15, 1980.

15. Aníbal Quijano, "Raza, etnia y nación en Mariátegui, cuestiones abiertas," in Forgues et al., *José Carlos Mariátegui y Europa*, Lima 1993 (Forgues et al 1993).

16. See the introduction.

17. Mariátegui 2012a, 495.

18. Mariátegui 2012a, 63.

19. Webber 2016.

20. "The problem of race," in Mariátegui 2012a, 354.

21. This topic takes us well beyond the scope of the present book. Jeffery Webber, as well as a helpful section on Mariátegui, addresses the wider problem in Webber 2016. See also my own *The End of the Pink Tide* (Pluto Press, London, 2018).

22. Mariátegui, preface to Ernesto Reyna 1932.

23. Marx-Zasulich correspondence, February–March 1881, available at www.marxists.org. This is from the third draft of his reply.

24. See Mariátegui 2012a, 349–404.

25. M. Löwy 2006, 34.

26. Flores Galindo 1980, 50.

27. "Anniversary and a balance sheet," in Mariátegui 2012a, 533.

28. Vitale 1997.

29. Mariátegui 2012a, 329.

30. Manrique 2000, 229.

31. "Reencuentro y debate," in *Siete Ensayos*, Clascso, Buenos Aires, 2014. available at www.clacso.edu.ar, consulted September 15, 2017.

32. Francisco Posadas 1968, published by Casa de las Américas and thus reflecting the official Cuban view, is particularly aggressive in this respect.

33. I address the last of these in chapter 8.

34. Mariátegui 2012a, 171.

35. González Prada, *Nuestros indios*.

36. Paulo Freire 2000.

Chapter Eight: Literature and Politics

1. Ricardo Palma's *Tradiciones peruanas* are to some extent an exception that proves the rule, according to Mariátegui.

2. Hence the enraged reaction of the Archbishop of Lima to Rouskaya's midnight ballet in the cemetery in 1916.

3. Quoted in J. Mojarro Romero. See also Vicky Unruh 1989.

4. "Order no. 2 to the Army of the Arts." I could not resist including this excerpt, though Mariátegui does not specifically mention it.
5. In his essay on Oliverio Girondo, the Argentine avant-garde poet, in *Variedades*, August 15, 1925.
6. M. Salinas in *Herramienta* 21.
7. Ibid.
8. Muñoz Navarrete 2012, 70.
9. Mariátegui 1964a, 11.
10. His interviews produced a series of articles spread across his *Complete Works*.
11. "The surrealist revolution and Clarté," in Mariátegui 1964b.
12. The Spanish term he uses here and frequently is "*disparate*," which translates as scandal, shock, wild behavior.
13. Julio Cortázar, *Rayuela*, Madrid 2006, 707; quoted in Muñoz Navarrete 2012, 83.
14. See Higa 372–5.
15. See "Biología del fascismo (Biology of fascism)," in Mariátegui 1925.
16. His "Couplets on the death of his father" are a classic of world literature.
17. Cf. "Heretodoxy of tradition," in Mariátegui 1970d.
18. See Hobsbawm 1983.
19. Mariátegui 2012, 253.
20. Martin Adán (1908–1985), "'La casa de cartón' de Martin Adan'" in Mariátegui 1970a, 150–4.
21. James Higgins 1989. See also Jean Franco 1976.
22. See Jean Franco 1976.
23. Mariátegui 2012.
24. "Literary populism and capitalist stabilisation," in *Amauta* no. 28, Jan 1930, 6–9.
25. Muñoz Navarrete 2012, 87.
26. Prologue to Luis Valcárcel 1927.
27. See Carlos Huaman 2004. See also Arguedas and W. Rowe (eds.), *Los rios profundos*, Pergamon, Oxford,1998.
28. "Lunacharsky," in Mariátegui 1925.
29. Raymond Williams 1977, 206.
30. Sánchez Vázquez 1973, 114.
31. "Towards an explanation of Chaplin," in Mariátegui 1964a, 55–62.

Chapter Nine: The Question of the Party

1. Cf. chapter 6.
2. Mariátegui 1969.
3. Mariátegui 1964c, 19–20.

4. See Antonio Melis, "Una carta de Cesar Falcón de 1923," in Melis 1999, 291.
5. Leon Trotsky available at www.marxists.org. My emphasis.
6. In *Amauta* no. 6, February 1927, 29.
7. "On a closed question" (Sobre un tópico superado), in *Amauta 28,* January 1930, 97.
8. See Ian Birchall's review of John Riddell's *To the Masses* (2015) in *Links International Journal of Socialist Renewal,* April 2015.
9. See above chapter 6.
10. V. I. Lenin, speech to the Congress of the Communist International, July 1921, available at www.marxists.org.
11. Lenin, *What Is to Be Done?* available at www.marxists.org. See too Lars Lih's groundbreaking work *Lenin Rediscovered: What Is to Be Done?* Lih 2009.
12. Higa 2013, 87.
13. Ibid, 120.
14. Mariátegui 1964c.
15. Rouillon, 267.
16. See chapter 4 on Mexican revolution.
17. Unfortunately the Lenin lecture notes are the briefest of the series.
18. Quoted in Vanden 1980, 75.
19. Ibid, 79.
20. Cf. Arico 1978.
21. Flores Galindo 1992, 20.
22. Letter of June 10, 1927, in *Mariátegui* (1994), cited by Flores Galindo 1992, 20.
23. On this period in Mariátegui's life, see Flores Galindo 1980.
24. Chang-Rodriguez 1957.
25. J. Portocarrero 1987, 176.
26. South American Secretariat 1929, 155–6, quoted in Vanden 1980, 82.
27. In IP.
28. Mariátegui 2012a, 412.
29. Flores Galindo *La agonía de Mariátegui,* 30–35.
30. Portocarrero, 158.
31. Moreshevski 1941.

Chapter Ten: Mariátegui's Marxism

1. "Message to the Workers' Congress," in Mariátegui 2012a, 424–5.
2. Mariátegui 1959a.
3. Ibid., 16.
4. Robert Paris, for example, described him as "an ambiguous Sorelian." See Paris 1973.

5. In Lukács 1967.
6. Löwy 1979, 174.
7. Mariátegui 1959a, 68.
8. Quijano 1981.
9. Posadas 1968 is especially brutal.
10. Benjamin 1970, 258–59. See also Löwy 2006, "Introduction."
11. Pearce 1977.
12. "Marxism and National Liberation," in A. Abdel Malek 1981, 84. My emphasis.
13. F. Claudin 1975, vol. 1, 265. Cf. A. Quijano 1977, 86.
14. Malek 1981, 263.
15. "The anti-imperialist perspective," in Mariátegui 2012a, 410.
16. Mariátegui 2012a, 51.
17. See Gilly 2006.
18. See, for example, Gilly 2006 and Knight 1990. See also chapter 9 above.
19. Mariátegui 1960, 69.
20. Mariátegui 2012a, 464–5.
21. Cf. program of PSP.
22. "Elogio a El Cemento," in Mariátegui 1950 ,"Trotsky on Lenin," in Amauta vol. 5, January 1927, "Trotsky y la oposición," in Mariâtegui 1970 and "El exilio de Trotsky" in vol. 3.
23. See Flores Galindo 1980, 85–86.
24. Mariátegui 1925.
25. M. Löwy 1979, 174.
26. Ibid., 175.
27. In Mariátegui 1959a.
28. Mariátegui 1959a, 66–7
29. "Two conceptions of life," in Mariátegui 1964a.
30. Karl Marx, "Afterword to the Second German Edition of Capital," 1873, quoted in Muñoz Navarrete 2012, 46.
31. Sánchez Vázquez 1977, 32–3.
32. Higa 2013, 111.
33. Ibid.
34. Mariátegui 1959a, 71.
35. Ibid., 57.
36. Massardo 2010.
37. "Gandhi," in Mariátegui 1925.

Index

Jirón de la Unión, 19, 36

Kautsky, Karl, 188
The Kingdom of This World (Carpentier),
    155
Klein, Naomi, 5, 8
Korsch, Karl, 44, 184, 188
Kropotkin, Peter, 150
Kuomintang, 102, 118, 172, 179

labor, 7, 16, 26, 28–31, 60, 69, 73,
    78–79, 85, 93, 96, 98, 103, 109,
    113, 117, 128–32, 136, 171, 175,
    176, 190
Lacandón Forest, 10
La Chira, Amalia, 23
Laite, Julian, 99
Lasalle, Ferdinand, 195
Laws of the Indies, 129
Left Opposition, 194
Lenin, V. I., 12, 33, 44, 50, 58, 60, 70,
    72, 75, 80, 82, 88, 109, 116, 149,
    163, 167, 169, 173, 174, 181, 184–
    85, 188–90, 192–94, 196–97, 201
Lévano, Delfino, 90
Ley de Vagancia, 90
Liebknecht, Karl, 12
Lima Group, 90, 100
Livorno, Congress of, 43, 50–51, 56, 58
López Albújar, Enrique, 112, 155
The Lost Steps (Carpentier), 154
Löwy, Michel, 16, 17, 44, 138, 196
Lukács, Georg, 4, 17, 44, 146–47, 158,
    184, 187–88, 195, 199, 201
Lulu, 25, 38
Lunacharsky, Anatoly, 154, 156
Luxemburg, Rosa, 12, 201

maize for ethanol, 8
Manhattan Transfer (Dos Passos), 157
Manrique, Jorge, 149

Manrique, Nelson, 139
manufacturing industry (Europe), 27,
    128, 175
Marcos, Subcomandante, 10
Mariátegui, Francisco Javier de, 23
Marinetti, Filippo, 144, 151
Marof, Tristán, 101
Martí, Farabundo, 8, 101
Martínez de la Torre, Ricardo, 32, 46,
    96, 114, 121, 181
Marxism, 1–7, 11–18, 20–21, 38–41,
    43–45, 47–48, 52, 57–59, 62, 64,
    69, 75, 77, 79–80, 100, 110–11,
    117, 124, 135–36, 139–40, 146,
    148, 154, 157, 172, 179, 181,
    183–91, 194–97, 199–202
Marx, Karl, 2, 6, 12, 16–17, 38, 44, 53,
    63, 75, 77, 79–80, 124, 126–28,
    135–37, 146, 183–88, 194–96, 198
Materialism and Empirio-criticism
    (Lenin), 75, 193
"Materialist Idealism" (Martiátegui), 76
Mayakovsky, Vladimir, 145
Mayer de Zulen, Dora, 112
Mella, Julio Antonio, 8, 115, 187
Menchú, Rigoberta, 10
Mexican Constitution, 191
Mill, John Stuart, 195
minerals, 8, 31
Minerva, 90, 99
mines, 27, 30, 85, 93–95, 97, 99, 120,
    128
mística, 76, 200
mito, 11, 15, 16, 35, 39, 112, 210
modernization, 14, 29, 31, 33, 42, 87,
    131, 140, 190
Moquegua, 23–24
Morelos Commune, 191
Moreshewski, 182
Morococha, 94–96, 99–100, 102, 120
Morris, William, 17, 136

About the Author

Mike Gonzalez is emeritus professor of Latin American studies at the University of Glasgow. He has written extensively on Latin American politics. His recent titles include *Hugo Chavez: Socialist for the Twenty-first Century*, *The Last Drop: The Politics of Water*, and *The Ebb of the Pink Tide: The Decline of the Left in Latin America*.

CPSIA information can be obtained
at www.ICGtesting.com
Printed in the USA
JSHW031907021221
20900JS00004B/6